There She Goes

Liverpool, a City on its Own

The Long Decade: 1979-1993

There She Goes

Liverpool, a City on its Own

The Long Decade: 1979-1993

BY SIMON HUGHES

First published as a hardback by deCoubertin Books Ltd in 2019

Published as a paperback in 2020

deCoubertin Books, 49 Jamaica Street, Baltic Triangle, Liverpool, L1 0AH.

www.decoubertin.co.uk

ISBN: 978-1-9162784-4-8

A CIP catalogue record for this book is available from the British Library.

Cover design by Thomas Regan

Typeset by Leslie Priestley

Printed and bound by Standart

In memory of Etta and Jo, whose wartime stories
introduced me to this city's history.

Contents

Another Cholera-Smitten City In India

THE CASA IS AN OLD SEA MERCHANT'S HOUSE ON LIVERPOOL'S HOPE Street, where there are vast Catholic and Protestant cathedrals at each end. The city's wealth is illustrated here, its entire existence succinctly explained in the Georgian Quarter – up on its rise and looking down into the centre and the docks beyond, where the real money was made and labourers, not knowing whether they'd be working from one day to the next, lived in squalor.

'Looking down,' Tony Nelson, thought, 'was a deliberate emotional decision by the powers that controlled the whole of Liverpool.' Nelson saw Liverpool's emergence as the most significant maritime port in the British empire differently to the majority of historians, whose focus had reliably been taken by the enormous provision towards the capitalist economic cycle rather than the consequences of a fairer redistribution.

Nelson had been a docker, though he was now the landlord of the Casa, more of a social club than a bar; a place born out of one of the longest and most heroic industrial struggles in the twentieth century, the 850-day dockers' dispute. It had raised a million pounds a year, providing a lifeline for people in need of help, the latest of whom had been Stephen Smith, a 64-year-old whose weight had dropped to six stone because of a range of health problems but was still denied benefits and told to find a job. When his story became public, it was Nelson and the Casa who came first to Smith's aid.

At the Merseyside Maritime Museum, there are walls filled with recollections which reflect what Liverpool used to be like. 'Ships filled the river, waiting their turn to gain access to fully packed berths,' one quote reads. 'The dock road was once again a daily confusion of traffic, while quays and warehouses were full to bursting with haphazard piles of crated, bundled, bagged and baled cargo.'

'The regions of the world were still sea-laned to Liverpool,' was another explanation. 'Within hailing distance of the Liver Building were small ships to Paris via Rouen, and a mere ten-minute walk took in ships of varying sizes loading for Limerick, Barcelona, New Orleans, Demerara, Lagos and Manaus... It was impossible to exaggerate how much the city of Liverpool was a sea port.'

History was illustrated on the walls of the Casa too. There was a framed plaque with all of the names of the Merseyside volunteers who fought against Franco in the Spanish Civil War. There was a photograph of Robbie Fowler whose support of the dockers strike, which ran between 1995 and 1997, coincided with his advent as a legendary goalscorer for Liverpool FC. There was also a glass case of pins donated by seafarers, demonstrating the multitude of shipping companies that once operated out of Liverpool.

In the corner of the lounge area beneath *'Let It Be'* sounding from the jukebox was a group of smartly-dressed bearded men, warmed by their duffle coats and leaning into one another in a sort of conspiratorial manner. They look like sailors and their presence confirmed that while in Liverpool there is religion, politics, football and music, the heart and lungs of the city was in the docks: the space where workers spent the most time, talked about the most and where the experience and personality of both its men and women was ultimately defined.

Liverpool had been one of the richest cities in the British Empire, producing more wealthy families in the nineteenth century than any other urban area outside London. Its golden era was between 1880 and 1899, when it was estimated that Liverpool produced as many millionaires as Greater Manchester, West Yorkshire, West Midlands, Tyneside and East Anglia combined. Over a longer period, 1804 to 1914, Merseyside produced almost twice as many millionaires as Manchester, and this showed just how lucrative shipping was compared to manufacturing. In the writing of this book, I would meet Michael Heseltine, a member of Margaret Thatcher's Conservative government who tried for Liverpool when it was at its lowest economically and nobody else within his party bothered. Heseltine spoke endearingly about the grandeur of Liverpool's buildings and other civic monuments, erected because of the endowment of its business people. The painting by Atkinson Grimshaw from 1887 showed Liverpool as it was widely viewed in its peak: a centre of trade, with tall men walking the streets dressed in elegant Victorian tailcoats; horses and carriages tapping and rolling across the oily cobbled dock streets, washed by seawater; bright lights in the shop fronts attracting customers and wine merchants inducing high-spiritedness.

Contrary to Heseltine's impression, Hugh Shimmin, the Tory radical, questioned intent, describing philanthropy in 1861 as 'a fashionable amusement'. If an old wealthy family of Liverpool donated funds for a new hospital or school it wasn't because they cared about the shocking levels of poverty that existed. 'It was because,' he wrote, 'it brought them into passing contact with this Bishop or that Earl.'

Liverpool's elites were more autocratic than philanthropic. Sir William Brown, who donated a free library as well as a museum to the city, was a millionaire cotton broker who sacked a footman for taking sympathy on a beggar by giving him a plate of food. Meanwhile, the 'public' parks were not really public at all; owned exclusively used by the carriage-owning classes who lived in grand residences close-by.

Hugh Farrie was a journalist at the Liverpool *Daily Post*. In 1899, the city had made more money than ever yet the gulf between the rich and the poor was stark. Farrie's reporting described a district around Scotland Road, which led north from the city centre towards Anfield and Walton. The area was, he wrote, 'dirty, tumble-down, and as unhealthy as any part of squalid Europe', despite its location less than a mile away from Liverpool's banks, cafes and commerce. On Dale Street, there was 'wealth and ambition ... of busy, happy men, all bent on winning some prize in the world.' He depicted a glorious place 'of ship windows, of gossiping politicians lounging on the steps, of carriages rattling past the Conservative Club'. Yet walk a few paces 'from this bright and cheering scene,' he concluded, 'and you will find gathered upon the very edge of it a deep fringe of suffering, helpless, hopeless poverty.'

The culture of casual labour allowed Liverpool's economy to boom for a born-into-privilege minority as well as a few entrepreneurs. According to Nelson, it could not be overestimated how profound an effect the culture of casualisation had on Liverpool's collective psyche. Every morning and afternoon, men would assemble at the gates of the shipyards not knowing whether they were going to work and whether they were going to get paid. Tides played a role on starting times and there was a lot of uncertainty. 'Unlike in manufacturing towns elsewhere in the north west where shift work was tough but reliable, there were no consistent patterns in Liverpool and this led to an undisciplined way of life,' Nelson said. 'It was uncommon for dockers in Liverpool to wear watches because they didn't live by the clock. Geography by its sheer nature meant that while being freer, we also had more to be concerned about because we didn't know for certain when the next pay was going to arrive and therefore had to be more creative in the way we worked.'

Nelson reasoned that because Liverpool's workers did not have a regular authority looking over them and because they were not constricted by contracts or shift-patterns, they were able to develop a single-mindedness, and a suspicion of anyone in authority telling them what to do developed from there.

The American novelist Nathaniel Hawthorne had not been in Liverpool for six months when, in 1854, he recalled observing on a Mersey ferry a labourer eating oysters using a jack knife from his pocket before throwing the shell overboard and wolfing down another. He then took out his clay pipe, filled it with rush and smoked the whole thing. Hawthorne considered the labourer as the embodiment of a Liverpool person because of his 'perfect coolness and independence' which was mirrored by other passengers. 'Here,' he wrote, 'a man does not seem to consider what other people will think of his conduct but whether it suits his convenience to do so.'

The extent of casual labour in Liverpool or anywhere else in Britain has never been established at any particular time. In 1921, a census revealed the number of workers who reported having no fixed workplace, though the figures did not include seafarers on voyage. This had also been the life for many men in Liverpool: a life at sea of casual relationships and few commitments on land. The census showed that there was twelve times as many men in Bootle, right next to Liverpool's dockland, without an address or a workplace than in St Helens', the glass-making manufacturing town twelve miles inland.

While the city was the first in Britain to appoint a Medical Officer of Health and amongst the first to build council housing at St Martin's Cottages in 1869, these developments did not represent progressive politics but rather, the desperation of Liverpool's situation. The deprivation in the docklands was astonishing. In 1880, more than 70,000 people lived in buildings already condemned as unfit for habitation and two years later, a new medical officer reported that 'whole districts were plagued as the cholera-smitten cities of India'.

By 1896, around the time Liverpool had more millionaires than anywhere outside London, new findings were stark: 'There is,' another report claimed emphatically, 'not a city in this country or in Europe, which could produce anything like the squalor that officials found in some of Liverpool's backstreets.'

TONY NELSON IS A TALL, THIN MAN WITH A PENETRATIVE STARE who took great care with the language he used, never swearing – an unusual trait amongst old school dockworkers in Liverpool. He described the docks as the 'destiny' he reached in 1973 when he was fifteen years-old. Nearly all of his family had worked there. His dad and his brothers were dockers and each of the girls on his mother's side had met dockers in the dockside pubs around Brasenose Road in Bootle. He was too young to lift and carry cargo and this meant he initially worked in the offices of Harrison Line, the Victorian shipping company which had started out 120 years before, as an importer of French brandy from Charente. Harrison Line's workforce had largely been the same group of men for decades, 'Fellas in their 70s,' Nelson said with affection. 'The whole place stunk of history from way before my time.'

Nelson was brought up on tales of industrial disputes. 'Dockers are storytellers,' he continued. 'There were great debates about the Russian Revolution so I learnt how to argue my case. I received a political history, how the communist party had developed in Great Britain. There were Stalinists and Trotskyists: a dense mix of socialist politics. It changed the way I thought about everything.'

The discussions in the canteen were usually led by former conscripted soldiers who had fought in the World War Two, a conflict which had dire consequences for Liverpool and its docks. Nelson was entering employment when Liverpool's port was just about keeping afloat in turbulent waters. Strategically, the city had been critical during the war effort and the Battle of the Atlantic was coordinated from a nerve centre deep below the Western Approaches on Rumford Street, close to the Royal Liver Building. Liverpool faced America and would act as the premier port for the convoys that kept the Allied war machine supplied. Hitler recognised Liverpool's importance and began to bomb the hell out of it from July 1940 onwards. Attacks eleven months later accounted for 1,300 deaths across just six weeks, almost half of all the casualties in the city during the course of the entire war.

In total, wartime raids destroyed 6,585 homes. A further 125,310 properties were seriously damaged. Liverpool was left with a housing crisis which reached into the 1970s and beyond when more than fifteen per-cent of properties were still derelict or vacant. In the docks, shipping companies such as the one Nelson worked for lost significant tonnage and it would take time to replace fleet and for lost markets to be re-established. In this crucial period, the world changed again.

Dramatic shifts in international transport and trading links impacted on Liverpool's significance. The earliest casualty was the lucrative transatlantic passenger lines which suffered as commercial air travel increased. The break-up of the Commonwealth and a reduction of trading partners made Britain look towards Europe following the creation of the EEC in the 1950s and this left Liverpool marooned on the wrong side of Britain. In 1966, Liverpool clung on to being the second biggest port in England but twenty years later it was sixth. While the share of ship arrivals in Liverpool halved, Dover's, for example, increased by four and a half times. When it came to new contracts, Southampton took many of those involving Asian countries from Liverpool. When United States Lines moved their ships, taking advantage of the faster turnaround times at the east coast ports despite being further away from the US, the signs for Liverpool were really ominous.

The east coast had been quicker to implement containerised docklands and this transformed the way goods were handled and transported. Previously, Liverpool's docks needed thousands of men to load ships and move whatever was arriving. By the late 1960s, large dockside cranes were hulking much bigger containers onto ships at a much faster speed and this heralded a new round the clock operation which heightened difficulties in relations with an already reducing labour force.

In 1970, the Mersey Docks and Harbour Board was already on the brink of bankruptcy. The south docks of Liverpool were redundant, the Mersey being too narrow and too shallow in parts to deal with the increase in ship sizes. As the area became off limits to the public, scavengers took timber for repairs and pig iron for ballast. At nights especially, as the last working lights flickered, a ghost town quietness became even eerier. Cats interbred at a frightening rate and supposedly, hundreds lived on an old fishing boat. 'You could smell them a fair distance downwind,' said a fisherman.

Seaforth in the north of Liverpool where the Mersey spills out into the Irish

Sea was designed to deal with the shift brought by containerisation but while that site was being developed, other towns in the south with more space were able to seize their opportunity, like Felixstowe, which was able to employ a new, more agreeable workforce which had not experienced the historic disputes like those in Liverpool and therefore made them easier to manage.

While Felixstowe became the largest container port in the country, employment in Liverpool's docks was slashed by more than half in the twelve years up to 1979, though it wasn't just the dockers who suffered. The impact on other industries which relied on the docks was also disastrous.

Before World War Two, manufacturing had overtaken shipping as the basis of Liverpool's wealth for the first time. Yet by the mid-1970s, only 35 per-cent of employment in Liverpool was involved in manufacturing compared with more than 50 per-cent nationally. The manufacturing trades, however, still relied on a functioning port, with sites located on or adjacent to the dock estates and food processing plants such as Crawford's Biscuits, Jacobs Crackers or Hartley's jam factory, further inland in newer areas like Aintree or further afield in Kirkby.

As the docks retreated, so did the manufacturing base. Opportunities in the merchant navy decreased because there was less space on newly mechanised ships that needed smaller crews. The repair firms that had operated out of the docks for centuries were suddenly rendered redundant because of the turnaround times and this impacted on the surrounding areas, with pubs and cafes initially shutting followed by the smaller dock firms who operated in rope and sacks. Between 1973 and 1983, male employment fell by 53 per-cent in Merseyside compared with 32 per-cent nationally. The women in Merseyside bore the brunt even more than the men as their workforce was slashed by 62 per-cent, compared with 33 per-cent elsewhere. In Kirkby alone, there were 13,000 job losses, which represented a 57 per-cent decline in overall employment.

The culture of ownership also partly explained the decline. Regional policies in the 1960s enabled a 20 per-cent rise in non-locally controlled firms by 1976 and this meant few bosses held any allegiance with Liverpool. Between 1966 and 1977, 350 factories in Liverpool closed down or moved elsewhere and forty-thousand jobs were lost over a ten-year period starting in 1971. By 1980, only one of the twenty largest manufacturing companies on Merseyside was controlled locally. The rest did not have any natural commitment to Liverpool or its workers. The city, therefore, had lost control of its economic future and became known as the

Bermuda Triangle of British capitalism. Tony Lane, in his evocative book, *City of the Sea*, would describe Liverpool as an 'Imperial mausoleum: an embarrassment to the post-colonial establishment.'

'Liverpool,' predicted one council survey, 'looks set to become the Jarrow of the 1980s,' after 17,000 jobs were lost in 1978 alone and it was discovered that unemployment was twice that of the national average having risen by 33 per-cent in less than a decade.

According to some politicians, Liverpool's dockworkers were partly to blame for the demise. In 1966, Harold Wilson condemned seamen from Liverpool as a 'band of communist agitators holding the country to ransom'. Two years later, Wilson spoke again about, 'strike after strike frustrating the efforts of the government; signalling a question mark to those industrialists who are attracted by the inducements and are considering establishing themselves here'. In 1967, Liverpool's dockers had maintained their strike for much longer than other ports over arguments during process of decasualisation and lost days amounted to twice the national average.

There had been prior warnings about Liverpool having to come to terms with a reduced workforce and when that workforce railed against the possibility, other politicians blamed them for not embracing progress, even though the evidence around them indicated the world was changing and Liverpool – by its geography – was never going to be able to keep up. Tony Nelson thought of Liverpool's resistance to change as an understandable reaction – that history sided with the workers because of the way the modern docks became, where fewer staff are still able to generate vast amounts of wealth for global companies.

'The fortune of each dockland community was bound in the number of ships that were in the docks and the trades that those ships stimulated,' Nelson said. 'Nobody was quite sure about the impact of global trends at the time but dock workers were feeling it. What are they supposed to do? Accept that the next 30 years will be bad for them or fight for everything they can claw back? When we were told that the resistance was putting off investment, where we supposed to be grateful for capitalists taking advantage of our weaker position?'

Capitalism would be a feature of the discussion with Nelson, as it would be with other dock workers when researching this book. Many felt let down by a system which they felt casts aside without feeling or sense of responsibility when the wind shifts, though not all felt as strongly as Nelson about the alternatives: 'It let Liverpool down – it has let lots of cities down,' he said. 'From there, it boils down to whether you want to do something about it.'

The sharpest focus of Nelson's disappointment was with the trade unions. He believed it was their failure to understand the difference in cultures that existed in the manufacturing industries and the docks which culminated in dockworkers feeling misrepresented and undervalued by the authorities supposed to be supporting them.

'Were we responsible for that being a bit insular?' Nelson would ask himself. 'Maybe so. We were behind a wall. We looked after each other. It was a bit of a cult to be honest with you. Maybe we could have let more people in and trusted a bit more but maybe we were right not to trust because by the 1980s, the government was encouraging everyone to look out for number one.'

Liverpool's docks would become important again, engendering more profit in the decade after 2010 than it ever has before, but it would never be the same. The Mersey came to terms with containerisation and the site at Seaforth flourished, with the annual tonnage initially increasing between 1991 and 1998 by 20 million tonnes. For that to be possible, though, Margaret Thatcher's Conservative government had quashed the National Dock Labour Board Scheme in 1989, an agreement which, after the end of decasualisation, had given registered dock workers jobs for life. When dockers went on strike nationally, the government offered each affected worker around a redundancy package of nearly £35,000. Though Liverpool's strike lasted longer than the rest, the tactic placed the future of all dockworkers in the hands of private firms and this preceded to the Torside walk-out in 1995 which began when five men were sacked and led to 500 more losing their jobs in one of the longest running strikes in history.

Nelson thought this dispute would blow over quickly but when Torside handed the strikers their notices for breach of contract, it went on, on and on. Nelson spoke of a 'sacred rule' in never crossing the picket line – 'Dockers before us had fought for better conditions and some had given their lives. We couldn't just go and throw away those rights and sell out on future generations.'

Twenty-two dock workers did, however, 'betray' the cause. 'Without going into much detail, but whenever anyone asks me about how this made me feel, I always say that they got the money but we got the city. What sort of life is that? Surely money is there to buy you freedom.'

For two and a half years, Nelson and hundreds of other dock workers stood in the wind, the rain and the cold knowing they were not taking home a wage. 'The duty when you're in dispute is to try and end it as soon as possible,' Nelson admitted. 'But then you get into a monotony and the longer it goes on the more gets said and the more difficult it becomes to end it. The first six months, there is a sense of independence: you've got no money but you're free. Then the economic reality sets in. Eighteen months in, stress levels became an issue. Five people died during the strike and another 50 have died since – all under 70.'

Nelson believed the strike succeeded in breaking down some social barriers. Dockers had previously been old-fashioned, rarely discussing their work or their problems at home. 'The strike changed everything,' he insisted. 'If we didn't explain the reasons behind the strike fully to our wives, we'd have been under pressure to go back. So, we had to get them involved in order to understand. They were absolutely brilliant.'

Suddenly, Nelson became emotional. He thought about his own wife, who drove him to the picket line every single day. Not long after the strike finished, she had died of cancer. He began to wonder: 'I'll never know whether stress had a role in what happened to her...' With that, Nelson looked away and fixed his gaze elsewhere, into the middle-distance. He would stop himself from speculating any more.

MY DAD WAS NOT A DOCKER BUT HE DID WORK FOR 33 YEARS IN THE same power station. Margaret Thatcher had been in charge of Britain for four of those years when I was born. I can remember my dad's reaction whenever she appeared on television. 'Not her again,' he'd say, reaching for the remote and pressing one of two buttons: mute or off. Hushed conversations would happen in the kitchen about redundancies and what might happen if Fiddlers Ferry closed down or fell into the hands of another company that wanted to make further cutbacks. Like every other major industry, Thatcher had denationalised the energy sector. Though big investors fired her economy, it came at the expense of workers and my dad was always hanging on. Though he just about did, it felt as though our existence was threatened.

We lived in a semi-detached house in Crosby. It was a middle-class looking home. My mum and dad were working class and had worked very hard. The issue of class never came up, though from the outside they'd probably have been viewed as lower middle-class by other families in Crosby, an affluent area seven miles north of Liverpool's city centre.

Between 1983 and 1997, Crosby had been controlled by a Conservative council led by Malcolm Thornton – one of the few in Merseyside. Above any other allegiance – even football – it was made clear to me that the only political party to follow was Labour. Yet Labour in Crosby from 1981 had fallen into third place, as residents turned away from a Michael Foot led leadership of the party and initially supported the Social Democrats. Shirley Williams had been one of the 'Gang of Four' Labour rebels who'd rejected Foot and in forming the Social Democratic Party (SDP), would take her constituency in Crosby from Labour. It was reflective of Tory dominance that before 1997, the best Labour could do in Crosby led to defeat five years earlier when Thornton maintained his control by taking nearly half of the vote.

In school, it had been an insult to describe 'yer ma' or 'yer da' as a docker. I have no idea why or where this started and I'm not sure it was used anywhere else in Merseyside but it did reflect, amongst other things, that by the start of the 1990s, dock working had become a trade of the past, certainly for families in Crosby, a town that must have felt a comfortable distance from the problem of unemployment. Waterloo separated Crosby from Seaforth and the enormous blue cranes of the new dock area pointed towards a different future, thus distancing those further down the coastline left wondering what to do next.

The politics of Crosby would change, however. No Conservative has come close to regaining Thornton's seat since 1997. The news in 2011 that all 90 members of the Crosby Conservative Club (essentially a snooker hall) had voted to de-affiliate themselves from the political party and rename the venue felt like the death notice for the Conservatives in Liverpool, a city which now feels like a no-go zone for the right.

It had not always been like this. In the 1959 local elections, when there were nine wards across Liverpool, six were led by the Conservatives and at least three were resolutely working class: Toxteth was Tory. Walton – though only briefly – was Tory. Wavertree was Tory. Sectarianism would largely explain this. Change came in the 1970s when Liverpool became Liberal and from there, the city swung between the parties.

The Liberals commitment to pavement politics during this period led to Labour losing voters and, in 1973, four Liberal seats became 48. When Militant then took control of Labour in 1983, indeed, the city council succeeded a Tory/ Liberal alliance. Thatcher had polarised the country by then and politicised so many people that many in Liverpool figured: 'I'm with Militant.'

Liverpool had been conspiratorial but never that radical a city, certainly not as much as Manchester, where Marx and Engels came and wrote about the living conditions of the working class. There was a transport strike in 1911 and a policeman's strike in 1919. Individuals like Jack Jones emerged as a leading politician and the unions slowly became more prevalent in working lives. Yet until the 1960s, Liverpool's dockers remained unorganised labour.

There had been a very individualistic trait in the people of Liverpool. Virtually everyone who came out of the city in the 1960s was a Tory – or not really bothered about Labour. The Beatles never spoke about politics, Ken Dodd was a Tory, Jimmy Tarbuck was a Tory. Leonard Rossiter was a rampant Tory. Though Cilla Black's brother was a communist councillor, when she married Bobby Willis, she became a Tory. Kenny Everett, who was educated in Crosby at St Bede's – the same school as both of my parents – later claimed that he was not really a Tory and rather a satirist but he did speak at a Tory rally in 1983, saying 'Let's bomb Russia,' before condemning Michael Foot. This was an era where class standing defined that if you had money in Liverpool, you were with the Tories.

For a common belief to emerge, there needed to be a fusion between an organised leadership with clear messages and a groundswell of resentment against the current authority. It was only by branding Liverpool entirely as a 'city possessed with a particularly violent nature' as Thatcher did the day after the Heysel disaster that the individual in Liverpool became the collective.

The history of modern politics in Liverpool is underpinned by the council being run by the opposite of whoever is in power. Even throughout most of New Labour, Liverpool was Liberal and it only became Labour again when the Conservatives took over nationally. For Liverpool, this meant it rarely had a champion of its cause in government. This reinforced the idea of it being an outside sort of place.

Part of me did wonder whether the death of Bill Shankly shifted Liverpool's political consciousness. It was only a few months after the riots in Toxteth. He had transformed Liverpool FC through his wisdom and deep socialist belief, though he never spouted Marx in a press conference and it never translated into a common thought of: 'I like this fella, let's vote Labour.' While others received honours for their achievements, Shankly did not and Liverpool only really came to think about that after his passing, thus heightening an anti-establishment sentiment.

In the same year, Norman Tebbit had told workers to 'get on their bikes'. Because of Liverpool's reputation for labour discord, a perception had already developed by then of its workers being idle – a perception that was perpetuated throughout the rest of the decade as the disharmony intensified. Yet the 1980s would see Liverpool's population decrease with many workers moving to other cities to find jobs. Liverpudlians, in reality, had passed Tebbit's test but in other places they were met with the sort of resentment that Poles or Romanians feel now.

Liverpool was always on the television. Impressions were beamed to a wider audience through dramas like *Boys' from the Blackstuff* and *Bread*. *Shirley Valentine* presented the Liverpudlian romantic, as did *Educating Rita*, though the latter was filmed in Dublin rather than Liverpool. *Brookside* would arrive with a harder more day-to-day edge: a constant reminder of how things supposedly were, only with an increased level of dramatic intensity to catch the viewers. At the start of the decade, the reading of Scousers had still been quite positive and Liverpudlians would play up to the reputation. John Lennon's death in 1980 seemed like both the end of a purer time and the start of something murkier. By the 1990s, the view of Liverpool had completely changed. What happened and the resulting media coverage of Militant, Heysel and Hillsborough presented the city in a darker light. Shifts in alternative comedy had a major role as well. In the 1970s there had been Irish jokes, Pakistani jokes and sexist jokes. The emergence of left-wing humour through satirists like Ben Elton began to challenge the acceptance of such supposed humour. This left a big gap in the market. Scousers in the main were not black or Asian – not the standard Jim Davidson target. Instead, they were robbing and lazy. If this was ever contested, Scousers also became sensitive and whingy – 'where is the famous Scouse sense of humour?' they'd ask – and this suppressant enabled the stereotype to endure.

The 1980s proved to be a defining decade in Liverpool's history, a city with a lifeblood in its docks. In writing this book, it became clear that Liverpool's problems were mounting before 1979 – the year Thatcher was elected. Liverpool, it is fair to say, needed help but her ascendancy brought a new set of opposing values. Thatcher possessed a fundamental distrust in the power of government and at the expense of state intervention believed in the primacy of competition and a free market.

This compounded Liverpool's position. How were an already deeply suspicious workforce supposed to react? What happens to a city when its existence breeds from one industry and that industry is told to lay down and change? Thatcher's government, it turned out, did discuss plans for Liverpool and in 2011, it was revealed that the city was targeted for 'managed decline'. Those still in a physical condition to speak about the memo, which was sent from the office of Geoffrey Howe – who was Thatcher's longest-serving cabinet minister – denied his suggestion evolved into a coherent plan. That Liverpool would fall the furthest of any urban area under Thatcher suggests otherwise. On her death in 2013, crowds would gather at the Casa, spilling outside onto Hope Street. They toasted the moment by drinking milk and setting off fireworks. The celebrations would carry until the next morning.

1

Looking After
Number One

'I'LL TRY NOT TO FART,' LORD TEBBIT PROMISED, WHEEZING WICKEDLY as I placed a recording device between one of his frail limbs and the quilted arm of his comfy chair as he sat in the study of his home in Suffolk. The cellar in Tebbit's townhouse dated back to 1080 when a fire ripped through Bury St Edmunds and though his mansion was re-built in a mock-Georgian style, the area was ecstatically bucolic. Nearby was a white hotel covered in ivy with a plaque on the wall announcing proudly that Charles Dickens once stayed there and the surrounding cobbled roads and lanes were restored with names like Angel, Athenaeum, Chequer and Hatter. There was a stillness, an impressive collection of red post boxes and old signs in the main square pointing towards Ipswich, Stowmarket and Sudbury in one direction, then Yarmouth, Mildenhall and Thetford in the other, as if they were the ends of the earth. In the ruins of the abbey in the shadow of the cathedral, a medley of conkers and berries lay scattered across the gravely footpaths and rare species of bird cackle in the aviaries. Not far away someone was roasting chestnuts and its bouquet filled the autumn air. Thankfully, poisonous gasses from Tebbit's study did not.

Bury St Edmunds is a long way from Liverpool and it was quite a distance from this Conservative politician's roots in north London – where he was known simply as Norm. He was keen to explain his family's heritage was, in fact, in East Anglia where the Tebbits worked as farmers and bell ringers or, the 'original rock stars', as he put it in a reedy quasi-Cockney twang. Nearly 88 years old, he walked unaided but was shrunken with a hunch and his skin was pallid. He was dressed smartly but with colours and shades that clash. There was an unavoidable turquoise V-necked jumper, the checked shirt, the green tie, the cream trousers, the mustard socks and the heavy brown shoes. In front of his eyes were enormous glasses which filled half of his face. His interest in art seemed to be limited to impressions of fighter planes, of which there were a dozen or so in the magnificent hallway. He introduced himself by pointing upwards at a Spitfire. 'A government's first duty is to defend its country's shores,' he warned, appearing to relish the challenge.

Tebbit's wife was upstairs in bed. She had sustained debilitating injuries from an IRA bomb blast in Brighton, meant for the other Margaret in Tebbit's life – Thatcher – at the Conservative Party conference in 1984. She was now suffering from dementia. All of this made Tebbit seem vulnerable. Yet he remained a Thatcherite bogeyman – a nationalist who voted for Brexit – someone who was keen to remind me that he still possessed, 'a very, very, very right-wing view,' which made me wonder how many verys you needed to reach extremism.

In his post front-line political career, Tebbit had condemned gay marriage and celibacy, saying, 'There's Ted Heath. He was celibate. But Ted wasn't a raving queer.' He denounced western aid to Africa, believing it went 'down in the same sink of iniquity, corruption and violence'. In November 2016, when Home Secretary Amber Rudd decided not to instigate an inquiry into the Battle of Orgreave, Tebbit praised her, describing a potential inquiry as something that 'could have been used as a stick with which to beat the Thatcher government', a government of which he was a major part at the very beginning.

It was right at the end of Thatcher's final term as Prime Minister, indeed, when he proposed a cricket test to determine whether immigrants were supportive of England or their native countries, a test he believed would then show whether they were significantly integrated into the United Kingdom. By then, he had become a hate figure of the British left. He was the Chingford skinhead, a union smasher and the scourge of state dependence. A *Spitting Image* character reflected his thuggish notoriety.

'It helped me enormously, particularly with young people undecided by the left,' Tebbit beamed. 'I owe a great deal to my creators at that show. They didn't intend it to be complimentary. I was the bovver boy – leather jacket; looking after Thatcher. I remember one programme where she was there with the French president of the day, Mitterrand. They were in the cab of a truck, struggling for the wheel. I was there and resolved it by bringing out a knuckle duster and sorting Mitterrand. I was always presented as being on the winning side…'

'I'd been up north of Merseyside one Saturday night when [John] Major was prime minister, poor little Major,' he suddenly remembered – Major being Thatcher's successor and pro-EU. 'I was coming back on the train and discovered there was no first class dining car. I needed something to eat so I wandered up to the buffet car and it was full of Millwall supporters… not only that but they'd lost that afternoon. They were a fairly sort of bolshie lot and I was waiting in the queue for my British Rail sarnie and half a bottle of red when one of them recognised me. It started with, "Hey Norm, where's you're jacket?" Interestingly, they started on at me at Major's proposal to privatise British Rail. I informed them it was right to privatise it but it would be a balls up because he'd been told by boys in Brussels that he'd have to split the ownership of the track. It would not work unless you had the ownership of the two under the same management because the responsibility would be in one place. I can't say I was winning the argument but we were having a sensible discussion. All of a sudden, there was a shout: "Norm, you're right mate." I said, "Of course I'm right, what's convinced you?" This bloke shouted back, "They've just ran out of fucking beer… only a nationalised fucking pub could run out of fucking beer on a fucking Saturday night."'

Tebbit used a wolfish smile whenever he wanted to emphasise something, but particularly whenever he swore.

'… after retiring to my compartment and then getting off the train at St Pancras, I was again surrounded my Millwall supporters on the concourse. I was a relatively elderly gentleman with a long blue coat, glasses and briefcase. Their leader said, "We're going to escort you to your car, Norm." I told them I didn't have a car waiting for me. "Then we shall escort you to your cab then…" You see, Norm the leather jacket wearing *Spitting Image* character had carried me through. I was one of them. I think that was one of the reasons we managed politics rather well when I was in a position to influence it.'

Tebbit talked about himself as a sort of everyman but Millwall were not everybody's sort of club. Like Tebbit, its Bushwhacker hooligan firm was white, aggressive and British. He had been born into a poor working-class family. I wondered what made him Conservative. He will always be associated with the 1980s but it became clear that the defining decades in Tebbit's consciousness were the 40s and 50s.

red his throat, as if this were a rehearsed speech. 'My grandfather came to make his fortune because he was not the eldest son and he did not .... family farm in East Anglia,' he explained. 'He died as a result of a traffic accident where he was tipped out of his pony and injured. I construe that he broke his ribs, caught pneumonia and that was that. The family was left in very difficult circumstances but that was made no easier when my father and his younger brother volunteered to join the Middlesex Regiment in the First World War. They were at Ypres and the Somme. It enormously damaged both of them and my mother had to take the decisions that needed to be taken thereafter because my father was not capable of doing so. I won a scholarship to go to grammar school in Edmonton. This was during the Second World War and fortunately, I received exceptionally good teaching. I gradually realised by the time I was 13 or 14 that I was instinctively anti-collectivist. I felt that I wasn't particularly tribal. I wanted to do things my way and was not prepared to go along with a consensus for which I was not part. I went in my direction. Some of it was enforced. The consensus was, to get on in the world you had to go to university. Well, that path was closed to me so I had to find another one. I went down the anti-collectivist path even to the extent of being a single-seat fighter pilot.'

During the 1945 general election, Tebbit stood as the Conservative candidate in his school form and lost. A year later, the Young Conservatives were formed and he entered the political arena in Enfield. Iain Macleod was standing in Enfield North, a man who according to Tebbit was 'from the right of the Tory right,' and someone who 'would have later got rid of Heath and seen things in a much more sensible light', had he not died in 1970.

Aged 16, Tebbit became a journalist at the *Financial Times* and two years later, he was called up by for military service. There was one occasion in 1954 when he had to break open the cockpit canopy of a Meteor 8 to escape it, fracturing two vertebrae. But he did not see combat. It was his later experience with British Overseas Airways Corporation (BOAC) that left him convinced that socialism did not work for him.

'I had an enormous sympathy for the management, in that they were not in a position to manage the assets for which they were responsible because of union power,' he explained. 'It leads to bad decisions, socialism. It leads to decisions taken on a political basis.' It became apparent that despite Tebbit's reputation for possessing forthright views, he still had a parliamentary knack for talking in smartly constructed sentences while not necessarily answering the question. He would lead on to a story about James Callaghan, the Labour Prime Minister who Thatcher knocked out of the way.

'I had a very strange friendship with him,' Tebbit admitted. 'He sometimes used to invite me to go back to his room in Westminster when we sat late as we did in those days, when the House of Commons was a full time place rather than part time as it is now with family friendly hours. He would sometimes ask me questions over a bottle of whisky. One evening he asked my advice about the prospects for an aircraft which was going to be produced by British Aerospace, which was state-owned. Jim said, "What do you think about the commercial prospects for it?" I said that it was a lovely looking aeroplane and I'd like to fly it but it would never make profit because it wouldn't sell enough. It was behind the times. The American DC-9 and the Boeing 727 had been in production. The market was already being filled and he said, "Yes, you're probably right – but it's difficult for me..." Helene Hayman sat for Hatfield, which was a marginal Labour seat, and this decision would impact on a lot of people within her community. A few weeks later, a decision was announced and Labour went ahead with it. Jim came up to me in the corridor by the library that day and said, "Seen the decision, Norman?" I said, "Wrong one I'm afraid." He said, "Yes, I think you're right but what else could I do?" That's the corruption – not in a financial sense of course because Jim Callaghan was a very considerable guy in my judgement. But it eats into making decisions on political grounds for political advantage as opposed to taking them on primarily economic grounds.'

Tebbit explained what he saw as 'the ridiculousness of socialism': 'Public ownership undermines respect for property,' he fired off. 'People in public housing may well neglect their property... somebody else's job to make sure they're looked after. When they become owners of property themselves, they look after that property.'

With the exception of Nigel Lawson, Tebbit was the only member of Thatcher's first cabinet still engaged in public life, still carrying the torch of Thatcherism, for which he defined by the roots of those leading the government.

'I think you have to look at where Thatcher came from to understand what Thatcherism was. Daughter of a lower middle-class shop keeper from middle England, devout non-conformist Christian and a scientist who'd actually worked as a scientist. She was on the team that created soft ice cream: her great gift to the nation. If you take those three things together you could usually see which way she was going to react to any issue. They were the three pillars that guided her. The scientist in her particularly was strong. I remember her saying in a cabinet meeting one day that the conversation was going off the rails. She was the only woman in the cabinet. "Gentlemen," she said, "shall we have the facts first and the discussions afterwards? It leads to better decisions." That was her way of doing things. She could be difficult to manage at times because she didn't have a particularly robust sense of humour. She was naïve. She didn't see double-meanings. We'd brief her ahead of PMs questions when she was the leader of the opposition and she'd be determined to make a point regardless of the consequences. It was left to me to say, "No Margaret, you can't say that." "Why can't I say that?" "Because they'd all laugh…"'

Tebbit says he did not really get to know Thatcher until he and a number of other Tories decided it was time to remove Heath as the party leader, 'because he was bloody useless'.

'All sorts of cabals were meeting as dining groups and I belonged to one or two of them. We had to sort Heath out. There were a number of people whose names were being carted around as potential successor to Heath. Airey Neave asked me what I thought and I was pretty damn puzzled. He said, "Why don't you talk to Margaret Thatcher?" I admitted that I hadn't really thought about her. This was 1970 – a woman leading a major political party? Everyone assumed it would happen at some time but it was almost certain that it would be a left-wing party, Barbara Castle leading Labour for example. The idea of the Conservative Party doing it was odd.'

Tebbit concluded Thatcher 'was the only one'. 'Principally because of her clarity of thought. Secondly because of her open-mindedness to ideas which hadn't occurred to her which she would then look at dispassionately.'

Tebbit joined Neave's 'little group' – a group referred to by Julia Langdon, a Labour journalist, as 'the Gang of Four.' During the Second World War, Neave had been the first British prisoner to succeed in escaping from Colditz and later worked for MI9. He was the Shadow Secretary of State for Northern Ireland when he was blown up and killed by the IRA outside the House of Commons in 1979, two months before Thatcher was elected.

'We became devoted to the idea of getting Margaret as party leader and then, for her to take the country. From there, things really did happen.'

*

TWO DAYS BEFORE POLLING COMMENCED IN THE 1979 GENERAL election, Ken Dodd was attacked as he campaigned for the Conservative Party on the streets of Speke, a tangle of council estates down near the airport where the city's slum clearances were rehoused twenty years earlier.

Though the Tories had controlled pockets of Liverpool earlier in the decade, the mood – partly due to the decline of the docks – had since changed. 'Ken Dodd was not tickled pink when he led a Tory showbiz campaign to Speke Market,' the *Liverpool Echo* reported playfully. 'The King of Knotty Ash' and his entourage had been kicked, punched, pushed and kneed, with an official complaint from the Conservatives being made to the police and the office of Garston Labour candidate Eddie Loyden. The party of twelve Conservative campaigners also had posters ripped from their van while hecklers shouted them down with loudhailers only feet from their faces. In his letter to the former dockworker, Loyden, the Conservative candidate Malcolm Thornton – a river pilot – claimed that 'Mr Dodd was subjected to the most vicious abuse I have had in fifteen years of election campaigning'. Loyden responded by insisting he was not at the demonstration. 'This is the sort of trivia the opposition tries to divert from the real issues,' he said. 'I don't believe my supporters had anything to do with it.'

Liverpool was simmering but over the next 48 hours, there would be more reminders that the city was not quite as aligned politically as it is now. Dodd may have felt the wrath of Speke but each of Liverpool's daily newspapers felt confident enough to tell its readers Labour's time was over and that Thatcher's Conservative party presented the way forward.

To understand how influential a regional newspaper could be – particularly in Liverpool – a history lesson is necessary. The *Liverpool Daily Post* had been running for 124 years by then. It had originally been printed to rival the *Liverpool Mercury*, a paper which had supported the successful bid by Thomas Colley Porter to become Liverpool's mayor in 1827, an election which parliamentary historian Margaret Escott described as being 'most expensive, venal and violent contest' ever. Porter would beat Nicholas Robinson by just fifteen votes. It was later found that Porter and Robinson had spent as much as £10,000 each in their attempts to gain office. After three electioneers were prosecuted and disenfranchised for bribery, Robinson was elected as mayor unopposed the following year.

The *Mercury* would eventually merge with the *Post* whose financiers by then had already started printing the *Liverpool Echo* as a cheaper evening edition to the morning *Post* out of the same city centre office building under the umbrella of Trinity Holdings. Until 1979 it had claimed to be centre left but it was more centre than left in its stance. Perhaps its editors could see which way the wind was blowing. No paper really wants to end up on the losing side. Both the *Liverpool Daily Post* and the *Liverpool Echo* supported Thatcher's Tory crusade.

It is unimaginable now that any would-be leader Conservative or otherwise would take the time to reply to readers' questions in any provincial newspaper but they did then, with the *Echo* leading on the challenge from Thatcher. Callaghan described Labour as 'a good friend to Merseyside' and called for loyalty to his cause, and sounded out a warning: 'The alternative is frightening, the Tories and their allies would begin immediately to axe all help for industry. Their philosophy of greed calls for the survival of the fattest – and that means a very thin time for areas like Merseyside.' Thatcher, meanwhile, did not refer to Liverpool directly at all in any of her answers, vowing instead to free Britain from 'overbearing state domination'.

The eve of the election reflected clearest the editorial standpoints. In the *Echo's* comment section under the headline of 'Time to get Britain moving again' Callaghan's Labour regime was castigated and he was described as a 'wheeler-dealer'. It remembered the previous months, the winter of discontent, when Britain faced the biggest industrial strike since 1926; when factories were brought to a standstill and thousands were laid off because the dead lay stored in rows because they could not be buried; when patients were denied the hospital attention they needed; when urban centres were overflowing with rotting rubbish. 'Where was the thrustful Mr. Callaghan then?' the *Echo* asked – and it is worth emphasising there was no byline on this and so, it must have been a sort of collective view. Callaghan had been in the Caribbean at the time of this crisis. 'For all the impact he had on the situation, he might as well have stayed there,' the *Echo* decided, accusing him of maintaining a low profile in the face of 'near-anarchy'. He had delayed an election before he was defeated in the commons – 'he wanted to put last winter as far behind him as possible... but we mustn't allow ourselves to be diverted.'

'It is the Tory party which is the party of change and Labour which offers the status quo,' the *Echo* continued. '... there is no reason why a Tory government should not be able to bring about reforms such as clear guidelines to control picketing and encouragement of postal ballots over industrial action – which could reduce the chances of wildcat stoppages and the sort of gross abuses we suffered last winter.' Its conclusion was less of a question and more of an answer. 'Do we really want another five years of the same – or even more socialist policies or is it time for a freer and less bureaucratic approach?'

That morning, the *Post* – a paper which had specialised in business matters, had been even more emphatic in its backing. One lengthy column entitled 'A vote for a better way' stated that Callaghan would have retired by now in any other form of employment. It felt a need to outline its position and sense of responsibility: 'The *Daily Post* is an independent newspaper. It has no alliance with any particular party. It is concerned with policies, which will benefit the nation in general and this region in particular.' Unusually, then, the column did not mention Thatcher's view on state intervention. Surely any newspaper that was able to reflect what was happening in Liverpool efficiently would have even then been able to assess the landscape and realise the city needed help rather than cutbacks to get its economy rolling again?

Instead, there was this: 'Before 1964 the Conservatives had 13 years in office and they were years of economic growth. Since 1964 Labour had provided the government for 12 years out of 15 and during this period unemployment has topped one and a half million and growth has been minimal, leaving us far behind our competitors. It is matters such as this which should concentrate the minds of the voters.'

'The state, insatiable, hacks away handsome slices from the rewards of corporate or individual achievement and distributes them among those who have failed to make it; this socialism is getting a bit out of hand,' it concluded. 'The *Daily Post* believes that today, as in 1964 and 1970, there is a strong desire for change, for something new and more invigorating, more challenging and more rewarding. Edward Heath failed to fulfil those hopes, Margaret Thatcher may be more successful. The *Daily Post* believes that she should be given that opportunity.'

The *Daily Post* would get their wish. 'IT'S MAGGIE,' was the front page headline on Friday 4 May, the report stating that 'Merseyside turned right with the Tories along with the rest of Britain', because Labour votes had been reduced, leaving casualties in Ellesmere Port and Garston, where Malcolm Thornton – supported by Ken Dodd – beat Eddie Loyden.

Caution came from Bob Parry, Labour's man in the Scotland Road area. His majority was down on 1974 but the three other contestants from the Conservatives,

Communists and Liberals lost their deposits and this reflected a wider reality: that Liverpool remained overwhelmingly Labour in spite of Conservative gains. 'I give warning to Mrs Thatcher from the Merseyside trade union movement that we are not prepared to put up with policies which will, in fact, mean a reduction in the living standards of people on Merseyside,' Parry said.

There was no whiff of concern in *Daily Post*. By the Saturday morning there was another triumphant headline. Under, 'Lady, You're the Greatest' came details of Thatcher's first cabinet which 'which will help put Britain on course for prosperity in the Eighties'.

Two years later, Norman Tebbit was in that cabinet.

BACK IN BURY ST EDMUNDS, AS MID-MORNING DRIFTED INTO afternoon, it became clear that all of the most right-wing views a man could have were possessed by Tebbit. He gave the impression that he enjoyed being interviewed by someone who might have opposing feelings about an important subject instead of someone who actually agreed with him. When I suggested he revelled in confrontation, he nodded zealously, but stressed this applied to Thatcher too, which explains why she gave him challenging roles, like in the autumn of 1981 when he became the Secretary of State for Employment just at the point where unemployment figures had tipped three million for the first time in British history.

Tebbit was also one of few people who dared stand up to Thatcher and told her when she was wrong. When she successfully negotiated a third term in 1987, she was more popular than ever before according to the vote. By then, according to Tebbit, her judgement was beginning to slide.

'When a Prime Minister first goes in to number 10 and the door closes behind, he or she turns back and the windows tend to be big,' he said. 'I think the windows get smaller as the years pass – there's a natural mechanism which militates against a Prime Minister being in office for eight to ten years consecutive years. The other thing that happens is that there are more and more people on the government backbenches who have been ministers and have been dropped. There are more and more on the back benches who have been ambitious to be in government but have never been asked. There are fewer and fewer on the back benches still with hopes of getting into government. The arithmetic is steadily moving against the PM. Under those circumstances Prime Ministers tend to become more defensive and aggressive. They tend to look more and more for people who will tell them what they want to hear.

'There was a fairly outspoken discussion between us where I made it plain to her that I would always do the job that she asked and if she didn't want me to do it, I would go away. But while she gave me the responsibility for an aspect of policy I would be grateful if she took advice from me and not from outsiders. Prime Ministers who are losing their grip tend to look to outsiders for answers.'

Tebbit took a pause, stood up and slowly wandered over to the shelf behind him. He reached for a heavy book bound in blue cloth. It was Thatcher's memoir, released in 1993. On the title page, beside the name Margaret Thatcher, the title 'Downing Street Years' and the Harper Collins logo, there was a message with a line from the second verse of a Rudyard Kipling poem. 'But the Thousandth Man will stand your friend,' she wrote. 'With the whole round world agin' you.'

He stood there blankly for a moment like a proud foot soldier who'd always remained loyal to a cause. He had famously been described by Michael Foot as Thatcher's 'house-trained polecat'.

'I was a particularly hard pusher,' Tebbit suggested back in the comfort of his seat. 'We did have people like Keith Joseph who was a man of decency and fair-mindedness to the point that that he found it difficult to come to a conclusion for action. He would walk around and around a problem, constantly seeing it but without getting to the point of saying, "That's it." I became his minister of state for a year, essentially to look after him. He had an extremely good secretary who occasionally would come bursting into my office, saying "Minister – you've got to get up there to the Secretary of State's office; those bastards are just not fair to him." These were his colleagues. They'd wheel me in to stiffen dear old Keith up. It was not because he couldn't think things through but he didn't want to come to a point where he'd have to make a decision that would cause concern to some people. There was a German general who said, "The worst generals are those who seek to avoid casualties."'

Tebbit was not one of those generals. He may have presented Joseph as a gentle soul but in 2011, it was revealed that he and Geoffrey Howe had recommended to Thatcher 'the unpalatable truth' that Michael Heseltine, the Tory minister sent to Liverpool, was wasting his time trying to find investment for the city, particularly from the government. While chancellor Howe warned her not to waste money trying to 'pump water uphill' and said that Merseyside was 'much the hardest nut to crack', Joseph was assertive enough then to propose a 'managed rundown' of Liverpool. Later, his private secretary asked for minutes of a meeting to be amended to exclude mention of any potential economic regeneration. Joseph believed 'it is by no means clear that any such strategy could lead to a viable economic entity'.

In another one of those moments controlled by a sort of inner-officialdom, Tebbit came across rather coldly. He could not remember reading any such memo from Joseph and Howe and he claimed the clearest insight he'd had into Merseyside was from one of his wife's nurses, someone known within his family as 'Old Scouse.' It seems impossible that Tebbit would not be privy to these discussions considering unemployment levels in Liverpool were higher than anywhere else just at the time he was stepping into the role as the Secretary of State for Employment.

'I do know,' he said quietly, 'that Merseyside did not have – and I still don't think it has – as good a reputation for employers to go as other areas, particularly Tyneside.' He had been the minister that negotiated the contract with Toyota Datsun when they started making cars in the UK. 'I know that one of the things that influenced them in going to Tyneside were the popular tales about industrial relations and how they were more stable up there. In that sense, Liverpool had not helped itself since the decline in the North Atlantic shipping trade, which moved quite a lot of wealth from Merseyside.'

Tebbit accused union leaders in Liverpool and elsewhere of 'fomenting industrial sabotage'. He believed that 'the giants of the TUC had an unhealthy relationship with Moscow – where they went on paid holidays'.

I wondered whether the Conservatives had any sort of positive plan for Liverpool. He responded by suggesting that 'trying to rescue a drowning man that insists on putting his head under water is quite difficult'. He also believed that strikes in the 1970s as containerisation grew and labour diminished 'was also because containers are a lot more difficult to steal from…'

'You couldn't dragoon industrialists into going to places they didn't want to go to and in general, they didn't want to go there,' he said. 'Vauxhall as a typical GM subsidiary was happy in sticking around the Luton area, though the labour market was much tighter there and lots of other costs were higher.

Why would an industrialist go to an area where they felt like they were not wanted? That was the real difficulty. In Liverpool, I thought there was an element of being anti-the-rest-of-the-country. That may have in part been influenced by immigration from Northern Ireland as well as the south of Ireland. There was a bit of grievance culture.'

It became clear he did not rate Michael Heseltine as a politician, the one-nation Tory who did his best to try and help Liverpool. He had been a threat to Thatcher because he was popular. Again, Tebbit would offer insight but not necessarily the insight relating to the question when asked whether Heseltine was allowed to go to Liverpool because Thatcher thought he would fail there, knowing it would impact on the way he was viewed and ultimately make it less likely that he could take the leadership from her.

'He didn't always conform to the Thatcher doctrine of facts first and discussion afterwards. This meant that people would switch off from what he was saying. Heseltine is what I call a one-ball juggler, which is why he was good in London on the docklands issue where he went at it methodically and clearly when it came to overcoming the barriers for regeneration. He did some good in that way too in Liverpool. But to be a really successful politician you have to be a multi-ball juggler and if someone throws you an extra ball you have to decide whether to take that one or drop one of the others. Michael was limited in this sense because he'd try and take one more ball and drop a few others in the act.'

Heseltine's arrival in Liverpool came in the aftermath of the Toxteth riots and there is more about how race, policing and unemployment caused this in the next chapter.

'It was criminality as far as I was concerned,' Tebbit said narrowly. 'I didn't have very much as a kid. I knew what it was to stay quiet because the rent man was knocking at the door when we didn't have the money to pay the bills. My instinct wasn't to go and smash the shop windows. My instinct was to do something to earn the money to pay the rent. So, I got up early every morning and delivered the local newspapers and *Radio Times*. Then on a Sunday I would go around and collect the money for the newsagent. This would help pay what needed to be paid. Which way is more likely to create wealth? Smashing things up? If I remember there was a picture of Toxteth with three shops in a row. The middle one was a book shop untouched. One was an off licence and the other was a food store, both looted. Come on...'

The riots prompted Tebbit's infamous 'On yer bike' speech at the Conservative party conference in Blackpool later in 1981 where he again stared inwardly for answers rather than listening. During the Depression of the 1930s, his father had not rioted but instead 'got on his bike and looked for work – and he kept looking 'til he found it'.

Contrary to popular opinion, Liverpudlians were not work shy. In fact, they heeded Tebbit's message to the point where the city's population almost diminished by half in the years after his speech, leading to campaigns in towns like Bournemouth where John Butterfill, a Tory MP, described Scousers as 'drop-outs pursuing parasitical lifestyles' for living off the area and taking the jobs of locals. One Bournemouth suburb became known as 'Boscombe bedsit land' because of the number of Liverpudlians living there but Tebbit did not see a flaw in his theory because 'capital and labour has to be free to go to where it can to get the best return', though that view did not extend to immigrants according to this arch-Brexiteer.

As I left, he showed me three more artefacts. The first was a Christmas card from a friend who had married a Caribbean lady, which for some reason he kept on his mantelpiece all year round. 'I'm dreaming of a white Christmas,' the card read, with a quotation from the pregnant black woman in the photograph. 'Yes darling, but think of the children.' The second was a sketch from the *London Evening Standard* in 1985 where two skinheads were walking past a billboard. 'Tebbit warns on violence' the billboard said, with the skinheads responding, 'I wouldn't like to meet him on a dark night.'

Finally, he reached into his bookcase again. 'There,' he said pulling out *Constitution of Liberty* by Freidrich Hayek, the economist whose Monetarist views underpinned Thatcherism. Tebbit explained that he only read it in hospital when that IRA bomb in Brighton changed the course of his life and that of his wife. He would retreat from the political front line and even then, he did not have the patience to 'plough all the way through this fellow, Hayek'.

Like Thatcher's memoir, the book was inscribed but only with a signature. 'I'm not sure whether even Thatcher sat down and read him from page to page,' Tebbit admitted. 'But she did listen to him through Minford. She was definitely influenced by Minford.'

*

PATRICK MINFORD WAS SALIVATING AT THE POSSIBILITIES OF BREXIT when I met him at the beginning of 2018 in the warmth of a Westminster coffee shop near the Home Office, where four protestors outside in the cold held placards denouncing the deportation of refugees. 'Look at them,' Minford observed without having to say anything else to reflect what he thought. Instead, he preferred to try and explain why he thought a departure from the European Union presented similar economic opportunities to those in 1979 when Margaret Thatcher embraced Monetarism and sent the country spinning on a new economic path.

It had seemed a good topic with which to engage him at the beginning of an interview. He immediately came alive, jolting forward from his seat which was placed near a doorway where businessmen and their chins nuzzled into the breasts of their long coats brought with them a winter draft as well as the exhaust fumes from the engines of London buses and Hackney cabs as they screeched past.

'It will be tremendous,' he predicted briskly. 'The EU is a very backward-looking institution. It's protectionist. It's idea of regulation is to store everything in sight. It's precautionary driven. It's quite interventionist. There are lots of what I would call socialist objectives in regulation. And, of course, it also has this peculiar thing where it insists that anybody can go anywhere. It's got the trappings of an empire, really. It's incredibly unpopular with a lot of countries including this one. It's behind the times. It's not pro-technology either really. There are lots of technologies that the EU are attempting to slow down. Medicine too. So, I think to be free of that is going to be very good. Britain has always been a free-trade country really and that's going to be restored while also taking control of our borders, which is very important.'

Minford was 74. He looked like a traditional banker. What was left of his white hair was swept away from his face. He wore a pair of black thick-rimmed glasses. His pinstripe shirt was pale blue and white, his tie burgundy and his heavy woollen scarf tartan in pattern. His voice was rasping and his accent was difficult to place. He was originally from Shrewsbury, he had studied at Oxford, he had worked at Whitehall, Washington DC and the former British colony of Malawi before moving to Liverpool and Cardiff, cities where he held key academic positions. You could imagine him as a long-term expat in a country that scarcely understood him as much as he did not understand it. He had a habit of smiling incongruously, particularly whenever he attempted to emphasise a point he believed to be important, perhaps an attempt to convince that his way of thinking was correct.

There was otherwise, however, a casualness in the way he led discussions around his specialist subject. He released an enormous laugh when delivering economic conclusions even if they had severe consequences, as if nothing was really that serious to him but numbers. He gave the impression that so long as the British economy was booming, it did not matter to him how many people really benefited even if the margin between the rich and poor was grotesquely substantial. Beneath the eccentric avuncular exterior was a hard-line right-wing Thatcherite.

Even Nigel Lawson, who was Thatcher's financial secretary for the treasury for the first two years of her first term, described Minford in his autobiography as an economist from 'the radical right', confirming him as being one of the Monetarists she listened to the most. Ian Gilmour, another member of Thatcher's first cabinet, described Minford as 'militantly monetarist'. Gilmour was later cast aside for not being zealous enough and was subsequently decried as a wet. Though Minford, as a treasury advisor, remained highly influential he largely operated in the shadows, living largely in blissful anonymity, untroubled by the turbulence in the city that offered him work, Liverpool.

It had been Minford's 'Liverpool Model' that brought him to Thatcher's attention. He was appointed at Liverpool University as a professor of economics in 1976. He was incredibly young, just 33 – leading a group of more experienced lecturers and a younger team of researchers from an old building long since demolished, which looked more like a Victorian school than a place that would prove to be the setting which recalibrated the future.

Minford described the financial landscape of the country then as 'such a mess – based on bad ideas, bad practices and terrible institutions. They all had to be recreated. We had to restore markets to get taxes down. We had to get rid of union power and create new industries while persuading people to work in them even though they weren't as well paid as before.'

Monetarist ideology formed the basis for Minford's model, a system which 'allowed people to do what they wanted rather than being told by the unions, cartels, big businesses, governments or regulation'. Instead, as Minford put it, 'you let the markets work – you don't create inflation by allowing governments to spend too much'. He would speak about 'the British disease', which he immediately targeted simply as too much state intervention but when pressed a little harder he dismissed as 'socialist ideas', citing that, 'the worst example of the British disease was in Liverpool which like the rest of the country had become very inward looking, obsessed with things like the NHS and the redistribution of wealth' after the Second World War.

Central to the Liverpool Model was 'rational expectation', an ingredient that leaned on human instinct, trusting that 'if you give people clear information about the environment they're operating in and if you leave them alone, they're smart. They'll do their stuff.'

It was a conclusion with populist appeal – that the little man knew best – one developed from John Muth, another academic from Pittsburgh who published a paper in 1961 about pig farmers in the American Midwest, where he discovered that the industry was not at the whim of country idiots but instead skilled and knowledgeable tradesmen who knew their market well enough to judge what to do to survive and sometimes flourish. To Minford, this confirmed that most competitive businesses are often smaller but better organised.

Minford had been commissioned to write about his ideas in a selection of national newspapers including the *Guardian* when Keith Joseph contacted him for the first time in, 'oh, I don't know – around 1978. Keith introduced me to Mrs Thatcher. What did I think of her? She was wonderful – made of steel. A real look about her. I liked this thing, Thatcherism.'

Thatcher, though, was no economist. 'She was no economist at all,' Minford emphasised gleefully, because this was where he came in. 'She had been a chemist, of course. So, she had a sort of scientific brain. She tried very hard to understand it. Instinctively she was very cautious. We had seminars and endless long meetings. We'd discuss things and she'd shout at a lot of people. She liked that sort of thing because she didn't really trust her civil servants. A lot of the civil servants were in the old mould. They backed the unions, they preferred nationalisation, they wanted government controlling policy all of the time. She didn't really like them at all. She trusted me. She trusted Hayek too. She trusted monetarism.'

TO UNDERSTAND THE RATHER DRY CONCEPT OF MONETARISM AND to understand the direction which Liverpool and the rest of Britain was heading in 1979, you have to retreat to the Swiss village of Mont Pèlerin 33 years earlier. Across Lake Geneva from the more famous town of Montreux, beside the pure blue waters, the green forests and the white mountaintops, the resort was the unlikely birthplace of an economic counter-movement that would take the world by storm.

It could have been the setting of an Ian Fleming spy novel. The Hôtel du Parc is a Belle Époque style residence where the ceilings of the rooms are high, the beds are enormous and the views from the windows of the conference centre particularly give stunning views of the lake beneath it. World War Two had finished not two years before when forty or so Western intellectuals assembled here in the spring of 1947 to debate the possibilities of a new global direction.

At the end of their discussions, the scholars – amongst them, academics, economists and journalists – would release a statement of aims, highlighting the dangers faced by civilization. 'Over large stretches of the Earth's surface the essential conditions of human dignity and freedom have already disappeared,' it read gloomily. 'In others, they are under constant menace from the development of current tendencies of policy. The position of the individual and the voluntary group are progressively undermined by extensions of arbitrary power. Even that most precious possession of Western Man, freedom of thought and expression, is threatened by the spread of creeds which, claiming the privilege of tolerance when in the position of a minority, seek only to establish a position of power in which they can suppress and obliterate all views but their own.'

The Mont Pèlerin Society was born and Freidrich Hayek had been one of its creators. His collective belief was purely economical: that politics, indeed should be shaped by economics and not the other way around; that governments can only control inflation, ensuring a healthy economy, if they control the amount of money in circulation. Considering inflation resulted in money being less valuable, the only way to make money more valuable was to contain its availability. In real terms, this eliminated state support and if carried out ruthlessly, would destroy socialism.

Hayek remarked that the battle for ideas would take at least a generation to win. He and the Monetarists of Mont Pèlerin would wait frustrated for three decades, as the world – where millions of workers were radicalised by the experience of two World Wars – embarked on a new economic trajectory at the expense of big business and the wealthy.

By the mid-1960s, Richard Nixon, the soon-to-be President of United States, was once forced to concede that 'we are all Keynesians now'. John Maynard Keynes had been a British bisexual campaigner for women's rights who treated economics as a matter for ethical judgements. He recognised prosperity liberated people to make their own choices, that the proper aim of work was to provide leisure. The love of money for its own sake seemed to him 'a somewhat disgusting morbidity, one of those semi-criminal, semi-pathological propensities which one hands over with a kind of shudder to the specialists in mental disease'. Traditional capitalism 'exalted some of the most distasteful human qualities into the position of the highest virtues'.

Having seen his task as saving capitalism from itself, he died a year before the formation of Mont Pèlerin and would miss the period up until 1979 when Keynesianism became the dominant economic belief, where the will of market forces were diverted or eliminated through legislation laid down by both Labour and Conservative governments in Britain.

Unlike Marx, Keynes had not promoted a substitute for capitalism. For him, the problem was laissez-faire capitalism; that unfettered markets had the potential to devastate capitalism if they were left to the selfish pursuit of individual profit without consideration for the rest of society and this had been proven in the Great Depression of the 1930s and the global conflict that followed. Most trade union leaders, having to answer the concerns of Westminster and their rank and file, found Keynesianism a tolerable form of controlled capitalism. It was amidst this scene of thought that Europe re-built itself in the mid-twentieth century, affording the development and expansion of the welfare state.

Hayek contradicted Keynes in his work, *The Road to Serfdom*, where he anticipated a post-war world that would reach a nadir of capitalist ideology. 'The prospects for Europe seem to me as dark as possible,' he wrote. Instead of controlling the markets, Hayek believed they must be unfastened and left to the natural order of the 'invisible hand'. According to Hayek it was government interference in the money supply which amplified inflation and dampened corporate profits. Hayek insisted all such deviations warped the markets which built on misleading capital, led to a swing of extremes and ultimately unending crisis.

Hayek was a lanky, erect, tweed-wearing Viennese professor who insisted on being called 'Von Hayek'. As respect for Keynesianism began to rise, he had been recruited to the London School of Economics where he was surrounded, in his own words, by 'foreigners', 'Orientals of all kinds' and 'Europeans of practically all nationalities, but very few of real intelligence'.

Hayek spent a year as a visiting fellow at the University of Arkansas before moving to the University of Chicago where he played a pivotal role in transforming how Milton Friedman and others thought about how society works.

Friedman was a squat, bespectacled figure who was born in Brooklyn and studied in New Jersey, describing socialism as 'absurd', warning 'there ain't such thing as a free lunch' in a folksy Midwest drawl. He would also compare inflation to alcoholism, saying: 'When you start drinking, or when you [the government] start printing too much money, the good effects come first. The bad effects only come later.' The cure, according to Friedman, was the other way around – 'when you stop drinking or you stop printing money, the good effects only come later. That's why it's so hard to persist with the cure.'

Hayek would publish *The Constitution of Liberty* in 1960 where he claimed unrestricted entrepreneurs would create the wealth that would trickle down to everyone while creating a natural hierarchy of winners and losers – a more efficient system than could ever be designed though planning or by design. He implied that regulation, trade union activity or state provision – basically anything that delayed this course – was counter-productive. This marked the moment Hayek transitioned from holding an honest if extreme philosophy to someone who created a racket led by political lobbyists generously funded by multimillionaires who saw the dogma as a means of shielding themselves against democracy.

One of Hayek's most notable early supporters was Barry Goldwater, an American conservative who opposed the Civil Rights Act of 1964. He emerged as a favoured political philosopher of Ronald Reagan. Then came Margaret Thatcher, who had become the leader of the Conservative party in 1975 when she invited Hayek to a private 30-minute meeting at the Institute for Economic Affairs in London. Thatcher's staff would ask Hayek what he had thought. Sensing his opportunity to crush Keynes and restore the world according to his vision, he replied: 'She's so beautiful.'

The story goes that one of Thatcher's colleagues would soon attempt to explain what he saw as the fundamental 'middle-way' pragmatic principles of conservativism when she reached for her briefcase, snapped it open and pulled out a worn-out book before slamming it in on the table. 'This,' she announced sternly, 'is what we believe.' The book was *The Constitution of Liberty* and with that, Hayek's free-market philosophy and Thatcher's Victorian values collided – changing the world.

Hayek would fade into a benign philosopher king unable to compete with

Friedman on style due to his clumsy English and thick Austrian accent. In a war movie, Hayek would surely have made a perfect villain while the younger Friedman, with his enthusiasm and homespun way of relating his thoughts, related to more Western audiences and thus became a frenetic man of business, jetting from the lecture theatre to presidential suite, all but omnipresent in the newspapers and across TV screens.

Friedman visited Chile, advising the brutal military dictator Colonel Augusto Pinochet to move the country even further away from the free spending policies of Salvador Allende's left-wing government in order to control inflation. Great social unrest followed austerity but when Pinochet used electric shocks, waterboarding, beatings, sexual abuse and state murder to maintain his control as well as the economic line advised by the Chicago School, Friedman kept quiet, neither supporting or reviling the tyranny that his strategies helped unleash.

Five months after Thatcher was voted in as Prime Minister, Friedman had called for Britain to experience the monetarist 'shock treatment'. He would serve as an adviser to Thatcher from 1979 to 1990, describing her government at the beginning as a 'kind of experiment' before helping develop a free-market economy where state-owned industries were sold off and interest rates were raised to reduce the amount of money in circulation. Upon his death in 2006, Thatcher remembered Friedman as 'an intellectual freedom fighter'.

THOUGH MARGARET THATCHER ESTABLISHED THE PURITANICAL Conservative ideology for the 1980s and used foot-soldiers like Norman Tebbit to enforce it both within and beyond party lines, their politics was underpinned by a right-wing financial dogma that tended to explain most things that happened.

Milton Friedman had won the Nobel Prize for economics in 1976 and as he spread his message by hopping from one part of the globe to next like a scholastic celebrity, most of Thatcher's consistent support in pursuit of this dangerous fiscal pursuit came from a small faction of lower-profile British monetarists. Alan Walters became Thatcher's chief economic advisor on New Year's Day, 1981 and he – like Friedman – had been a sympathiser of Pinochet's Chile. Walters had been Minford's PHD supervisor. When meetings were held at Chequers, Minford was there.

Thatcherites accepted monetarist propositions as conclusive laws. In 1980, Sir Henry Phelps Brown, an economist who applied social science to his theories, was disturbed to find that Geoffrey Howe, the Chancellor of the Exchequer that advocated the managed decline of Liverpool, had 'treated monetarism not as one theory among others but as an unarguable principle like the law of gravitation'. Another treasury minister was even more confident. In the House of Lords, the minister likened monetarism to the simple truth that, 'If twice one is two, then twice two is four.'

Ian Gilmour and other 'wets' believed Thatcher's faith in Friedman and Minford was not based on profound knowledge, research or even consultation with the Bank of England. He revealed that Lord Rothschild used to refer to one of the more intellectual cabinet members with a penchant for forceful pro-monetarist observation as 'A-level economics.'

'Thatcherites had been frequently warned by moderate Conservatives of the dangers of slavishly following fashion and of wholeheartedly embracing economic doctrine,' Gilmour wrote. 'Just as Christian fundamentalists remain impervious to modern biblical criticism, the monetarist zealots in the new Conservative government did not allow irksome facts or the existence of differing monetarist sects to disturb their faith in the Chicago prophet.'

While Tebbit admitted that he did not care to read Hayek until 1984 and had boasted of propping up dear old Keith Joseph years before as he struggled to control those operating below him, Gilmour's view of Joseph was of someone who had undergone a conversion to a Thatcherite zealot, despite him serving previous Tory governments that had been different to this one.

'Belief in monetarism, it emerged, was now a prerequisite not only for controlling inflation but for being a real Conservative,' Gilmour added. He described Thatcher's first cabinet, '... with its complement of wets, dries, and those who were too intelligent, cautious, fearful or uncommitted to be either, was palpably not a happy and united body'. Jim Prior, who Tebbit succeeded as the Secretary of State for Employment, believed that the government from 1979 to 1981 was, 'the most divided Conservative cabinet ever', and this gained a response from Thatcher: 'As Prime Minister,' she said, 'I could not waste time having any internal arguments.'

Voices like Gilmour and Prior would be replaced by the Tebbits and the Minfords, who was described by Gilmour as 'the arch-monetarist' – the professor who suggested that over the three years between 1982 and 1984, real social security benefits should be reduced by 15 per-cent and the money saved used to cut income tax on lower-income taxpayers, 'in order to reinforce the incentive effect of reducing benefit'. Minford described unemployment to me as being, 'the biggest problem and the area we spent the most time working on'.

'We devised a lot of changes that needed to be made, particularly on unemployment benefit,' he remembered proudly. 'In the end, they didn't cut benefit as enthusiastically as we wanted them to but they did make it much, much tougher to get it. You had to get a job. It is people who work that should be rewarded not those who don't bother.'

It became clear that one of Minford's central beliefs was that for monetarism to drive on, unemployment needed to fall and for that to happen, the benefit system had to be quashed. 'We made it clear, "Look, you've got to reduce what you pay people when they're unemployed – or you've got to make it much tougher to get it, and give them more money when they're instead employed."'

The figures confirm that Minford did not find a solution. Initially, unemployment fell from 1,089,100 in May 1979 but that was before monetarism kicked in. By July 1986, unemployment had reached a peak of 3,133,200. Between August 1986 and the start of 1988, it would fall by half before rising to 1,763,000 in November 1990. By May 1992 it had risen again to 2,717,000. While Thatcher was in Downing Street unemployment was below two million for only 45 months. It was above three million for 26 months – a record. Even at its lowest in 1990, figures were fifteen per-cent higher than the Thatcher government had inherited.

Considering the percentage of all families with dependent children headed by lone parents had risen to fourteen per-cent and were almost double the proportion in 1971, it seems clear that the burying of state industry and the rocketing of unemployment contributed if not entirely explained the collapse of relationships in those communities that struggled the most. The consequence of this was the emergence of an underclass: a group paralysed by poverty to the extent that they retreated from the places they once thrived in, ultimately depriving them of the chance to participate in the supposed new freedoms Thatcher was so convinced by.

'Those who remain unemployed will be worse off,' warned Minford in 1981, before he released the most depressing of all his assertions as if it were a mission statement capable of convincing people. 'The decision to remain unemployed will be a voluntary one,' he said.

Monetarism was the Thatcherite equivalent of the Marxist materialist conception of history. As much as the dawn of socialism would transform social, political and economic relations, so too would the introduction of monetarism revolutionise the British economy and in doing so, it would profoundly alter the principles and positions of society.

Incentives to work are pointless unless there are opportunities to work. Thatcherites constantly claimed that under them choice in Britain would be unlimited and yet, providing greater choice does not automatically translate as greater access. Monetarism became popular because it promised to deliver a simple solution to the problems of inflation, the power of the trade unions and the decline of certain industries. It failed because the attempt to govern the growth of money was in conflict with the gradual deregulation of the financial system and the resultant growth of credit. This stimulated an exceptionally large, rapid and enduring rise in unemployment. With that came unprecedented social unrest.

In Liverpool, more than 50,000 people living inside its city boundaries were unemployed by 1981. A forecast by the City Planning department suggested that by 1986 this was likely to rise to a figure between 70,500 and 90,900, or between 32 per-cent and 41 per-cent across wider Merseyside. On that basis, an approximate grossing up of figures suggested that unemployment in some city wards would range between 60 per-cent and 80 per-cent by 1986.

In Liverpool, amongst those who took the time to assess Thatcher's economics, Minford became known as Professor Wrong. By 1983 there were eighteen unemployed candidates available for every managerial vacancy on Merseyside and more than 1,700 for each labourer's job.

Minford's dogmatic assumption that the labour market always straightens out – and therefore employment was, indeed, a voluntary decision – blotted out such dull facts from his vision, permitting him to go on contentedly lounging in theories which blamed the jobless for not discovering positions that did not exist.

By 1981, he had moved home across the River Mersey to Birkenhead, close to the ground of Tranmere Rovers Football Club. There, he received some threatening anonymous phone calls but going ex-directory was as dramatic as it got for him in Liverpool. Some weekdays, he would go for lunch in a pub on the northern fringes of Toxteth, where the Granby ward's male unemployment rates, at 39.3 per-cent, were the second worst in the city. From such a vantage point, Professor Minford might have been able to see what was coming next. 'The riots...' he pondered briefly without further need for discussion, copying Lord Tebbit: 'the work of criminals.'

2

Burn After Midnight

IT WAS A BROILING MID-SUMMER'S AFTERNOON AND JOE FARRAG was acting as the unofficial tour guide of Liverpool 8. As the wheels of the car rolled slowly up Granby Street passing underneath the green, white and red bunting that he'd attached between two wooden telephone poles on opposite sides of the road earlier that week to encourage residents in the area to celebrate a national holiday in Somaliland, he explained his heritage in detail and it would involve the sort of complexities that many of his neighbours could relate to.

Farrag's first name used to be Yussuf. His mother's Lancastrian family were Protestants, originally from Ireland. He was brought up a fully-fledged member of Liverpool's Orange Lodge. When Orangemen asked, 'What are you doing here?' during those marches on Upper Parliament Street, it was code for: 'You don't look like one of us.' This was because Farrag resembled his father, who was from an Egyptian village in the Nubian desert, close to Wadi Halfa on the Sudanese border. His identity would take on new meaning when he was told by a Jesuit scholar, as he gathered with his mates outside a nearby synagogue, that in Hebrew Yussuf translated as Joseph. It was around the time the Black Panther movement was gathering in popularity across Britain's black inner-city areas 'Everyone was changing their name to either Mohamed or Yussuf,' Farrag remembered. So, he did what Liverpudlians tend to do when something becomes popular: they do something else, something opposite. Yussuf became Joseph – or Joe.

To reach Liverpool 8 from the Royal Liver Building at the Pier Head, you pass the restored handsomeness of the Albert Dock and the busy warehouses of the Baltic Triangle before Chinatown appears out towards the left, where the streets have Cantonese names, scents of sesame oil emit from open doors, and a few luridly painted restaurants have ducks roasting in the front windows. At the top of a grassy slope stands the bloody sandstone of the Anglican cathedral, marking a ridge which overlooks all of Merseyside. There is a row of glorious Grade II listed Georgian townhouses named after James Gambier – a Royal Navy captain who fought in the American War of Independence and the French Revolution. John Lennon once lived there at number three. Behind that terrace is a square which has a history as a pick-up point for prostitutes. Then, there is the beginning of Liverpool 8.

Ethnic communities had been in the district for generations, arriving not because of slavery as it is commonly thought, but through shipping and the desire to work. Farrag's father had been one of those seamen to pass through the city's docks with aspirations of staying. Toxteth's black population had increased by the substantial recruitment of sailors from all parts of the British Empire and Commonwealth during the two world wars and, of course, by the process of unlimited immigration from Africa, the West Indies and the Indian sub-continent that prevailed until 1962.

Liverpool has been described as the world in one city but in Toxteth – or Liverpool 8, specifically the area called the Granby triangle – could be the world in one neighbourhood. In 1981, the much larger part of Liverpool 8 and Toxteth was west and south of Princes Avenue, back towards the old south docks. Princes Park, Brunswick and the Dingle was almost entirely white working-class population, with their own schools, separate shopping streets and distinct communities. To the west was Mill Street, with streets dropping steeply into derelict docks and the Mersey. On North Hill, the Dickens streets of Weller, Micawber and Dorrit were facing the bulldozer; meanwhile the Welsh Streets had their own residents' association who successfully opposed demolition and had encouraged the revitalisation of the terraces. Coaches stopped at Madryn Street for tourists to see the birthplace of Ringo Starr. Windsor Street, with its community centre, was known as the 'Holy Land' and had street names after David, Isaac and Jacob. Closer to the city, Brunswick bore the burden of tenements set up in seas of tarmac.

On the eastern boundary of Liverpool 8, Kingsley Road had a Catholic church and a Catholic school. In Liverpool 8 alone, there were more than 20 residents' associations, five of them in the Granby triangle. Strung along Upper Parliament

Street, or 'Parli', were the Charles Wooton Adult Education Centre, the Merseyside Caribbean Centre, Stanley House youth club, the Ibo club, the Ghana union social club, the Merseyside Somali Community Centre, the Sierra Leone social club, a Somali restaurant and a Nigerian club. Close by was the Pakistani Association and a mosque.

It was therefore irresponsible to use 'black' as an umbrella word to describe non-white people in Liverpool 8 because the description ignored the different races and religions that existed there. No such bonding existed. Those with origins in different parts of Africa, the West Indies, the Indian sub-continent or elsewhere in Asia had little, if anything, in common. There was no view from within that this was one homogenous group. It meant that in the Granby triangle, with its collection of communities, there was no single group able to speak for all.

In the decade before 1981, the population of Granby and the Princes Park area declined from 24,000 to 15,000. Neighbouring Dingle fell from 15,000 to 12,000. 'The human effects of such rapid movement leave people who feel hemmed in,' wrote Michael LeRoy, a Baptist minister who studied the area after 1981. 'Those who do move consider that they are improving themselves but some choose to stay. Many, who would like to get out, feel trapped. They have a sense of being held captive.' LeRoy cited one local planner who had worked in Toxteth as well as the Old Swan area where he was placed under considerably greater pressure by lower-middle class residents despite the people of Toxteth having more issues to raise.

In the 1830s, the American writer Herman Melville contrasted the position of black people in Liverpool with that of black people in the United States during the same period. 'In Liverpool the Negro steps with a prouder pace, and lifts his head like a man; for here, no such exaggerated feeling exists in respect to him, as in America.'

By the 1970s, Liverpool 8 had become a ghetto, segregated from much of Toxteth and the rest of the city. Melville had seen black people within the confines of the own communities but not elsewhere. Howard Gayle, the first black footballer to play for Liverpool, recalled growing up in Norris Green, the sink estate to Liverpool's east, where he was routinely bullied by white kids in his class and invited to fight on a village green. When a teacher molested him as a teenager, he concluded it happened because he was 'exotic'.

Joe Farrag brought with him experiences of being a young black man, attempting to fit in. He was an Everton supporter and one of only a few black faces on the terraces of Goodison Park around the time Cliff Marshall became the first locally born black player to represent the club. 'Cliffy took terrible abuse from the crowd,' Farrag remembered. 'He could have been a great footballer but he only played seven times. It didn't seem to matter whether he was doing well or doing badly, the crowd would be at him.'

Farrag describes his love for football and love for Everton as 'unrequited – why should I let the words of bigots stop me going to a place that I want to go to?' Liverpool city centre, though, was a different matter. When shopping for clothes, he felt more comfortable in Manchester where there was a bigger black community. 'Ideally, I'd get the things I needed on Granby Street,' he reflected. 'At one time, it had everything anybody ever needed.'

Though efforts had been made to recharge Granby Street to the place it used to be, it was quiet in the middle of the day with many of the steel-shuttered storefronts closed for some time. Farrag believes the sense of containment in Liverpool intensified because of poor council planning in attempts to enhance transport links with the fading docks. By the mid-1970s, diggers were in the ground for a new road to the M62 which had implications for Upper Parliament Street, resulting in the closure of nearby roads. Whereas traffic used to flow directly from Liverpool's city centre into Granby Street, enabling easy access to shops, it was now cut off by the newly created Selbourne Street, ironically the setting for the starting gun of the riots that followed a few years later.

Liverpool 8 was once reachable and visible but suddenly it was hidden away. In the 1968 Gore's Directory, more than 70 shops were registered on Granby Street. A decade later, that number had reduced by half. 'It used to take 40 minutes to an hour to walk down Granby because all of the shops were open and people stopped to talk,' Farrag recalled. 'With the creation of Selbourne Street blocking the way for cars, fewer shoppers went there and gradually, the place closed down.'

Liverpool 8's connection with Liverpool was gone and the area's main source of employment taken away, coinciding with the decline of the port. Toxteth was a working-class community, with sixty per-cent of its inhabitants white, but because it was the area of the city with the highest percentage of black people in a city which had just one black community, it was regarded as Liverpool's black area. As technology advanced, there were implications for residents whether white or black, but with racism at its root.

'There was an increasing reliance on the telephone as a way of communicating, particularly for job interviews,' Farrag remembered. 'It started to affect the white people in our community. When you phoned up for an interview they'd ask for a name and an address. "Liverpool 8," you'd say. As soon as you said the postcode, the opportunity was lost. It meant there was high unemployment in the area for white people as well.'

In 1979, the Conservative candidate for Toxteth was a 41-year-old flour mill owner called Anthony Shone. He was married with three children and his promise two days before the general election proved to be absolutely accurate but for one final detail. 'Conservative policies will progressively dismantle state control, reduce public spending and restore incentives to private industries,' he claimed. '... giving Toxteth the opportunity to prosper again.'

Margaret Simey, the Glasgow-born community activist and long-time councillor of the Granby ward, described in her memoir the mounting tensions in Liverpool 8. 'Increasing demands for the police to assert their powers of control on the streets only added to their sense of alienation: Granby was habitually referred to them as a criminal community and policed as such.'

In the 1999 documentary, *Riot*, Simey recounted having warned the authorities in Liverpool 8 that a disturbance was inevitable. The police, she remembered, had been closing down nightclubs in the city centre where young black people would socialise. Another contributor to the documentary told a story on his late mother's behalf, how she was called 'a breeder of mongrels' by the police and how that changed her views on the way things were. Previously, she'd been a law-abiding citizen and suddenly she was being abused on her own doorstep, not by one policeman, but many.

There were other stories of 'middle aged white women making petrol bombs for kids to throw in 1981'. 'Before 1981, nobody called the area Toxteth,' Farrag said ruefully, as we turned left into Upper Parliament Street where the worst fighting would happen. 'It had always been known as the South End, L8 or L1... now if you Google the name Toxteth, the first thing that comes up relates to what happened 1981.'

JIMI JAGNE LIVES A FEW DOORS DOWN FROM JOE FARRAG ON Beaconsfield Street. His father had arrived in Liverpool from The Gambia as a seafarer, his mother's roots were Chinese and his grandmother, an Irish catholic, lived in Chinatown, sleeping next to an oil picture of St Patrick that was decorated by tea lights on her bedside cabinet. 'She's been over there for most of her life,' Jagne said, as if Liverpool's Chinatown was another land when really, it was a mile or so away from where he grew up.

'I felt great in Liverpool 8,' Jagne thought. 'It was easy for me to make friends. I wasn't aware that being born into a secure nuclear family was even an alternative: to be treated to trappings, being able to have access to material things. I did not think it was possible to go to a school where you did not have to prove yourself in unreasonable ways. You were expected to grow up very quickly and not complain. If you did complain you'd more than likely be reprimanded. It was only when I learnt about how life was for other people outside the community as I got older that I started to realise how entitlement was the norm and that we were actually deprived.'

Jagne was born in 1964, the year before The Gambia declared independence from Britain. His parents were separated by the time he was one. He would not see his father often while his mother re-settled in London, leaving him with another grandmother and her St Lucian husband – not his maternal grandfather – in a busy house filled with cousins on Egerton Street.

Despite being surrounded by all sorts of ethnicities and religions, faith did not play a role in his upbringing. 'It was the same for most kids my age. We were descendants from African seaman, whose lives were fast with a certain degree of cultural disconnection because of the job they did. Sea does something to people. They might leave Africa as religious people but by the time they get here, sea changes them. Seamen – wherever they are from – develop an easy set of values, they don't necessarily have a home. They set down in a port, they make acquaintances then they move on. The lifestyle involves casual relationships; drink and music. There's a distinction between Africans who came here through the port and Caribbeans who came as part of the Windrush generation. Unique to Liverpool, of course, was the long line of Africans who'd been here for generations.'

Jagne passed the 11-plus but lacked the belief in himself that he could go to a grammar school and flourish. He would instead leave an overwhelmingly white secondary modern with enough O-levels to have been assured of securing a job had he not been black and had it not been 1980, the year that sandwiched Margaret Thatcher's rise to power and the riots in a small section of the district in Liverpool that he called home. Between 1979 and 1981 the rate of unemployment in Liverpool accelerated to a frightening level, rising to 51 per-cent. By 1982, there were just 49 opportunities on offer for the 13,505 youngsters without work. Deindustrialisation was turning Liverpool into a 'graphic illustration of urban dereliction', as Tony Dickson, an author in social studies, put it. It was no coincidence that the 'People's March for Jobs' in May 1981 began at the Pier Head. Jagne remembers a conversation with a careers officer warning him of the perils that awaited.

'He was worried for me because the chances of getting an apprenticeship and a trade were reducing by the month. Companies like ICI and Pilkington's were nearby but they were scaling down and reducing training opportunities, putting more money instead into the business of selling stuff to people that did not necessarily have the money to buy. This meant they went into credit.'

While unemployment had rocketed because of Thatcher's failing monetarist policies, police relations with Liverpool 8 were appalling, but they had been for decades. Jagne's introduction to their ferocious methods had been as a 12-year-old walking home from school. The incident had a profound impact on the rest of his life.

'It happened just there,' he said, pointing out the stretch of tarmac where Upper Duke Street merges into the grandeur of Hope Street near the Anglican Cathedral. 'I've got my school uniform on and my Gola kitbag with me, with my PE kit and my exercise books. The police used to drive around in a Black Maria or Panda type cars – Austin Allegros. One of these started crawling alongside me. The driver was looking at me carefully then he sped up and parked 15 yards in front. The officer in the passenger seat got out and he did not introduce himself or explain why he needed to talk to me. He said, "Where do you think you're going?" It was letting out time so I replied, without any tone in my voice, "I've just finished school, I'm going home."

'He asked me what I had in the bag. Because I had no history with the police, I had no reason to question why he might be asking me this question. I told him that I had my school books and my PE kit. He snatched the bag off me, opened it up and rummaged through. He zipped it back up then asked where I lived. "Just along there, 38b Windsor Street." He looked at the driver, the driver shrugged his shoulders – whatever that meant, I don't know – then he said, "You're coming with us."

"Why, what have I done wrong? I haven't done anything wrong...

"Get in the fucking car..."

'I was now starting to get upset. "Are you going to take me to a police station?" I asked. "Get in the fucking car you little black swine," he shouted. In fear, actually I ran into the car because I thought I'd upset him. To my untrained mind, only people that did wrong were troubled by the police.

'I sat in the back seat and he slammed the door. The driver sped past where I lived and carried on. I said to them, "That's where I live… aren't we going to see my mum (who'd moved back from London)?" One of them told me to shut up. "You're coming with us." I stayed quiet for a couple of minutes before asking whether we were going to a police station. I pleaded with them to tell me what I'd done wrong. I told him I was scared. "Scared, are you? Well wait and see what fucking happens next…"

'I started crying. They drove past the police station and kept on going all the way down to where Speke Retail Park is now. It was a wasteland, covered in mud and puddles. It was wintertime and starting to get dark. They drove off road and stopped as far away from any footpath as possible. Both of the officers got out, the passenger flipped his seat and dragged me out by my blazer. He swung me around and I fell back into a puddle, completely soaked in dirt. The driver took my bag, opened it and threw everything into a puddle. They both started laughing and they were joking amongst themselves.

'I burst out crying. "I want to go home, you're frightening me, I don't know what I've done wrong." They carried on laughing, they got into the car and as the passenger got in he turned to me and said, "Remember this you, you black bastard; if you ever think you can grow up and rob from decent white people or cause any trouble, we'll be back to fucking get you."

'Then, they drove off and left me there.'

It took Jagne several hours to walk the six miles back to Toxteth in filthy, sodden clothes, carrying a wet sack of ruined books. His mother died several years later not knowing what had happened that day because he was afraid to tell her. He thought he'd done something terribly wrong – that he was to blame. In the loneliness, Jagne started to think differently about his status within society. He allowed the injustices of the world seep into his consciousness and politicisation followed. He would read history books. He followed *Roots*, the American television series which broke viewing records and prompted a national conversation about race. The programme's release came just a year after the police had taken him to that murky piece of wasteland in Speke and the experience of watching it was a sort of awakening, because it started to explain a landscape he was previously unaware of.

Meeting new Rastafarian friends in his later teens filled in more of the gaps. They had all the answers he was looking for: 'Like how colonialism was a continuation of slavery.' Haile Selassie had died in 1975 and Jagne's understanding increased again, learning how Selassie, according to the legend, had led Ethiopia against Italian colonisation armed only with spears and the terrain know-how of tribesmen at the Battle of Adwa. Though some of the stories were wrapped up in mythology, they were empowering. 'As black Britons, we felt like we were the latest in a long line of people who struggled against racism. The done thing was to challenge it. You don't allow yourself to become a victim.'

Though Liverpool 8 was united by collective struggle, it was divided in so many ways, not just by nationality or religion. Jagne refers to his younger self as a 'black youth – because racism was a problem for us', and though it was for his parents as well, they dealt with it in a totally different way. A generational split existed. Jagne's ancestors in Liverpool 8 could not have come to Britain without investing a certain amount of faith in the opportunities that were supposedly there. Having been born in Britain, Jagne instead would learn that he was a British citizen in the making, that his status was questionable – and he was certainly less willing to accept discrimination than the generations that went before him. 'My granddad worked as a joiner for the city council and was a fully-fledged member of the Labour party. He never missed an election. He'd have a *Vote Labour* poster in his window. I didn't feel quite the same. Whereas people like my granddad had arrived in the country as an adult determined to fit in at whatever cost, the only way to move up in the world by 1981 was to take loan from a bank. You used to have collateral and of course, many black people didn't have anything to show the bank as insurance.'

Few black people were able to demonstrate they were a safe investment. Key institutions were therefore not as supportive of people of Liverpool 8 as they were somewhere like Allerton.

'We lived marginalised lives.'

IN 1988, KENNETH OXFORD WAS KNIGHTED. TEN YEARS EARLIER, when he was the chief constable of Merseyside Police, he had written in the

BBC *Listener* magazine about '... the problem of half-castes in Liverpool'.

He concluded that these had been the product of liaisons between black seamen and white prostitutes in Liverpool 8, which he roundly referred to as 'the red light district.'

Worse still, in his opinion, '... the negroes will not accept them as blacks and the whites just assume they are coloureds. As a result, the half-caste community of Liverpool is well outside recognised society.'

There may have been some truth in Oxford's final observation but the basis for his argument was sweeping and clearly, he had little time for sensitivities around language.

His 42-year police career in three of Britain's major forces was saturated in controversy. Authoritarian and socially conservative, he resented any call independent or otherwise to justify his actions, taking it, for example, as a personal attack when his case for an increase in manpower was met by the financial consequences being pointed out to him.

From the moment of his appointment on Merseyside in 1975, criticisms by elected councillors on the Police Committee were interpreted as a political assault upon the police service.

Thatcher's promises must surely have encouraged Oxford, who in 1989 briefed the prime minister four days after the Hillsborough disaster where he blamed ticketless Liverpool supporters that turned up in large numbers for the crush that led to 96 deaths.

In those discussions, Oxford also commented on how he felt 'uneasy about the way in which Anfield was being turned into a shrine'.

A decade earlier, Thatcher had said, 'The police will not only be properly paid but will also be given full-hearted moral support. We will restore respect for law and order.'

By 1981, under Oxford's guidance and according to his wishes, Merseyside possessed the highest police to population ratio outside of London having improved command and control facilities as well as huge capital expenditure from Thatcher's government.

Oxford's personality was projected into the police force that he led. The relationship between the police and working-class communities in Liverpool had plummeted, particularly in Huyton where the death of Jimmy Kelly in police custody after being arrested for supposedly being drunk and disorderly in June 1979 followed a series of violent incidents.

Allegations of police brutality in the notorious K Division led to Harold Wilson, the local MP and former prime minister, calling for a public inquiry which resulted in Oxford, amidst a wave of critical pressure, staunchly refusing to discuss the case with democratically elected representatives from both Labour and Conservatives groups.

The loudest of these critics was Margaret Simey, who led the Labour Group on the Police Committee. When Simey pushed hard for an inquiry Oxford responded in his annual report by referring to her as 'vituperative' and 'misinformed'.

After a Panorama television programme stirred a similar defence, the results of an internal investigation of K Division were not placed into the public domain and nine months after Kelly's death three pathologists gave a verdict of death by misadventure, enabling the Home Office to reject demands for a public investigation.

The unresolved debate over Kelly's death characterised what was to come in Liverpool as Oxford continued to shoot down anyone who questioned his attempts to increase the efficiency of his leadership.

Oxford had been warned for several years about the rising tensions in the city's poorest areas, not least in Liverpool 8, where Simey was a resident. Oxford responded to complainants by accusing them of 'criminal negligence'. When a crime reporter called James McClure asked whether he could spend twelve months interviewing and writing about the officers of Liverpool's A Division, Oxford agreed. The outcome was *Spike Island*, a book released in 1980 that defined McClure's career even though it amounted to nothing more than police propaganda.

The A Division was a tiny patch but the busiest on Merseyside, where several thousand revellers disgorged into the city centre at 2.30 in the morning from 500 pubs and clubs, as one senior officer explained to McClure, to 'pinch our cars and bust our windows and break into our shops'.

Spike Island was famed for another quote from another officer who described the turf as 'the bit of Liverpool that's like a band-aid stuck over where they ripped the heart out'. If an officer from Liverpool really did say that, it is more likely he used the term plaster.

Oxford had contributed a preface to the project where he congratulated McClure on producing 'a most readable book' of 533 pages. Though there were some references to homophobia and occasional sexism, it seemed incredible that in such a detailed and prolonged search into the realities of police officers' lives – but for describing the 'Yellow people' of Chinatown – there should not be another racist reference, despite Britain's oldest black community sitting uncomfortably in the first district south of the city centre.

What were the police trying to hide? In 1981, just a year after the release of *Spike Island*, Merseyside Police had just four black officers in a force of 5,000.

Under the laws of the Vagrancy Act of 1824, Oxford had, in the 1970s, dramatically increased the use of 'stop and search' powers, which as its name suggests, allowed the police to use their own discretion on the street in order to inspect the person of possession of illegal material. Under Oxford, Liverpool 8 was under constant surveillance and regularly his units swooped down on the area like an invading force.

Joe Farrag kept with him a file entitled *Riots in Liverpool 8: Some Christian Responses*. The author, Michael LeRoy, was a Baptist minister from Bridgnorth and it was his independent view that Liverpool's police officers were feared rather than respected. In a far-ranging and balanced study of the 1981 riots, he retold a story from seven years earlier when outside a Christian youth centre, the police tried to arrest a black youngster suspected of attempting to steal a car. The black youngster's friends rushed back into the centre to tell of his arrest at which point the club emptied onto the street where the officer found himself surrounded by a hostile and suspicious crowd. This turned into a medium-scale disturbance according to police records and when other officers in their wagons turned up, all of the civilians present ended up being arrested. Having been found guilty in court and then cleared after several prominent local people spoke in his defence, the youth leader, who was white, made a significant conclusion: 'If it had been a black youngster, I would not have been acquitted.'

Michael Heseltine, the government minister sent by Thatcher to Liverpool in 1981, concluded at the time that 'relations between the police and the community are virtually non-existent'. In his autobiography, he wrote about his long conversations with Oxford at the city centre police headquarters, who had told him that 'crimes of every sort were organised by the powerful and ruthless gang leaders operating from Toxteth,' for whom 'there were examples of conspicuous wealth for which there could be no legitimate explanation.'

Heseltine took a sympathetic view on the residents of Liverpool 8, however, recognising that crime and associated and drug businesses offered the easiest way out of the hopelessness of the situation they perceived themselves to be in. 'The police were an alien presence.'

'At night, when the personal radio alerted the local police patrol to a snatched bag or mugged pedestrian, "some black youth running up Parliament Street," would become the prelude to a stop and search of every young black in the area,' Heseltine assessed. 'Time and again they would be questioned for no apparent reason, simply because they were part of the anonymous group of local kids that could be identified by one distinguishing characteristic: they were black.'

'The police had identified black youths as criminals in the making,' Jagne believed. 'In other words, if you get them off the street, if you demoralise as many of them as possible maybe they'll think twice about resorting to criminality. Whether or not they saw that as a fail-safe strategy or whether they genuinely believed there was something criminal about our existence, I don't know. It meant that stop and search became the critical point of contact between us and them. This has a psychological impact on the person or people you are dealing with.'

Jagne would describe a typical stop and search from the point of view of a young black man. His frustration with the hopelessness of this process remained evident.

'You could be walking alone or with a group of lads. Particularly in the wintertime when it was dark, we moved about in numbers. A skinhead movement was lurking in Wavertree. You have more safety in numbers because if something bad does happen, there's more of a chance of at least one person escaping and telling someone else about it.

'As soon as you notice a police vehicle every decision becomes critical. What you do next either encourages them or makes it appear normal. If they see you and you switch directions, they're coming after you because it appears suspicious. They can say, "Why are you avoiding us?" If you continue, especially in a group, there's every chance you are going to get stopped anyway. From the first moment you see them there's a problem. You take a chance, you carry on walking... inevitably an officer gets out of the vehicle. From here, the questions are always along the same lines. "Where are you going?" Depending on how you answer that question, they'll know how to react. Even if you play it smart and say you are going down the youth centre, they'll then ask, "Where have you just come from then?" The questions continue, whichever answer you give, until they make an accusation.

"Going to score there, are you?"

'They're attempting to start an argument which then provokes a reaction. They want to reach a point where they can poke you in the chest and say, "Who do you think you are? You don't talk to a police officer like that." They'll keep poking until someone tries to stop them poking. At this point one or two of the others will grab you. You either allow yourself to be flung into the police vehicle or you resist. If you resist, you then get a slap and the one thing you don't want to do is strike an officer because the moment that happens all hell breaks loose. You are going down. You will stand before a judge who will hear about a decent, hard-working police officer who stands in the rain on a cold night in an undesirable area on behalf of a decent civil society, facing a black scallywag with no care for authority. If you think I'm exaggerating about the use of language and the reference of the scallywag being black, I'm not. Police officers would use racial semantics in court to appeal to a judge, a jury or a magistrate. Black youths were frowned upon in conventional society to this extent.'

'The police were a threat to the existence of our community,' Jagne continued. 'It was more unsafe for us to walk the street with the police there than if they weren't. Their actions not only had an impact on our present but our future as well. You might get battered and left in hospital. You might end up with a criminal record. The consequences were dire and affected not only the person involved. What if one of these guys from our community has a child and he's got to go to jail for five years – what future does that child have? What happens if one of the guys has a place in college and that opportunity gets swept away? Life unravels very quickly. Then, what about the 17-year-old whose life has amounted to nothing so far – the one who might have few qualifications and a limited amount of work experience – but within twelve months is a little bit older and wiser? After five years in jail, he's a black criminal and stigmatised forever. He's got no chances of getting work. And the chances were slim anyway.'

RAY DAVENPORT WAS A CONSTABLE WITH MERSEYSIDE POLICE. ONE humid evening on Friday 3 July 1981, he stopped a car near Lime Street in the centre of Liverpool, believing it was stolen. As he leaned into the vehicle the driver accelerated, dragging him two hundred yards before smashing into a glass bus shelter. Two hours later, Ray Davenport was dead.

The newspaper report of this dramatic incident was covered across just four paragraphs in the next edition of the *Liverpool Daily Post* when it was printed the following Monday. Instead, the front page was ceded to coverage of what had happened less than a mile away over the weekend, with headlines such as '*Riot City*' accompanied by stories about how fifty policemen had been hurt, with one of them detailing '*My Night of Terror*'. Further analysis was provided under '*The Tightening Circle of Hopelessness*'.

There were photographs of policemen in helmets ducking behind riot shields and a phalanx of officers standing in three rows shoulder to shoulder across the width of Upper Parliament Street. Facing them were mainly black youths throwing stones, bricks and whatever else lay within reach on the bloodied tarmac. To those outside the city, it was known as the Toxteth Riots. To those in the city but outside the ward where they happened, it was the Liverpool 8 Riots. Those who were involved call it 'The Uprising'.

The violence had started at around 9.45pm as police in an unmarked car chased a motorcyclist they suspected of theft. On the corner of Selborne Street and Granby Street, the young man fell and an arrest was attempted in front of a congregation of people who had previously been chatting away – passing the time.

Leroy Cooper, a 20-year-old photography student, whose brother had been acquitted 24 hours earlier from a crown court case where the verdict included mention of 'unwarranted police attention', had been at a youth club close to Selbourne Street when the news of the 'police being at it again' came through. He went to look, 'someone opened the door of the van', the arrested youngster got away and in the skirmish that followed, an officer's nose was broken.

Swiftly, eight police vehicles were on the scene, and in one of those vehicles Cooper was carted away. On the advice of his legal team and knowing he could get three to five years in prison, he pleaded guilty to assaulting three officers, though thirty years later, he still claimed those allegations were 'ridiculous'.

Cooper would hear about what happened next in Liverpool 8 from a remand centre in Risley. Until 1.45 the next morning, police vehicles patrolled the area and half a dozen had their windscreens smashed by bricks and bottles. This prompted a build-up of police presence. They had received an anonymous tip-off there would be a 'bloodbath'. On Saturday afternoon, police were fronted by a small group on Myrtle Street and a larger group – perhaps as strong as 150 white

53

and black youths – on Upper Parliament Street. This prompted the erection of barricades. The fighting escalated and by 11pm, two lines of police were advancing eastward along Upper Parliament Street. A full-scale battle commenced.

The first full night of rioting did not subside until 7.30 on the Sunday morning. While there are no official records that detail the full extent of civilian injuries, by this time seventy policemen had been injured, seven of them hospitalised.

Cars were set on fire and used as protection. Railings were ripped out and used as weapons, buildings were lit and a car was driven at police lines with its accelerator jammed until it crashed into a wall. Petrol bombs were thrown for the first time and some of them penetrated riot shields, setting fire to police uniforms.

There was a lull on the Sunday until the rioting resumed to the smell of burning tyres taken from the Kenning's tyre depot. When police retreated back to the traffic lights by the old Rialto cinema, the most destructive night of the riots ensued. The Rialto, the Racquet Club, a National Westminster bank and several other buildings were burned to the ground. Two fire engines were captured and damaged, one of them driven at police. Rioters used a bulldozer to lift a police car and plough through scaffolding at the front of some houses. Until reinforcements arrived from Cheshire, Lancashire and Greater Manchester forces, police lines were held at bay by throwing stones, bottles and petrol bombs. Only when CS gas was used for the first time on the British mainland did the rioters start to give way.

By Monday night, nearly 1,000 police were on the streets of Liverpool 8. Rioting in Moss Side and Wood Green would divert the attention of the national media while local reporters moved to other trouble spots across Merseyside like on the peripheral estates in Netherley, Speke and Halewood, or other inner-city areas like Walton and Kirkdale. The most prolonged conflict would happen on the Cantril Farm estate.

'This was not a racial issue,' Kenneth Oxford said, when he spoke particularly of what happened in Liverpool 8. 'It was exclusively a crowd of black hooligans intent on making life unbearable and indulging in criminality.' He would ignore the glaring fact that only small proportion of those arrested – in spite of the increased possibilities – had criminal records. In the *Liverpool Echo*, the photographs included the angry faces of both black and white young men.

Michael LeRoy believed that at the height of the rioting there had been a mood of anger and violence mixed with an excitement running through the community that some described as being like a carnival comparable to the emotions of Guy

Fawkes night. The ferocity with which youngsters threw missiles at police disturbed the local people who knew them. Aged 17, Jimi Jagne remembers the sound of reggae and disco music playing from the back of an estate car fixed with a generator and some speakers. The car's owner had driven to Liverpool 8 to sell booze and make some money out of the gathering crowds, some of whom were hippies and students who stood around dancing in the street as battles went on around them. A Thatcherite entrepreneurial spirit was well and truly alive in these desperate times.

Jagne was in a closer position than someone like Lord Tebbit to explain why some buildings were attacked and others were left intact. While looters tended to be white opportunists that quickly sensed police attentions were elsewhere in the area and quickly took pricey items such as rugs and other furniture away from shops on nearby Lodge Lane, the worst damage was at national chains like Tesco's and Kwiksave. The mood of retribution also provided the chance to settle grievances and one of these may have been at Swainbank's, a furniture store run by a councillor whose antagonism towards local people had been documented six years earlier when he was quoted as saying: 'I've tried to get on with the coloured people in the area – my god I've tried. It just doesn't work. Especially with those half-caste kids. They break into my place nearly every day now and steal something... I've paid my takes, I work long hours every day. All I see around me is layabouts, whom I'm supporting. They've got an easy life, I'm telling you.'

Symbolically, the Racquet Club, the Rialto Theatre and the Natwest Bank would burn at the same time. Jagne says he would have left two of the buildings alone but admits congratulating those who torched the Racquet Club. 'It was a private members place that was frequented by people from all the usual establishment professions. You had magistrates, judges and high-ranking police officers. We knew this because we often saw them go in wearing their uniform. This was a cruel irony because the only time the police had anything to do with our area otherwise was to brutalise us. And yet they would come and socialise on our turf and hobnob with people of their own ilk when it suited them. We couldn't get a membership. There were rumours that persisted: "They've got gold in there that was stolen from our countries during colonial times," or, "They've got ivory and furniture that kings and emperors used to sit in." Some of this might have been myth but people were primed to do away with that building and it was significant that it was torched before the other two.'

Jagne spoke with a sense of anticipation when he heard about the demise of the 107-year-old Racquet Club, explaining how he ran down Kingsley Road to look inside before it collapsed. 'There were a lot of expensive things in there. The rumours were not altogether untrue.'

The following morning, the club's chairman Richard McCullagh detailed some of its most cherished items of value. These included a precious painting of Istanbul called the Golden Horn, five 'prestigious' paintings on loan from the Walker Art Gallery, a library holding a 'priceless' collection of records and book volumes, as well as fine furniture, sculptures, silverware, an indoor tennis court and three squash courts.

McCullagh described it as 'an extremely sad day for Liverpool. So much history and tradition has been destroyed in one fell swoop.' To escape from the blaze, he had fled through the back door and jumped over a wall into the private quarters of St Margaret's church where he sought refuge for the night. On the same stretch of Princes Avenue was a Greek Orthodox church, a synagogue, a mosque, and a Caribbean Community Centre. This district of dense ethnicities had endured enough.

THE ATLANTIC TOWER WAS DESIGNED TO RESEMBLE THE PROW OF A ship to mark Liverpool's maritime history. Ten days after the first wave of riots in Toxteth, Michael Heseltine had taken residence in the Port of Liverpool Suite on the hotel's sixteenth floor, a mile or so away from the most violent clashes on Upper Parliament Street. By day, he held crisis meetings across the road in the Liver Buildings and alone at night, when the pressure was off, he would stand with a glass of red wine looking out at the magnificent view over the river, asking himself a question: 'How had this great British city fallen so far?'

Lord Heseltine, as he had become, was peering through another window when I met him at his rented space on the fifteenth floor of a wealth management firm's glass-plated office block in the Victoria area of London. For the first time in his 52-year political career, he had been sacked from government having rallied against Theresa May by supporting a House of Lords vote on any Brexit deal. At 83, he'd become one of the oldest rebels in history. Night was falling and it was close to Christmas. Street decorations twinkled and so did his pale blue eyes.

Heseltine had been either a one nation Conservative who tried to help

Liverpool when no other leading figure in his party was willing to, or he was the Tory with aspirations of becoming Prime Minister who saw an opportunity when the recklessness of Monetarism caused unemployment and subsequent social disturbances, gambling that he could probably convince the rest of the country to follow him if he could convince Liverpool. Perhaps Thatcher recognised Heseltine's threat because of the popularity of this 'vivid, preening carnivore', as Andrew Marr later described him, and decided his ambition might make suicide out of his own political career.

'I have very early memories of Merseyside, albeit in very unfortunate circumstances,' Heseltine would say, staring down towards the scudding dark waters of the Thames. 'It was 1941 and my father was in command of a Royal Engineer company in Northern Ireland. My mother took my sister and I to stay in a village called Dundrum, a few miles south of Belfast. I remember sailing from Heysham. Before an air raid, you could hear the warning systems all the way from Liverpool.'

Heseltine returned to his leather executive chair and leaned back into it with his arms behind his head, as if he was speaking to a psychiatrist about the past. He was seven in 1941 and twice that age in 1948, the year he saw Liverpool for the first time, then as a pupil from Shrewsbury School on a missionary trip. What had struck him?

'Oh, the grandeur,' he smiled quirkily. 'It had been a hugely wealthy Victorian city enormously endowed by its business people. The names were there: The Walker Art Gallery, the magnificent St. George's Hall, the Adelphi Hotel complex, Lime Street railway station, the Royal Liver Buildings. There was a huge magnificence in its architectural inheritance. But of course, what a contrast with the relative poverty of the surroundings. The dynamism had gone. The spirit was going.'

Heseltine was a dyslexic schoolboy who made a £300million fortune in low-rent hotels and magazines. Born in Swansea, he was the president of the Oxford Union at 21, chairman of Haymarket Publishing at 33 and the Conservative MP for Henley-on-Thames at 41. His presence in front line politics grew as Liverpool's grace disappeared. By 1981 the world's premier ocean liner port was defined as a ghost town of abandoned warehouses, silted docklands and exhausted tower blocks, having haemorrhaged almost a fifth of its population since 1971.

'It's a much-misunderstood point that I went there because of the riots, this was not true,' he stressed, explaining that he had frequently been to Liverpool in the two years prior in his ministerial role. He credits Labour's Secretary of State, Peter Shaw, for creating a series of partnerships in places that suffered from difficult social conditions. 'I was asked whether my ministerial team would like to continue with that project and I said yes. Peter had associated himself with Liverpool and I was asked if I wished to continue with the same responsibility. Again, I said yes. So, from 1979 I was involved in an unusual cabinet role that involved regular contact with the city.

'It was because of this relationship, I had to try and do something when the riots took place in '81,' he continued. 'I didn't just say, "This is one of those unfortunate things," and that the police would sort it out. I felt a personal responsibility because I'd been around for the best part of two years doing what I believed to be necessary and helpful, and the place had burned. So, I said to the Prime Minster, "We can treat this in a simplistic way – it's just a case of better policing and let them get on with it." Or I could take a rather different view: that something there was not quite right. I wanted to walk the streets to try and figure out what it was. The Prime Minister agreed and so for three weeks, I walked the streets. That is when a much more indelible impression was formed.'

From London, Heseltine had seen how many Liverpudlians had moved to the capital for work. Liverpool's port trade had transferred principally to Europe but also to the south of England. He believed that the switch had been hastened by a destructive breakdown between 'generally incompetent management and consistently belligerent dock unions'. In his autobiography, he would conclude that Liverpool had lost too many of its leaders. 'Toxteth, a tiny microcosm in terms of location and population, became a very misleading symbol, though still a symbol of spreading disease,' he wrote.

'There was,' he paused inside his office in Victoria, 'a deeply divided society. They all shouted at each other, abuse from the tops of mountains. They never talked to each other. They never sat down and said, "Okay, we might disagree about this but let's try and sort something." It was so easy to blame someone else. And of course, of the cities that was most scarred by the breakdown of order in the face of trade union militancy, Liverpool was probably the worst. They literally couldn't bury the dead. The bodies were stacked up in mortuaries because of strikes. This had happened under a Labour government, although Liverpool wasn't absolutely a Labour seat because the Conservatives controlled the county council.'

'No one ultimately was really in charge,' he concluded. 'Everybody knew what was wrong. But it was you and them and him and her and never me. There was no common cause of how to pull the thing out of the despondency into which it had fallen. It started off like this. "What are you doing here?" I'd get asked. "Well, I've come to listen." They'd respond to that by pointing out politicians never listen. "Well here I am." That lasted for about three days until people started asking me about what I thought. I knew then I couldn't leave the city after three weeks and say, "I've learned a lot, thank you very much and goodbye."'

This had been an option. Thatcher had agreed that Heseltine should be in Liverpool but Willie Whitelaw, the home secretary, 'seemed wary'.

Whitelaw sent Tim Raison, his minister of state, to accompany him and watch over his department's interest in police matters – though Heseltine insists he welcomed that decision because he believed it might avoid misreporting from Liverpool to London.

Heseltine was told by Conservatives in the prosperous suburbs that he was wasting his time in Toxteth, that 'there are no votes for us to win there'. Having walked the street he requested supplicants to bring him solutions rather than problems, preferably summarised on a single sheet of A4 paper.

'I was unwilling to accept the all-too-easy assertions that saw such outbreaks either in stark terms of disgruntled troublemakers on one hand or police intolerance on the other. There was a political menace in the relatively small-scale disturbances which no responsible government should ignore.'

He spoke of '... a shared feeling of hopelessness born of low attainment and encouraged by the inevitability that anyone who had actually prospered would have long since moved away; a sense of grievance against the police and a belief that even a home address in Toxteth was a certain barrier to employment.'

When the Treasury put forward proposals to cut public spending by another £5million a month after Toxteth, the cabinet revolted. The soon-to-be sacked Ian Gilmour quoted Winston Churchill, 'however beautiful the strategy, you should occasionally look at the results,' pointing out that the cuts would increase unemployment and lead to a rise in domestic disturbances. 'The Prime Minister found herself virtually isolated, alone in a laager with Keith Joseph and the two Treasury ministers, Geoffrey Howe and Leon Brittan,' Gilmour remembered. Thatcher either had to change her policy or her cabinet. Gilmour and several others would be dismissed, though Heseltine was not one of them.

'It was much easier to throw moderates overboard than jettison dogma,' Gilmour wrote. 'Michael Heseltine was no Monetarist but he was sensibly selective in opposition.'

'I was arguing against cuts in investment in the public sector and in favour of cutting consumption,' Heseltine insisted. 'When it came to industrial intervention I had no problems at all using what powers I had as a politician to help pursue strategic objectives.' Like Gilmour he too would quote Churchill: 'My thought was always this and I am not saying anything that Churchill didn't put better: "We are all free to rise, though none must fall."'

It had been Churchill, of course, who reacted to the General Strike of 1911 by sending gun boats up the Mersey, ordering them to face the Royal Liver Buildings.

JOE FARRAG HAD BEEN ON THE LIVERPOOL 8 DEFENCE COMMITTEE that was set up in the aftermath of the riots, meeting with Heseltine after he'd been escorted by armed policemen from the Atlantic Tower to the door of a one-time bourgeois property on Princes Street. There, Farrag remembered him 'listening more than he spoke'. Somehow, a Special Branch constable made it in with Heseltine, having hidden a pistol in a brown envelope. Heseltine recalled sitting in a packed basement room with his back to the window, far away from the door that gave him entry and offered escape. Some of the men staring at him had cuts and bruises sustained from the recent events. He described the subsequent discussion as 'the most demanding I have ever chaired', though the scene was brittle rather than ill-tempered. Back at the Atlantic Tower, 'We all agreed we felt as though we were sitting on a powder keg. The wrong gesture, the wrong remark and the whole thing could have exploded...'

The Royal Wedding meant this explosion was widely ignored. On 27 July, a smaller number of youths assembled in the middle of Upper Parliament Street, this time faced by double the number of policemen who banged their riot shields as if they were preparing to enter war. The authorities were much more on the offensive, with convoys of police proceeding to drive through the area at speed. Kenneth Oxford, stung by criticism of his previous tactics argued that this 'form of dispersal' was 'preferable to CS gas'.

David Moore, a 23-year-old from Wavertree, was visiting family in Liverpool 8 the following night when he was unable to get out of the way of a police van as it charged across some wasteland, targeting a crowd that had suddenly ran towards him. Moore walked with a heavy limp, the result of an earlier car accident, and he was unable to get away, sustaining the back injuries that would take his life. The incident prompted the *Daily Post* to print a front page of contrasts where 'In Love' was proclaimed in bold, large type above an image of Charles and Diana kissing on the balcony of Buckingham Palace. Next to the fairytale romance was a smudgy image of Moore with a sobering warning: 'New Riot Fears as Man Dies.'

Heseltine referred to Moore's death simply as a 'tragedy' for which two police officers were acquitted of manslaughter eighteen months later on the direction of the judge. As for Kenneth Oxford, who died in 1998, Heseltine remembered him as a 'dour, unbending personality', though he had made a conscious decision not to judge anyone in Liverpool, and rather 'find the solutions that I'd asked the people to bring me'.

Heseltine asked his private secretary to ring the chairmen of the fifteen largest financial institutions and banks in the country, taking the CEOs on a dark tourism bus ride around Liverpool's most extreme areas of Modernist failure: the unfinished peripheral Radburn housing estates of Cantril Farm and Netherley, and the abandoned Piggeries of high-rise housing that had not so long before replaced the classic Georgian terraces of Everton. 'Liverpool might seem a long way away to them, but if Liverpool could burn, so could other cities and as the cities burned their assets would go up in smoke as well,' he thought. 'This was not just my problem, or the governments problem. It was their problem too.'

In 1981, the people of Liverpool were not the only ones unconvinced by his intentions or approach. 'There has been something ludicrous in Mr Heseltine's professions of concern about the problems he has seen on Merseyside, when it was he who savaged the Housing Investment Programme and recalculated the Rate Support Grant to favour the shire counties at the expense of the inner cities,' noted the housing charity Shelter in 1981.

Heseltine recognised that property markets would not recover in a contaminated environment and he set in motion plans to clean up the Mersey – 'an affront to a civilised society' – integrating the German idea of garden festivals to reclaim polluted land first in Liverpool and later in Stoke, Glasgow and Gateshead. The International Garden Festival, which opened in 1984, would scarcely benefit the unemployed population of Toxteth despite the area being only a mile away from the site. Many like Howard Gayle, the first black footballer to play for Liverpool, believe Heseltine 'planted a few trees' and little else, that his contribution had been a classic Conservative policy of 'scattering crumbs and seeing people fight over them'. The festival site did not prove to be an advert for market forces and 34 years later, its long-demolished dome remained undeveloped and returned to dereliction.

Heseltine had more success with initiatives like the Albert Dock, which had been described in 1978 by the socialist councillor and writer Tony Lane as 'the Imperial mausoleum', and an embarrassment to the post-colonial establishment. Heseltine's efforts would earn him the Freedom of Liverpool in 2012. He did not get everything right but he was able to construct some sort of framework for regional revival against the scepticism of Thatcher and many Conservative colleagues.

I suggested to him that one of those colleagues may have been Geoffrey Howe, the chancellor who had urged Thatcher to instead abandon Liverpool. 'I fear that Merseyside is going to be much the hardest nut to crack,' Howe wrote in a memo, which continued with assertion: 'We do not want to find ourselves concentrating all the limited cash that may have to be made available into Liverpool and having nothing left for possibly more promising areas such as the West Midlands or, even, the North East. It would be even more regrettable if some of the brighter ideas for renewing economic activity were to be sown only on relatively stony ground on the banks of the Mersey. I cannot help feeling that the option of managed decline is one which we should not forget altogether. We must not expend all our limited resources in trying to make water flow uphill.'

Howe acknowledged any public suggestion that Liverpool could be left allowed to slide was potentially damaging to the Conservatives. 'This is not a term for use, even privately,' he warned Thatcher.

A coldness came over Heseltine when I read this back to him.

'I do dismiss it,' he said flatly. 'If you were chancellor, every day you would see bids – painful, tear-jerking bids – for more money from all over Whitehall. They'd be couched in the most gut-wrenching language about the disaster about to befall to the least fortunate members of society. That's your job: you have to cope with it.

'Geoffrey, who was a good friend of mine, came from a South Wales background, was a one nation Tory if ever there was one,' Heseltine insisted, speaking rapidly for the first time. 'He'd have done absolutely the same sort of thing as I did if he'd been in my position. But he wasn't. He was chancellor. In the most awful of economic situations, let's not underestimate that. Inflation was running at 16 to 17 per-cent. And so, a letter came round – I don't even remember it being mentioned at all, let alone discussed.'

Was Howe's immediate view shared by others in the Conservative party?

'You've got no evidence of that and nor have I, except for this one letter,' Heseltine fired back. He recommended that I listen to his speech at the Tory party conference in the autumn of 1981 to gauge whether members agreed with his direction for Liverpool or Howe's. 'It was probably the finest speech of my life,' he reflected. 'David Dimbleby said, "Michael Heseltine picked up the Tory party, shook it and put it down where he wanted it to be." That was when I explained to the bulk of the Tory party the issues and traumas of Liverpool.'

Could he understand why Howe's words were so damaging?

'Yes, of course I can. But in politics in each decision, every spectrum of opinion is expressed all of the time. All parties are coalitions. The great trick of running a great party is to draw those coalitions into a collective set of policies. In anything that you do there will be people – a tiny number often – who say the most appalling things about the consequences on what is being proposed. The impressive thing is how the party survives even with this extremity of view from either left or right and come up with sensible policies that actually ignore both the extremes.

'I honestly don't remember this letter of Geoffrey's. But I'll never forget the Tory who said to me, "I don't know why you are wasting your time there. There will be no votes for us." I was appalled! Here you had a cabinet minister who was appalled as opposed to a non-entity cabinet member who no one gave a toss about expressing the extreme view. This is what made the party fascinating.'

Heseltine defined one-nation Toryism as 'the obligations of privilege. Its critics would call it noblesse oblige. I don't find any problem with that phrase. I think if you have privilege you have obligations. A great deal of the charitable foundations and social traditions of Liverpool reflect the desire of the people that had made their money in the city to endow it with hospitals, museums, universities...'

And yet by 1979, Liverpool was being described as an 'Imperial mausoleum.' Had capitalism ultimately failed Liverpool?

'Preposterous!' he shot back. 'The great thing about the capitalist system is that it finds itself out faster than the socialist system. Both make mistakes. But under the capitalist system there tends to be a limitation on the scale of the mistakes because the money runs out. With the socialist system, there is far less discipline because the politicians throw money at their mistakes and pretend it can be alright tomorrow. And so, the capitalist system is much more disciplined in that sense.'

Heseltine was certainly a capitalist but sometimes he sounded like a liberal rather than a Conservative.

'Liverpool's position had nothing to do with the capitalist system, a system that harnesses human energies and ingenuities and it does so more effectively than the socialist or communist alternatives,' he concluded. 'The market knows no morality so extreme capitalism is no more attractive to me than extreme socialism. Civilisation is built on regulation and intervention, the creation of codes and the imposition of moralities. That's something in my view which the Conservative Party has a remarkable record of pioneering. It doesn't make it perfect but it's better than anything else. It also generates the wealth to pay for aspirations so I don't have any time for those who look for the simplistic extremes of politics. No success is associated with either of them. Enlightened capitalism or one-nation Conservatism, as I would describe it, is the most satisfying of human arrangements.'

IRENE AFFUL'S AUNTIE COLETTE LIVED ON ST. NATHANIEL STREET, where the backs of the houses verged on a grass mound which acted as a separator from Upper Parliament Street and the rest of Liverpool 8. When the uprising started, Irene and her sister pleaded with their mum to allow them to go to there and watch.

'She had a balcony,' Afful remembered. 'We were far enough away from the petrol bombs. It was kind of exciting. We were like, "Oh, wow! This is happening on our estate!" But it was terrifying as well. People were being hurt on both sides. There was fire. There were lines and lines of police officers and you could see the riot shields. You could see stuff getting lobbed both ways; each side surging forward then being pushed back. It didn't feel real. But it was real. You could smell the petrol and the burning tyres. You could see the orange, the red and the darkness. You could hear the shouting, the truncheons banging on the shields. It was like being in a film set.'

Irene was 15 but experienced enough to understand why this was happening.

'We used to play out on the street, hopscotch and games like that. The Black

Marias would drive into the estate and police officers would hang out of the windows shouting racial abuse at us. We were just kids. It was "Nigger," this and "Nigger," that. "Black arses," and "get back to where you came from." They'd make monkey noises. I was completely shocked. I was scared. I thought that the police were supposed to be there to help us. But if I was ever in trouble, I realised I should never turn to a police officer because I'd probably get worse treatment in their hands than whoever it was I was trying to run away from. It was a really bad atmosphere and I did fear the police. You'd hear stories about the police picking up so-and-so, slinging him in the back of the van, beating him up and taking him out to a field and left.'

Irene, with her mother, her brother and her sister had lived in a maisonette.

'Though the Falkner Estate was almost brand new the housing quality was very poor. It was infested with rats. It only lasted for twelve years then the place was knocked down. It was a predominantly black community and there was a lot of tension between the community and the police. The tension did not come from the people who lived there. The tension came from the police.

'... people on the estate looked out for each other. Nobody looked down on anyone else. Everyone knew who the druggies were and everyone knew who the prostitutes were. My mum would know if I was out after dark, I'd be okay. I could walk through the community and feel as safe as houses. I never felt unsafe unless the police were there. There are parts of the city where I would feel unsafe but Toxteth wasn't one of them. The badness came from outside, people bringing trouble into the community.

'The riots happened because of the heavy-handed policing and the oppression happening in Toxteth. There was a lot of unemployment and this fed into the dissatisfaction because there was no attempt to revive the area and no opportunities, certainly if you were a black person. You'd walk through the city centre and no black faces were working in the shops.'

The segregation of Liverpool 8 had created a ghetto. Irene passed the 11-plus and this gave her options. She went to grammar school in Woolton, one of the most prosperous areas of Liverpool. Of the 1,100 pupils, only a handful were black. She was one of three in the 180 students across her year. She can remember having stones thrown at her while waiting at the bus stop. For a while, the family lived in Wavertree, an overwhelmingly white area where there was a National Front presence. As a six-year-old, she was chased down the street by the dogs of racist families. Irene had self-worth issues to overcome.

'When people put you down for something you can't help you start to think you aren't good enough, you're not intelligent enough or skilled. People who know me wouldn't think I it, maybe I hid it well, but I had massive confidence issues about not feeling good enough. I went through a phase as a teenager when I wanted to be white. I hated being black and I hated the way I looked. A lot of the people I mixed with were from more affluent families from more affluent parts of the city. I wished we had our own house and wished we lived somewhere that was a bit nicer than Toxteth.'

After nine years as a child protection officer, Irene was looking for something else. She had met a couple of CID officers through work. 'I'd got to know them quite well; they were really funny, really down to earth and they were a good laugh. They seemed normal – nice people. I thought, "There must be some nice people in the police, they can't all be horrible."'

When they suggested she train to join the police Irene thought about it and was concerned about the reaction of her family. The pay was better and she believed she could change attitudes from within. She also remembered the time during the riots a crowd sang Larry Graham's 'One in a Million You' to a lone black policeman amongst a force of powerful looking white officers.

'I felt sorry for him, he was certainly very brave,' she reflected. 'One or two of my uncles had been arrested and roughed up by the police. There was a fear and a mistrust. I dreaded telling my family that I was thinking about joining the police. They were horrified at first. It was an act of crossing enemy lines. Half of the people I asked said I shouldn't do it and the other half said I should. My mother? I think she was more worried about the abuse I'd suffer walking the beat through a white area rather than becoming a turncoat. In the end, I decided to join. I gave myself two years. If I didn't like it, I could always leave if I didn't.'

Irene would rise to become the first black female detective inspector on Merseyside, standing as the only one for eight years. Since her retirement there three other women have followed her as well as two men.

'I was still on my probation and I'd just come out of training school. You get allocated what they call an ATO [Area Training Officer]. They walk you through the procedures of being a police officer. The ATO at the time was a sergeant. At the station where I was working there was a bridewell, a custody suite then a little office where the officers congregated and had a cup of tea before they went out on patrol. The training officer had his back to me as I arrived in the room and he was telling a racist joke. I stood behind him at the counter and a couple of officers listening in saw me. He carried on with the joke, "Nigger," this, "Nigger" that. The ones listening put their head down and looked visibly uncomfortable. When he delivered his punchline, there were a few muffled laughs. He asked, "Why aren't you laughing?" in the way they normally would laugh. And then he turned around and saw me. He went bright red.

'He said, "Oh, Irene, can we have a word?" Then he took me into his office. "I'm so sorry, you should never have heard that..." I went, "No, I shouldn't have heard that really but more importantly, you should never have told it." He said that if I wanted to make a complaint, he'd explain how to do it. I told him that I wouldn't make a complaint, "But if I heard anything like that ever again, I'll have your job." I wasn't a teenager wet behind the ears. I was 25 years old and I was a line manager in my previous job. I'd been to court. I thought, "I'm not listening to this shit." Inside it made me feel sick. Although I expected to receive racist abuse with the job, I didn't expect it to come from someone who was meant to be teaching me, someone who was meant to be a bit more knowledgeable. It never happened again from him, while I was there at least. It did with others.'

There were occasions on van patrol when Irene was still on probation and the driver would say, 'There's a car full of spooks, let's have them over...' She knew one black officer who worked in Kirkby had bananas placed in his locker.

'I never got that level of abuse and if I did, I would have made a complaint. I wonder whether it's because I'm a woman. I think black men got more racist stick. Men will always give stick to other men but as a black woman you're not part of the male majority and you're not part of the white majority. It tends to come more from the sexist angle. You were seen as an object and because I was black I was a bit different or even exotic. The abuse ranged from being told to make the tea because that was a "woman's job" – which I'd deliberately make as unpalatable as possible so they wouldn't ask me again – to being severely stalked by two colleagues.'

In moments of confrontation or violence, she'd regularly be asked to step back – occasionally because she was a woman and colleagues were genuinely concerned, but reliably because many thought being a woman automatically meant she was somehow weaker – even though she did martial arts. This was the type of attitude that could hold someone back when career promotions are at stake. 'I just wanted them to let me get on with what needed to be done. If I needed help, I'd ask for it. I didn't want anyone else to make that call for me.'

Irene campaigned from inside the police force for better treatment of black officers, as well as black communities. 'I didn't want young people to think they couldn't approach the police if they were in trouble or consider it as a potential career. It's a good job, it's solid – the pay's not too bad. Why should any section of society be closed down from an opportunity like that? It most certainly was closed down because of the way the black community was policed and because of the way the black community perceived the police. There's kind of fault on both sides because the black community didn't make it easy either. Sometimes they lived up to the stereotypical views that the police had of them but more often than not they didn't: they were perceived that way, treated that way and therefore started to behave that way. It's a Liverpool trait to push back if you think something is wrong.'

THERE HAD BEEN ANOTHER INCIDENT IN LIVERPOOL 8. DAVID SCOTT, a police officer, was holding on to Leslie Bruce Thompson, a black teenager; succeeding in his attempts to calm him down. 'He was a local lad who had just successfully got a job with my help and nobody wanted him to get into any bother,' Scott wrote in a signed affidavit supplied to the Gifford Inquiry which examined what had happened in 1981.

When Scott later discovered that other officers at the scene had mistaken Thompson for Leroy Thomas, another black youth who was actually arrested that night, 'It was obvious to me that a serious miscarriage of justice was going to be done.' He was determined to put the matter straight and after he accused the other officers present of compiling inaccurate notebook entries, Scott was called a 'Nigger lover' in a police station corridor.

He recalled another incident when a black youth called Darryl Husband came to the station with a collecting tin for the children's bonfire that was being held on Granby Street. Scott would pass the tin around and when it came back, a senior officer had written '*Darryl's coke fund*' across it. Scott's evidence would get the case against Thompson dismissed but before leaving the court, a magistrate warned him, 'Officer, think about your position.'

David Scott was born into a white Toxteth family in 1942. He had served in the army for twelve years, and was based in United States, before joining Merseyside Police, where he served from 1975 to 1988. Scott's wife, Michelle, was born in Liverpool 8 and her father was Jamaican. This background led to Scott's helmet being daubed inside with the words 'Yankee Nigger Lover'.

He recalled conversations over police radio control when the officer responding on the other end of the line would say, 'It's shithead,' or 'It's the nigger lover.' One senior officer, with Scott's wife present said, 'Your husband is doing a good job with those niggers down there.' Another senior officer told him, 'Your wife is not a nigger. She's got a black father but he's a half-caste, she's not a nigger so take no notice of what the other officers say.'

Scott continued: 'Use of the word nigger was commonplace. When we were sent for riot training the instructor would say, "When these niggers come at us…" At meetings with the police federation whenever a police officer had been injured within the division people would say, "We've got to deal with these niggers." There was a particular chief inspector who had a ferocious hatred of "those fucking niggers".'

Scott would find himself isolated, with other officers refusing to work with him or pass on relevant information. His testimony to Gifford contradicted Kenneth Oxford's belief that the Merseyside force was understaffed and over-worked. According to Scott, the opposite was true, particularly in Toxteth where the section consisted of four shifts, each containing one inspector, two sergeants and 20 constables. In addition, there would be a day inspector and a chief inspector. With CID also present, there was also a detective inspector, four detective sergeants and ten detective constables. 'Because there were so many officers, they were often terribly bored,' and yet, they would still take on the considerable over-time, which was on offer because of the supposed challenges of working in the area.

'If available overtime dropped, officers would fill in what were known as tension indicators on a form, saying, for example, that bottles and bricks had been thrown in Granby Street the previous night.' On the basis of such fallacies, overtime would be reinstated and officers from outside Toxteth put on standby duty resulting in further overtime. When Scott detailed his concerns to senior officers that some incidents simply hadn't happened, he was told that if such reports upped the overtime, it was good for officers' morale and that bobbies would not work in Toxteth without the option of overtime.

It might not have been a policing policy but officers were capitalising on

Toxteth's reputation, intensifying corkscrew of decline in the district. Officers, though, were not the only people looking – or were allowed – to make money out of Toxteth's problems.

'At community meetings of police officers held at Admiral Street, all the emphasis was upon targeting black people or clubs and there was no discussion of tackling major crime and the real criminals,' Scott wrote. There had been no will within the force to tackle and eliminate the use of hard drugs during this period but there was a concerted effort to bring local people before the courts on public order charges 'even if the evidence was not all it should be'.

Scott had been assigned to the Toxteth Division two years after the riots. His duties had been to collect intelligence about drug dealing and active criminality. Based in Hope Street, his beat was on Granby Street. He would submit a full report into his findings and he was told they were going directly to the Chief Constable, Kenneth Oxford. It had become clear to him that every person in Toxteth had the potential to be treated as an offender regardless of their history after he was asked to set up a gallery in Hope Street and some of the photographs were taken from the files of local people who did not have criminal records.

In 1983, Scott had relayed that no hard drugs were in circulation. Cannabis was widely available and largely tolerated because it did not appear to lead to violence or anti-social behaviour. It had been his brief to watch for the possible introduction of hard drugs such as heroin and cocaine, 'which was already prevalent in other parts of Liverpool'.

Gradually he noticed a change, and the 'Liverpool men from outside the area' who were masterminding the circulation of drugs and beginning to 'use black people in Liverpool 8 to sell them'. It was his conclusion that 'had a police action been taken at this time, a halt could have been called to the escalation of the use of hard drugs...'

'It was hard to understand why the intelligence I was obtaining and passing on was not put to use,' he wondered. 'It seemed that the only intelligence that was wanted was that concerning small local people and not the major dealers or criminals from outside the division.'

In some cases, two years passed between the filing of reports and arrest. By that point hard drugs had become so entrenched that in the process of one conviction, a relative or associate would be able to take over the same business and so the issue was not going away.

Though he understood inter-departmental jealously within the force meant that while individual officers wanted to work with their own informants and different sections wished to maintain control of different areas of crime, he could not fathom why he was not encouraged to deal forcefully with the problem of hard drugs.

'We felt it was a dereliction of our duty,' he wrote. 'Some of the drug dealers appeared to be making individual deals with individual police officers so that their own activities would not be curtailed.'

Scott believed the Merseyside force recognised after 1981 that anything was better than another public order confrontation in Liverpool 8. Perhaps too the government realised that it could not afford risks around the negative headlines. It suited the Conservatives to portray what had happened in Liverpool 8 as a riot rather than an uprising, that black criminals had caused it rather than raging black youths fed up with racism and ultimately, unemployment that Monetarism had brought.

'The community would be left to *dope itself up...*' Scott concluded and this meant that a community which might otherwise cause problems for the police would be 'suppressed' by its new focus on drug use and circulation.

Scott's affidavit was shocking and damning, yet the headlines after the Gifford report related to Liverpool itself, where the racial discrimination was 'uniquely horrific', though it would be if the supposed minders' of the peace were approaching the city's most deprived area in such a brutal way.

At best for the police, Scott's testimony accused the police of low-level corruption but at worst it gave insight into the minds of the authorities at the time. Had the police and the government colluded to allow Toxteth to slide the same way as Liverpool entirely, just like Geoffrey Howe suggested?

For Toxteth and for Liverpool, the horrors of cocaine would follow. Scott became aware of Liverpool 8's first 'crack victim' in 1983. A nineteen-year-old was in such a state, he was able to snap a pair of handcuffs. Before long, drug dealers started coming from London to buy heroin and cocaine to re-sell. Large quantities arriving through Garston Dock and Bootle had made Liverpool prices cheap. When Scott reported that this new drug must have arrived in the area he was told by one of his superiors to 'stop being a clown'. Soon, the first crack factory in the United Kingdom was discovered at Kelvin Grove, Liverpool 8.

3

It's Just Smack

'I'D GROWN UP IN THE ALMOST ALL WHITE NORTH END, SO THERE was something cool about moving down there. You could get cheap flats. It was a bit edgy. It was the sort of place where artists had the space to thrive. There were lots of musicians, actors, poets and lunatics. You didn't need a plan, a path or an education. You had the freedom to make mistakes...'

And then, Pete Wylie interrupted his own flow: 'I'm sounding like I went to the University of Life, now aren't I? Fuck, I'm not turning into one of those people...'

Wylie had rented a flat in Kelvin Grove until his dog ran off and stopped in front of another property not too far away on the last road before Toxteth becomes Aigburth. It would become Disgraceland, his home of the next 35 years. 'A woman came out and asked if I was there for the viewing,' he remembered. 'There was no for sale sign. It was a detached house with big windows and you could see a big fire place inside. "I couldn't afford something like this," I said. She told me it was going up for £34,000. We had just enough to buy it. I love it. It's my safe place. Elsewhere in the country, it might cost a million or two. But in Toxteth...'

Wylie called it Disgraceland because by then, a title of his own had stuck and he was known as the Punk Rock Elvis. It was 1984 and his hit 'Story of the Blues' had reached number three in the charts. 'Suddenly, everyone was clamouring for the follow-up but I'd say, 'Nah, there is no follow-up.' We weren't a pop group churning out hit after hit on an industrial scale. Though they try to do that now, I never felt that sort of responsibility at all. In fact, I felt a commitment to do the opposite.'

Wylie's Twitter handle was 'Part Time Rock Star. Full Time Legend...'

a deliberate exaggeration, he reasoned; a laugh at his own expense, he continued – just the same as calling himself Peteloaf on stage. There was, however, some truth in the statement. He never quite became the star he could have been but in Liverpool – the city he refused to leave, especially for London, the city he 'detested' – his reputation remained legendary.

An interview with him is an explosion of stories, scurrying parallel conversations, immediate thoughts and long rants. He comes at you and then falls back. He is serious and maudlin. He is thoughtful and abrupt. You are not quite sure what is going to happen. I thought of him as being the ultimate Liverpudlian: the ultimate outsider in a city that existed on the outside, beyond the boundaries of acceptability. He liked that when I told him.

His first band was called the Crucial Three and it lasted for six weeks. The other members were Ian McCulloch, who would form Echo and the Bunnymen, and Julian Cope, who formed Teardrop Explodes. Wylie remained friends with McCulloch but not with Cope, though he could understand it when Cope later said: 'Someone like Pete Wylie would have been bigger if he had come from almost any other city except Liverpool.'

I sat with him by the window of the Monro pub in Liverpool's Duke Street which ran up a hill and southwards towards Chinatown and Toxteth. Beneath a pair of red-rimmed spectacles, his eyes sharpened when he spoke about his childhood. His whole life, he thought, could be explained by what happened in Walton.

He started off: 'I've got a fantasy version of my upbringing, one where I was born in Oxford Street the day after Buddy Holly played in the Philharmonic Hall. Elvis and Betty Page are my parents and they have sent me over here because they knew I would have ruined their careers.'

'The reality was,' he quickly carried on, 'I grew up in the last street before Norris Green. The house backed on to a railway line and trains rattled past. It was a dysfunctional working-class family where I was fat, shy and freaked out. In a three-bedroom house I lived with me mam, me dad, me nan, two brothers and a lodger. Me mam, I think now, had post-natal depression which impacted on me then and still does. I've been to therapy for that. Me mam and dad never spoke. She would ask me to ask me dad to fix the washing machine. He was a lot more mellow than me mam and looked like Norman Wisdom, without being as intellectual. I was academically bright. I went to a county primary school and they moved me up a year. I was ahead of other kids but too self-conscious and shy at that age to meet new friends. I was bullied when I was young. I didn't know my family was different to any other family until much later, more or less when I met McCulloch. His family were more loving and supportive.'

Further information came flying my way: he studied French, Latin and ancient Greek and teachers at his school, Alsop Comprehensive, suggested that he should go to university at Cambridge or Oxford. But he feared being away from the familiarity of Liverpool and he was more into music by the time he did his A levels. His mum had worked at Birdseye in Kirkby and, having joined a record club which entitled her to pick six new records every six weeks from Kirkby market, Wylie would choose the vinyls. He could remember fondly, the times his father who worked as a postman, would take him to Banners record shop in Broadway, Norris Green.

In 1971, Tony Blackburn's record of the week was 'Changes' by David Bowie. A year later he performed 'Starman' on *Top of the Pops* and from there, Wylie knew exactly what he wanted to be. 'When he stared into the camera and pointed, it felt as though he was pointing at me.' He submerged himself in music, swallowing every fact he could find and every lyric, which he later found ironic because by then he'd completely lost interest in the music created by other artists. 'Music became my escape route and it allowed me to be smart.' At Alsop, he eventually gained a reputation for being funny because he learned to laugh at himself, 'though I was still a fat get'. Though the bullies stopped bothering him, he remained self-conscious. 'I'm 60 now and if someone looks at me in TJ Hughes's it still scares the shit out of me.'

On stage, it would be different. His first gig was Black Sabbath in 1971. His favourite gig was Bowie a few years later. He started studying at Liverpool University on Monday 1 October, 1976. The previous Friday, a new nightclub called Eric's opened, one of 235 in Liverpool. After the closure of the Cavern, the venue associated closely with the rise of The Beatles, it became the cellar on Mathew Street where Liverpool's music scene roused itself once more. The Stranglers played on its first night and it was 60 pence to get in. Wylie went with his friend, McCulloch. 'The timing was crucial. The opening of Eric's also shaped my life,' he thought. 'Suddenly, I was meeting loads of people I had a natural rapport with, sharing ideas. Punk Rock was starting and when I went to see the Sex Pistols in November '76, Pete Burns was there. Has was dressed in PVC and I wore me trench coat. I'd never seen anyone like him in Liverpool. We hit it off. Eric's became everything.'

Wylie actively avoided employment, having worked eight days one summer at a rice mill which he hated because of the rats scurrying around the factory. He received a grant to study and figured out that he could just about survive on this and income from Probe, the famous record shop just down the road from Eric's. 'The freedom allowed me to have my own identity and be whoever I wanted to be. No commitments to anything.' He wanted to be a guitarist rather than a singer. 'I'd had a go doing backing vocals but I had a particularly loud voice and sometimes ended up being louder than the actual singer. As a child, I was taken to hospital because I talked loudly. My mum thought I was deaf. The doctor said, "he's not deaf, he's just fucking loud."'

Wylie loved Burns who along with spectacular fashion choices, possessed an ambiguous sexuality and was a master of androgyny. With Julian Cope, he joined one of Wylie's many early bands, the *Mystery Girls*. Burns would have a number one hit in Dead or Alive with 'You Spin Me Round' but before all of that, he worked in Probe with Wylie where he treated customers with disdain, sometimes throwing their purchases at them when he disapproved of their selection. 'Pete was jumped a few times for being who he wanted to be,' Wylie said. 'He wasn't a little fella; he could have been a docker. He'd face people down and challenge them and that's why we got on so well.' Holly Johnson from Frankie Goes to Hollywood was also in their social circle and he was a similarly punchy character. When Johnson later called the Queen a moron and it was splashed all over the *Sun* newspaper, it was Wylie who ended up getting headbutted. 'I've still got the blood on my clothes,' he stressed, proudly.

Gradually, the creative scenes at Eric's and the Everyman theatre would merge. Wylie met stage producers, film makers, actors like Pete Postlethwaite and Julie Walters as well as journalists. It was a fifteen-minute walk from Eric's up to Hope Street and the bar at the Everyman was open later. In 1980, John Lennon was shot dead in New York but Wylie was not one of the mourners. He had seen how The Beatles had moved on from Liverpool but how other bands from the city were expected to replicate their sound. From 1966 onwards, he believed, Liverpool's music industry was dead because of it.

'I'd tell reporters that we hated The Beatles, not because we absolutely did but because otherwise the story would lead on a line about us wanting to follow them when really, we wanted to create our own thing. They'd also left Liverpool and weren't quite as loved by everyone in Liverpool as people outside the city would imagine. It was a conscious decision to reject them. It was important for us to be able to say that we were going to write our own history.'

When a music journalist called Pete Frame helped produce a rock family tree about Liverpool as part of a BBC series involving other cities as well, he said that Liverpool's was the hardest to make – particularly as the 1970s became the 1980s and relationships in the punk rock scene that Wylie was a part of were so volatile and transient. Wylie alone separately formed Wah!, Wah! Heat, Shambeko Say! Wah!, Wah! The Mongrel and JF Wah!

'Though I didn't really think about making records,' he insisted. 'I just liked being in the scene. You'd go to a Clash gig then see them in a bar afterwards and think, "We're not that different." It was one of those scenes where you'd meet someone one night, become their mates and then form a band with them the next day only for it to all fall apart soon after, then you'd make up and rise again.'

'Smalltown Boy' by Bronski Beat was playing on the Monro's speakers, and then came Spandau Ballet's 'True'. 'These?' Wylie asked himself. 'Shite!' In one of his bands with Julian Cope called the Nova Mob, the chief aim was not to sell records at all and rather demand that Big in Japan split up. The petition earned nine signatures, at least three of which were from Big in Japan members, and the campaign ended with the Nova Mob's drummer Budgie defecting to the enemy.

'The rest of the world became the enemy,' Wylie reasoned. 'Though we weren't aggressive to other bands we didn't like. We took the piss and then ignored them. My mission was to go and take the piss out of Wham! because they represented a trendy, espadrilles wearing nonsense. But I met George Michael and he was fucking sound. He was really disarming. A lot of our ideas were based on supposition rather than research. George's heart was in the right place politically. Groups like Duran Duran represented everything that was bad in the early 80s. All they sang about was money and status.'

There were members of other Liverpool bands who claim Wylie wasn't politically minded then as he later became, but he boiled at that suggestion, suggesting that aside from China Crisis and Cook da Books, he was one of the few writers that described what was going on in a city divided by race and suffering horrendously from unemployment. By the time 'Story of the Blues' was released, he insisted that his primary creative influence was Alan Bleasdale, the screenwriter who captured the city's decline when he wrote *Boys from the Blackstuff*, the bleakly funny call-to-arms about the impact of Thatcher's Britain on Liverpool. 'The Story of the Blues was the story of the oppressed,' Wylie said. 'I may not have mentioned Liverpool directly but the song, I think, has gained a phenomenal sense of a city fighting back. It was *Boys from the Blackstuff*, the musical. Alan didn't shout from a box going, "Thatcher is bad," instead he showed the human impact of what was happening. He made me think differently and showed there were other approaches other than sloganeering.'

Wylie's music reflected his personality: big gestures and grand emotions, ballads that could go on and on though you did not necessarily want them to ever stop. He returned to Cope's idea that it could have been different for him had he come from elsewhere. Cope was born in Wales but went to school in the Midlands before careering towards the bright lights of Liverpool and Eric's. Cope defined Liverpool as a Celtic city and Manchester as Anglo-Saxon. 'There's a pragmatism about Manchester,' he said.

'That's true,' Wylie nodded. 'We're not like the rest of the country. There's a kinship with Glasgow and Belfast but there isn't with Manchester even though they're thirty miles apart. The way people talk and think are very different. What I am goes way before me, with the docks. A mate of mine wrote a book which discussed seafaring, the way every night in Liverpool people were either coming home or going away. There was either a sense of celebration because you've just arrived or despondency because you were departing; you could never get too attached but when you did, the loyalty was intense. It has always been far more emotional than other English cities as well as creative because of the uncertainty.'

No period was more uncertain than the 1980s, a decade Wylie spoke fondly of in terms of football because his beloved Liverpool FC were top of the league most of the time but also because Everton emerged as their closest rivals for domestic trophies and 'it felt like Merseyside ruled the world and that pissed everyone else off, particularly those who wanted to put the place down'. Though he could not remember the date, he thought there was at least one week when the top 40 music chart had eighteen bands with links to Merseyside.

'But,' he admitted, 'the emotion could yield different results because sometimes, we're not tactical enough.' He raced through stories covering the periods where he went on strike against the record company's wishes for weeks on end if he felt they were not listening. Apparently, there were board meeting minutes at Virgin that read: 'Pete Wylie would sacrifice his career over a small point of principle.'

'It wasn't meant as a compliment but I took it as one,' he grinned. 'It was the best fucking headstone I could ever have.'

His logic about London stemmed to his views about authority and being told what to do. 'It's a place which holds few morals,' he said. 'If they can make money out of you, they don't care if you're Adolf Hitler. This lot could justify anything. If you've got charm and charisma, it works for them. I never had a problem getting record deals because they looked at me and thought, "Yeah, he could be a massive star." You could see the dollar signs spinning through their eyes like the wheels on a fruit machine. But what drives them towards me also ended up driving them away. What they forget is, I'm an outsider. When I acted in a way they considered to be rebellious, they act surprised. "Well, you were warned."'

Rather than promote the next single after 'Story of the Blues', he sang 'Hope' on a television show called *The Tube*. He had argued the day before with someone from the record company, Warner. 'It was the least commercial song we had and I did it just to fuck them off,' he recalled, moving on to another tale, this one about Frankie Goes to Hollywood who became one of the biggest bands in the world in the mid-eighties but in Wylie's words were 'booting each other's arses as they went on stage at Wembley' a year later.

'We all shot ourselves in the foot to some degree,' he concluded. 'Pete Burns was the same, he only became a household name after he'd pissed everyone off in music because was televisual gold: so funny, quick-witted and cruel, a monster almost. We came from a city that is good at self-sabotage, at least if you're an outsider that's what it looks like. Here, it looks heroic.'

To Wylie, nobody symbolised this more than Derek Hatton, Militant's deputy leader of Liverpool Council who in 1984 stood up to the Conservative government and won, by finding a way to extract £20million of central funding when no other councils were able to. Wylie thought he was absolutely the hero Liverpool needed to ride the tide of Thatcherism and in the fade at the end of his song, 'Come Back,' Wylie whispered, 'Hats off to Hatton.'

'He was a hero for saying, "Fuck off, we're going our own way." But within a year when the specifics of policy started getting looked at more closely, the sort of stuff people weren't interested in before, they were coming up to me, going: 'What's happened with your mate Derek Hatton?' even though I didn't know the fella. Everyone thought it was going to be one long heroic stance without ever

THE LONG DECADE: 1979-1993

stopping to think about the details. He was vilified on the outside and vilified a lot on the inside as well but I think his stance alongside Tony Mulhearn was vital at that point in time.'

Wylie believed that it is ingrained in Liverpudlians to try and prove others wrong and that was what 'Come Back' was actually about, after a producer had told him years before to contact him again after he'd experienced success.

'Come Back' was about the city of Liverpool and how its desolation contrasted with other parts of the country. It was also about Liverpool FC, and the dreams its team inspired. 'Down by the docks the talking turned: As some are striving to survive, the others thrive,' came the first verse and then the second:

'Well did you ever hear of hope?
Yeah! Yeah! Yeah!
A small belief can mean
You'll never walk alone
And did you ever hear of faith?
Encouragement! Development!
And it's all to you!
Yes, it's all to you!'

John Peel described the song as a 'record that knocks your socks off' even though it only made it to twenty in the charts. Peel, though, operated in a parallel world. A journalist, a disc jockey, a radio presenter, and a record producer, he had been born into an upper-middle class family on the Wirral peninsula and had been educated at Shrewsbury at the same time as Michael Palin, the future star of *Monty Python*. Aged 21, he had moved to the United States to work for a cotton producer who had business dealings with his father and was in Dallas when President Kennedy was shot dead, filing copy through to the *Liverpool Echo*. As Beatlemania struck America, he passed himself off as an expert on the band due to his own connections with Liverpool and from there, a career in radio flourished.

'He played music that you wouldn't normally hear and a range of music you wouldn't normally hear,' Wylie said fondly. 'He had that weird accent that wasn't Liverpool but was as close as you could get.' Without Peel's influence, Wylie isn't sure whether Liverpool musicians like him would have had their platform to perform. He had first criticised Peel in an interview for not playing enough early

Pink Floyd and Peel invited him to Manchester to speak to him about music. 'He was a pretty important figure in the music industry by then and I thought he'd be surrounded by loads of Dave Lee Travis style bouncers ready to jump me for having a go at him but instead he was really humble. Because of the affection he developed for me, he was often disappointed because I didn't fit his fantasy way of approaching music. One of his things was to tell you early on that he was really good friends with Marc Bolan and as soon as he had a hit he didn't want to know him. Rod Stewart was the same. I think he thought that once we had our hit we'd leave him behind. But I wasn't like that. He'd call me and I'd be too shy to call back. He was the only music producer I utterly respected.'

Aside from calling his daughter Mersey, the most obvious thing Wylie could do to reflect his love for the city was write a ballad lasting nearly eight minutes in 1998 called 'Heart as Big as Liverpool.' Sony had thrown a million pounds at him after he nearly killed himself by falling onto railings in 1991, breaking his back. A convalescence lasting seven years encouraged him to go along with everything the record company suggested: 'Signings, interviews, interference; the lot – I thought, "I'm not going to be obnoxious anymore and I'll play the game."'

When he was told that the song would not sell anywhere other than Liverpool, he joked, 'It won't even sell there.' He was also told it was too sentimental. 'But I kept quiet and thought to myself, "Sentimental is throwing sugar on it to make it all sound nice." Liverpool's story is not necessarily nice.'

With two days left in a publicity tour, Sony dropped him. 'Even when I tried to fit into their world, it didn't really work,' he reflected before racing away with a story which had dozens of strands reduced to the following sequence of events: they gave him the LP for nothing, he found a distributor, he released it two years later and it sold 30,000 copies – many of them 'probably' in Liverpool. There was also a period on the dole, depression, and the mention of an incident where he 'shagged a chocolate cake in front of a load of pensioners'. Unusually, Wylie rarely drank in his early days at Eric's because he did not need alcohol to stimulate his creative juices. 'They just came.' It was always assumed that his path in music was punctured by drug use but he denied that emphatically. 'It was one of my great achievements in life, especially in that part of the 1980s when heroin was like spice is now.' He saw the heroin epidemic in Liverpool as a consequence of the hopelessness created by Thatcherism. He could remember being at an anti-heroin gig organised by the drummer of Wah! where this new, mysterious drug was still getting sold from behind the bar. 'Loads of people were on it, it was that fucking bad,' he said. 'Everyone was telling each other, "Go on, it's no trouble."'

'It was,' Wylie emphasised, suddenly turning grave, 'Nasty, nasty stuff.'

JOHN POWER WAS TALKING ABOUT HIS EXPERIENCES OF HEROIN. 'When you're scagged out, the stuff is bliss,' he confirmed. 'A mate who was heavily into the gear told me, "What you've got to remember, John, is that when you've had your hit and you're lying on the bed, if the house was on fire, you'd think, 'fuck it...' You'd stay on the bed because it's fucking great." That's how it was.'

Power had seen how heroin controlled entire lives: 'Heroin encompasses everything,' he continued. 'You lose all feeling for anything else. Everything revolves around getting that next hit because it's physically addictive and mentally addictive. That's why you read stories of addicts selling their property and going behind their family, they cease being described as loved ones because there's only one thing you love when you're on heroin and that's the gear. I've got mates who've lost their parents when they were on heroin and they've still not cried a tear because when you're on heroin, you're immune to emotion. You become a selfish bastard. If your best friend was dying from withdrawals and you needed it too, you wouldn't give it to him. Caring goes out of the window.'

I wondered whether Power was trying to tell me something in code about Lee Mavers, the 'golden-haired beat prophet' as *NME* called him – indisputably the greatest Mersey songsmith since Lennon and McCartney. I would put it to Power that Mavers was the most high-profile victim in Liverpool of the heroin epidemic. He would neither confirm nor deny the The La's split was ultimately because of drug abuse. 'You'd have to ask Lee about that,' was Power's instinctive response.

It was believed that 'There She Goes', the record that sent The La's on their way to stardom, was about heroin addiction but that too remained one of music's mysteries. Nobody knew for certain. Mavers had written the song and he liked to keep it that way. Power became slightly more forthcoming with reason and context, though he was happy conclude with a sense of the unknown.

'It's well documented that The La's had chapters of drug use,' Power admitted. 'Did it influence the song writing? I wouldn't like to be the one who put it on the record saying that it did because the only person who could ever answer that question would be Lee himself.

'In my view, the themes in all of our songs were too varied to be held down as being about one thing. It's up to the person listening to decide what the song means. If the listener thinks it's about heroin, then so be it. There She Goes is a very euphoric shout, like a geyser in Iceland... THERE SHE BLOWS! I'm going to say on the record that it's about a euphoric feeling of the heart when for a moment it all jumps and everything becomes beyond the rationale and reason of reality...

'We were off our heads for a long time,' he continued. 'Most bands are taking things to give them an alternative view. But a lot of people were taking drugs in Liverpool because life was shit. There was a real sense of hopelessness. It still happens now. If you speak to anyone on the street who's homeless, they're getting off their face because, Jesus, the reality of kipping on the pavement is horrendous. Liverpool and a lot of northern towns had their industries pulled out of them by Thatcher and that impacts on the community and the sense of self-worth. It all fell apart. It's outrageous thinking the government were sitting around a table discussing tactics and methods of how to dismantle Liverpool as a city and let it slide in a controlled way. It sounds medieval, like something the Romans did to the Greeks or the Babylonians: "What we do is put blood in the air and salt in the ground."'

Power was the youngest member of The La's and a month short of being five years Mavers's junior. The pair had been introduced through an older friend, Mike Badger, who Power had met at a music training scheme set up by Liverpool's Militant city council.

When heroin flooded Liverpool's streets between 1983 and 1984, Power was turning sixteen. It was crucial, he thought, because had he not been in school and had he been unemployed, 'heroin could have hit me a lot harder – like some of my mates' older brothers'.

'Heroin was rife,' he said. 'Later, I hung out at the Brookhouse on Smithdown Road, or one of the pubs on Penny Lane. There was a lot of people on the gear, generally three or four years senior to me, though there were lads in my age group who got into it as well once they hit sixteen. A lot of people already smoking weed went down that path, which involved burglaries and robbing. There seemed to be a moral line which said scag 'ed and house thieves were not accepted. Pot heads were alright. But once someone got a name as a scag 'ed, they'd get the big steer.'

I met Power at his home in Stoke Newington, London. The soles of his

Birkenstock sandals slapped against the floor as he guided me towards the kitchen, which would have smelled even stronger of coffee had the patio doors not been open on a warm summer's afternoon. He was otherwise dressed in a checked shirt and shorts and his hair was a distinctive mop of curls, just as it was when The La's formed. He detailed all of his life changes since moving to London sixteen years earlier. Most recently, he'd cut down on alcohol but before that there was a switch to veganism as well as the shedding of all forms of technology that he believed interfered with, if not entirely dominated, society's time. Mavers had been fiercely protective over the sound of his records and hostile towards studio machinery to the point where there were tales of him demanding that engineers working on guitars 'capture the sound of the tree it was made from'.

Listening to Power at this point of the discussion, it could have been Mavers. In place of a television in the corner of a living area was a guitar. He made a conscious effort to access his phone only once every couple of days to respond to emails and text messages. Power did not have such distractions as a teenager. He was a loner and liked it that way, spending hours looking through the window at the rain. 'Creativity comes from being at ease in your own company and daydreaming,' he said, describing himself as a 'sociable recluse', someone who likes to meet people but is not easy to reach. 'Constant distractions mean everyone only ever ends up doing the same thing,' he went on. 'It erodes knowledge of yourself. How can you ponder and question your own existence and other people's being if you're constantly in this false reality? Reality is malleable. It doesn't exist in one solid scope because we've all got the ability to interpret things differently. If you're troubled and the world is askew, everything can feel frantic. If you are top of the world, blissed up and in the moment, the fucking ugliest thing in the world is beautiful. That's why certain artists can create something out of nothing – something others cannot see.'

There was meaningfulness to his thoughts, though occasionally they would drift towards the sort of psychobabble Mavers was also famous for. He admitted that London had taken him to some extent, that although he liked himself more since getting away from Liverpool – explainable because of the separation from the torment of relationships where there was once love, he did wonder whether the capital had removed his edge. This had been the sum of all Pete Wylie's fears.

'When you're in Liverpool, you don't want to be a victim and so, you walk in a certain way and act a certain way,' he reasoned. 'In London, you can be a bit of a ponce and it's alright.'

'The La's,' Power said, 'didn't try to be anything we weren't. Used to your advantage, Liverpool can be a strength. You think you are better than the rest. It can get you a long way. It can help you get through stuff and past obstacles. You've got a bit of foresight and wit. Nobody's going to take the piss.

'But then,' he added, 'this was viewed by a middle-class press as being too much as well as the middle-class nowhere across the rest of middle-England. A lot of journalists were great. But we also came across a lot who were probably from the Home Counties, probably with Tory backgrounds; quite posh. They just didn't get where we were coming from. They didn't like the way we presented ourselves, didn't like the angle and couldn't relate to that Liverpool scally that was in me. I kept a front on and I wouldn't have known it at the time but when I look back, it was a quite unfulfilling experience. My most successful time musically was probably the most stressful and the least enjoyable. I've blanked it out; it was like a bad childhood.'

His father was born in Waterford and when he was six years old, he travelled by boat to live in a tenement block that overlooked Liverpool's Chinatown, sleeping to six in a bed in his school uniform. The death of his father's mother led to abandonment by his 'sod' of a grandfather but despite being forced onto the streets, where he lived in abandoned Victorian houses, Power's father was eventually able to enrol at the Open University. Though he studied sociology, he would spend most of his working life at the Ford car plant in Halewood, 'which he fuckin' hated', because he believed night shifts were detrimental to living standards and psychology. 'Your body clock goes to pot – you live to work, you don't work to live.' Power considers himself fortunate that unlike lots of other Liverpool musicians, his father did not demand that he followed a traditional working man's path.

'When I was sixteen and hanging around on the streets, I asked my dad to get me an application form for Ford because the pay was actually quite good. He came back and said, "There's no forms left, they're all gone." It was only years later that he admitted that he'd lied. He wanted something better for me. He was a dreamer. In a different environment, it might have been different for him. I'm trying not to sound patronising because if you're skint and you have to pay the rent, Ford is steady. But he did make me realise there is more to life.'

One of Power's earliest memories was of his father explaining the difference between the rock and roll of John Lennon and the pop music of Paul McCartney. Lennon's first home had been at 9 Newcastle Road in Wavertree, less than a mile away from the Powers, who lived in a crescent of neatly appointed houses formerly owned by the fire service and police authorities. McCartney was originally from Speke but like Power, would grow up in Allerton, at 20 Forthlin Road. Liverpool's South End was the city's musical beat. 'My dad was a rock'n'roller... he loved Chuck Berry and Eddie Cochran.'

When Power displayed an interest in joining the cadets because a barracks was just around the corner, his father intervened: '"No chance," he said. He's anti-army. He's Irish. He went: "You go through school hating being told what to do then you want to join the army?" He wouldn't sign the forms. He instilled in me the idea we shouldn't be shaped by authority and that actually, individualism should be championed in a creative sense but not necessarily in an economic way.'

Power moved temporarily to Croydon after leaving school and at his home in Stoke Newington he still had the elastic band ball that he made at the Home Office as a reminder to the direction he was heading. 'I was opening letters all day with a bunch of aul' women. They were sound! But I was, like, "If I don't get out of here, I'll be here for the next forty years..."'

The job earned him £86 a week and he bought a bass guitar with one of his first wage packets, which he'd carry with him a bin bag when he went home at weekends using the National Express bus route. Back in Liverpool, he'd hang out at the attic floor of a friend's house on Smithdown Road opposite the cemetery. Amidst a haze of marijuana smoke, Power learned the basic three chords of the bass and following an interview to join a youth scheme set up by Militant, he came away with a determination to prove at least one person wrong.

'Two guys were there, one called Terry and another guy who was a git – I can't remember his name. I found out later that he was exactly what my intuition said. I came clean and told them that although I was into music I could only play three notes on bass. My spirit got me through the door. Terry liked me. But the git of a fella didn't. He was a show off, getting out his own bass, going *biddly-diddly-biddly-diddly- biddly-diddly*. He turned to me and said, "I bet you wish you could play like that, son..." I thought, "Fuck off you, you fat bastard." He was one of those sorts of fellas: probably a racist and a shithouse who'd snitch on you.'

The 'git', it transpired, was embezzling funds and before it was able to have a real impact on the youth of Liverpool, the scheme was shut down. Power appeared in the *Liverpool Echo* underneath the headline: POP FLOPS. 'It was our first bit of fame. The photographer asked us to all look sad so there we were, all glum.' The scheme nevertheless brought about the beginning of crucial friendships.

'Straight away, you could see the creative types. There was a lad in Chinese slippers, a goof. Another lad who was brilliant on the guitar. Then there was Mike Badger, who I took to because he looked cool. He had '50s clobber on, shades n' all that. We hit it off over smokes at lunchtime. It turned out he knew Lee Mavers.'

When Badger went to Mavers, who was looking for a new bass guitarist, and told him that he knew 'this sound lad', before warning him that he was still learning how to play, Mavers apparently replied: "Brilliant, that's what I want – someone I can teach."

After the post-punk rock of Wylie, and the dance pop of Frankie Goes to Hollywood, The La's brought the most authentic Liverpool sound. In 1991 during an interview in Japan, Mavers would suggest there were only four routes to success if you came from Liverpool and those routes involved football, boxing, criminality or music. Power loathed the sound of the previous decade from musicians like Julian Cope, who thought 'let's put eye-liner on, dark overcoats and act like it's all too much to handle,' before Mavers claimed it was 'not serious music'. Cope and 'all of them' Mavers said, were 'dead end', and by listening to The La's, 'you've got to come out of that alley way and into the main road'. Six months later, however, Power had left the band, frustrated with playing the same set of songs. In 1987, they had been tipped as a newer and better version of The Smiths but four years had yielded just a couple of single releases and an album Mavers hated.

At the beginning, the Pen and Wig pub had been their residency and Power was keen to stressed that The La's worked really hard to get their sound heard. 'It was to the point where some people were sick of us.' It helped, though, that The La's looked and sounded like they were from Liverpool: a truly representative band of the city at a certain point in history, just like Oasis were later for Manchester. The La's was pronounced Laa's and not Larze while Mavers was pronounced Mavvers not Mayvers. A dress sense had emerged from the scally culture on football terraces. It was at this point Power did reveal something about Mavers, who would only speak about Everton – his one true love supposedly – in later interviews. 'The reason Lee likes Everton is because of Ever... tone... Evert... tone,' Power would say, insisting that he had previously supported

Liverpool before the music scene took his interest away and melted it altogether. 'I think he might have even had a shake on the head off Bill Shankly,' added Power. He remembered a festival called Earth Beat in the early days of The La's when the Stone Roses were performing, 'dressed like goths in long coats – like the Bunnymen'.

When Jo Whiley introduced Power's next band as 'Carst', Power – wearing a Berghaus mountain coat – jumped in, announcing: 'We're Cast...'

'I was uptight, a bit too aggressive,' he reflected. 'You know how Liverpool lads are... got a bit of a front.' Despite Cast's success (two albums which went platinum), Power believed that the middle-class music press never took to Cast in the same way they did Oasis because scally culture had its roots in Liverpool and not Manchester and by then, Liverpool felt a lot more disconnected to the rest of England than Manchester, which culturally felt as though it had already started to overtake Birmingham as the country's second city.

'Snobbery,' Power called it. 'We got a lot of stick by the doyens of the music writing scene for wearing a checked shirt with cords and adidas trainers. They wanted everyone to look like Pulp instead. They tried to frame Cast as hooligans.'

Cast would prove to be far more productive than The La's, releasing nine singles across three years where there were two albums. Noel Gallagher described watching Cast play live as 'a religious experience.' The La's, however, are still regarded as one of the greatest bands that never quite got it together.

'There She Goes' had been a masterful display of songwriting. The video, shot on a hand-held camera in the sidestreets of Liverpool's South End, opened in a blur of psychedelia, with a young attractive girl appearing before fading away. Soon there were rumours about it being an ode to heroin, thanks to the line, '*There* she goes, *pulsing through my vein.*'

By the time the song was re-released in October 1990, reaching number thirteen in the charts, the band's reputation had also spread. Mavers was fiercely protective over the sound of his records, and his attitude towards interest in his own abilities was well known, too. Having sacked three producers, Mavers was reported to have rejected the use of a vintage mixing desk because 'it hasn't got the original Sixties dust on it'. When the self-titled The La's was finally released in October 1990, Mavers said that he 'hated' the album because of the sound, which was, 'All fucked up like a snake with a broken back.'

'We jibbed it three months in,' Mavers explained. 'It's a croke.'

He did not like the business of music, speaking about 'the red tape, the cooks spoiling the broth', and most of all, 'being told what to do'.

Barely a word would be spoken onstage. All that was important to Mavers was the music. When a young presenter in New York tried to get to know The La's by suggesting, 'You guys are like the Beatles, right?' Mavers did respond but only succinctly: 'Nah.'

'The La's had issues with themselves,' Power reasoned. 'Lee was definitely the most naturally gifted songwriter of a generation. No doubt about it. I've met a lot of people and nobody comes close to Lee. It was his full understanding of rhythm and melody. He can be the most charming guy in the world but he can also be closed and unforthcoming. There's a lot of bullshit in the industry. You've got to do a lot of things you'd prefer not to. He'd reach that point pretty quickly and in fairness, so did I. That's why The La's remain underground. They never did the tours. They made one album, which Lee still absolutely despises.'

Power had 'hated Thatcher from the moment I first heard her speak'. He listened to his father, who was pro-Arthur Scargill when she took on the miners. Her ideal was influential in the music industry. 'Quickly – if you're not careful – you end up making a lot of money for the man,' Power admitted. The La's were signed to *Go! Discs*, an independent record company that also had Billy Bragg, The Housemartins and Portishead. It was different with Polydor, a major label that had Jimi Hendrix, The Who and the Jam. 'If a movie was to be made about the music industry at this time it would be like the *Wolf of Wall Street* because there was so much money sloshing about and everyone was coked off their heads. Everyone was fucking everyone else over. The majority of the people in the industry were non-musical – corporate fat cats, who'd drop you tomorrow if the smelt money somewhere else.'

Power realised that drugs had always been a part of the arts, 'whether it was in the jazz age where musicians have taken things to bring themselves down or taken things to help give them an alternative perception and kick off a new creative flow'. Though he admitted smoking lots of weed, that he did a lot of speed and then acid, he rejected smack. 'I think it had been instilled in me that scag 'eads were meffs,' he said. 'You had to keep it at arms' length because a couple of toots and you'll be wanting some more.'

✳

Scotland Road, 1895. Liverpool was an incredibly wealthy city, but the divide between rich and poor was stark. In 1899, Daily Post journalist Hugh Farrie described Scotland Road as 'dirt, tumble-down, and as unhealthy as any part of squalid Europe'. [GETTY]

The general transport strike of 1911, involving dockers, railway workers and sailors. Until the 1960s, Liverpool's dockers remained largely unorganised labour, and at this point it was more of a conspiratorial rather than radical city. [GETTY]

In 1976, a nightclub named Eric's opened in the centre. Following the closure of the Cavern, this is where Liverpool's music scene roused itself once more. [MIRRORPIX]

A policeman stands stationary as a building burns to the ground during the Toxteth riots, which started in July 1981. [GETTY]

Four young boys stand outside a building. The building in question is the furniture store Swainbank's, run by a councillor whose antagonism to local people had been documented six years earlier. [MIRRORPIX]

Looting on Lodge Lane the morning after the first wave of riots. [HOMER SYKES]

Kenneth Oxford leaves after a meeting with community leaders during the riots and is protected by members of the police as he returns to his car. Oxford was chief constable of Merseyside police from 1976 to 1989, a controversial figure who was close to Conservative prime minster Margaret Thatcher. [REPORT DIGITAL]

Conservative MP Michael Heseltine walks around Toxteth following the riots. Despite being a key member of Thatcher's government, Heseltine enjoyed a largely amicable relationship with the people of the city due to his willingness to listen. In 2012, he was granted the Freedom of Liverpool. [MIRRORPIX]

Thatcher and her Secretary of State for Employment Norman Tebbit were far less willing to listen than Heseltine. Here they are at the 1981 Conservative Party Conference in Blackpool, where Tebbit gave his infamous 'On yer bike' speech. [ALAMY]

In 1981, the *Guardian* visited the Ford Estate in Birkenhead to do a feature on the children living there, two of whom had won literary prizes for the poetry, detailing the anguish of their upbringing. They would visit twenty years later, to discover that only three of the children lying on this grassy verge were not using drugs. Four from the photo had passed away. [ALAMY]

The Ford Estate from above, pictured in 1981. By the mid-1980s, it was by far and away at the top of Wirral Council's Multiple Deprivation Index. Like much of Liverpool and Wirral, it was a place badly affected by the heroin epidemic. [ALAMY]

Amid the political and social chaos in Liverpool during this era, music continued to thrive. Pete Wylie, guitarist and leader of Wah!, was one of the most influential figures, and in 1998 wrote the song 'Heart As Big As Liverpool.' [MIRRORPIX]

The La's rose to prominence in the second half of the 80s and receive critical acclaim for their self-titled album released in 1990, but the band and in particular frontman Lee Mavers (second from left) wanted nothing to do with it, and they would release nothing else. Bassist John Power (second from right) would go on to form Cast, who released two platinum albums. [GETTY]

Liverpool players line up to face AS Roma in the 1984 European Cup final, in Rome. The violence in the Italian capital would set the mood for the terrible events of Heysel twelve months later. [GETTY]

The fight back begins. Plagued by astonishing unemployment, civil unrest and a heroin epidemic, Derek Hatton and Militant go on the campaign trail. [PA]

A young girl on roller skates shows her support for the Militant led Liverpool council in 1985. [ALAMY]

Derek Hatton and Tony Mulhearn, two pillars of the Militant movement, address thousands of trade union members at a demonstration in support of the council in front of city hall. [ALAMY]

Hatton commanded support across much of the city but was not universally popular. In 1986, he was thrown out of the Labour Party, and plenty of people had already shown their displeasure. [GETTY]

Kevin Ratcliffe, Everton's inspirational captain, celebrates securing the 1984/85 league title. Soon after Everton would win the European Cup Winners' Cup and looked primed for European Cup glory. [GETTY]

Their chance would never come following the Heysel disaster, which ended in the expulsion of English teams from European competition. Trouble at the European Cup final between Liverpool and Juventus fans led to a collapsed wall and the death of 39 Juventus fans. [MIRRORPIX]

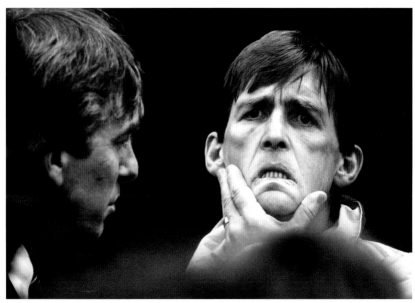

Kenny Dalglish, Liverpool's inspirational manager, looks on in anguish as the unthinkable unfolds at the Hillsborough, a disaster which took the lives of 96 Liverpool fans who had travelled down to Hillsborough for their FA Cup semi-final with Nottingham Forest. [GETTY]

Labour's Peter Kilfoyle is congratulated by his daughters after victory in the controversial 1991 Walton by-election, which was marred by accusations of rigging. Kilfoyle did not get on at all with the Militant council, describing Hatton as 'loathsome'. [PA]

The murder of two-year-old Jamie Bulger on 12 February 1993, abducted and tortured by ten-year-old boys Jon Venables and Robert Thompson was another shock for the city to process. There was serious anger as well, and here a man is prevented by police from charging at a van carrying the two boys to court. [PA]

There was unrelenting media attention, with many publications using it as an opportunity to paint the city in a negative light. There were cameras everywhere, even at the funeral. [MIRRORPIX]

The landing stage at Liverpool docks in the early 20th century. The docks once made the city one of the most prosperous in the UK, behind only London around this time. [ALAMY]

WHEN HE WAS TAKEN ON A TOUR OF CANTRIL FARM IN 1981 BY JIM Lloyd, the Labour leader of Knowsley Council, Michael Heseltine saw 'a classic post-war concrete jungle' – a badly designed and poorly built estate with nine tower blocks, deck-access maisonettes and a derelict shopping centre on top of a vast underground car park. A third of properties were empty and Lloyd predicted to Heseltine that ten years later, the last family to leave would have to 'turn off the lights'.

Heseltine's solution was monetarist, persuading the Abbey National Building Society and Barclays Bank to invest into a trust and this resulted in the 1986 launch of Stockbridge Village. The initiative in Heseltine's eyes had been 'a pioneer in the harnessing of private sector finance', as he roared with satisfaction: 'What had once been a monolithic public sector housing estate known locally as Cannibal Farm, was now a decent multi-tenure modern estate with its own waiting list. The queue to get out became a queue to get in.'

Before Peter Hooton became the lead singer in The Farm, he was a youth worker in the district of Liverpool where the band took their name. Like a lot of people in Liverpool, Hooton was suspicious of Heseltine and his motives, recognising that he was a threat to Margaret Thatcher and by sending him to deal with a problem city where he might have failed, he would be out of her way at a moment where unemployment was at its highest and the resistance against her was growing. Though he admitted Heseltine did find some solutions like at the Albert Dock, which transformed Liverpool's waterfront, Hooton thought Heseltine's take on the development of Stockbridge was too simplistic. The village certainly looked tidier at the end of the investment but some of the better houses were owned privately and few of the residents could afford to purchase one of them. Those that did were bound by Margaret Thatcher's right-to-buy scheme, which promised discounted housing only to see interest rates soar quickly, reducing the chances of them striking if they were fortunate enough to have had a job in the first place because there was a mortgage to pay.

'The appearance papered over the cracks,' Hooton suggested, and a Labour government survey eighteen years later would agree with him, reflecting rather differently on Heseltine's achievements in Cantril Farm. He had found a way to tear down many of the buildings, replacing them with additional housing, but by 2004 Stockbridge Village and the surrounding area remained a centre of urban poverty, ranked as the third most deprived district in the country. 'Now, nearly

30-years on,' Hooton stressed, 'we have Rachman-type landlords who have benefited the most from right-to-buy. Her supporters would say Thatcher was clever. I would say it was devious.'

Housing had not only been central to the heroin epidemic in Cantril Farm, it was central to all of Liverpool's problems – and ultimately its relationship with Westminster. Housing was linked to drugs. Drugs were linked to unemployment. Unemployment was linked to the docks and distance from the docks was linked to the housing problem. Meanwhile, unemployment was directly linked to the monetarist policies of the Conservative government. It was an atrocious economic and social tangle, with one issue compounded by the next – though it had been a collection of the main political groups that had initially failed Liverpool decades before by not solving the housing crisis when it was at its deepest.

Labour, the Conservatives and the Liberals traded control at the head of the city's council with none either willing or able to make progress on another's measures. There had been other Cantril Farms; like the Braddocks, towers which for just 29 years stood over Everton heights as monuments to Jack Jones and Bessie Braddock – the Labour politicians and their policies that dominated Liverpool's post-war era after wrestling control from the Conservatives for the first time in the city's history. Having been built in 1958, by the early 1980s tenants were left 'feeling like prisoners' when the lifts failed or when the condensation made views of the River Mersey invisible through the narrow windows. Labour's high-rise urban renewal programme had alienated voters and this allowed the Liberals to emerge, taking seats from Labour and decimating the Conservatives. For a decade, no single party held a majority on a council run by a minority of Liverpool administrators with the reluctant support of the Conservatives. In his 1985 book *Liverpool on the Brink*, Michael Parkinson – a professor at the University of Liverpool – concluded that the period was a recipe for 'confusion, delay and drift'.

Even before World War Two, there had been a necessity to clear Liverpool's slums and the 1936 Liverpool Corporation Act approved in parliament was followed by the Merseyside Plan of 1944. Bombing had worsened the city's condition, not least because of the number of damaged properties but also because of the inadequacy of construction materials and skilled labour, as well as demobilisation and a rising birth rate. By 1947, there were more than 20,000 unfit buildings in the centre of Liverpool and 33,000 applicants on the waiting list for accommodation. The political issue of the era led to party promises and immediate solutions, like the building of 3,000 bungalows, 1,100 of which were on the estate of Belle Vale. Over the next decade, close to 150,000 Liverpudlians would move homes on sites towards the edge of the city, heralding a new term 'overspill.'

While Speke's population rose from 4,000 in 1921 to 27,000 by the end of the 1960s, Kirkby became the fastest growing township in Britain – its boom emphasised in 1967 by the creation of a fourth housing estate called Tower Hill in addition to the ones in Northwood, Westvale and Southdene. Such haste resulted in a lack of comprehensive planning. A *Guardian* article from 1967 described Halewood, 'the rural idyll of hedges, broccoli and carrots,' which had already 'disappeared underneath Liverpool's bricks and concrete'. A photograph showed a street where the sign Pleasant View had been graffitied and named instead, Peasant View. The wider mood was summed up by a housing development officer at a council meeting when he said: 'There was a tendency to redevelop simply the housing. Partly because of necessity in the desperate housing shortage and because we can think about the rest of the stuff afterwards... people howl like hell that we must build more houses and as soon as they have got a house they say: "This is a bloody awful area. There are no schools or places for children to play. Why aren't these things happening?" You mention them before and they say, "Oh those are frivolities, they must wait..."'

In Cantril Farm, there had been a five to ten-year gap between the first wave of residents and the completion of the principal shopping and leisure facilities. This meant families were forced to use a select few shops, some of which added a premium to the price of goods. Restrictions in public transport compounded the sense of isolation. In Kirkby, workers relied on a tram service to reach the docks that ended in Fazakerley, adding extra travel time and inconvenience to their working day. In Cantril Farm, 69 per-cent of households did not have a car and there were complaints about the irregularity of the bus service. Much of Liverpool's working opportunity remained on the docks and there was only a small amount of manual work in the new areas. In Kirkby, the first manufacturing firms had arrived six years before the creation of new housing and so, there was already an established workforce. In Cantril Farm, only eleven per-cent changed their jobs on relocation. It resulted in workers feeling cut off from where they needed to really be. 'For many, in the early days life consisted entirely of sleep and work,' noted one council report.

An underfunded and divided council without one dominant party had been unable to maintain the properties and the complaints mounted. A housing committee chairman in Netherley described the development there as a 'mistake' before an estate had even been completed and within four years, a set of mid-rise flats nicknamed locally as 'Alcatraz' were suffering from water penetration. The Netherley Flat Dwellers Action Group was formed, and the discoveries were bleak, relating to drainage, vermin and the ill-effects on mental health due to poor social and transport networks. Meanwhile, in Cantril Farm a common grievance related to the thickness of the walls – that noise carried.

By 1983, the English House Condition Survey – conducted in 1981 – revealed that nearly a quarter of the housing in Liverpool was in poor condition. This included the Granby Ward where the riots had happened that year and many of the unfit dwellings had not been cleared with the same urgency or scale as the white areas like Scotland Road, north of the city. Sir Trevor Jones, a Liberal Democrat who served as leader of Liverpool's County Council from 1981 to 1983, would then emphasise the gap between politicians and residents, saying, 'You can't say the cause was bad housing because the whole area is redeveloped to a high standard.' Housing had improved in Granby but not all that is new marks progress. The flats of the Falkner Estate over the road from the Triangle were deeply unpopular, a place where just a few sets of curtains marked the homes of those who were trapped amidst otherwise smashed or boarded up windows.

The results of the clearance – despite the good intentions to wipe out some of the worst housing conditions anywhere in Britain – were disastrous both economically and socially. While people were stacked vertically when they were used to living horizontally, many families did not have a real choice in where they were relocated and this meant that old social networks which defined relationships as well as street culture were destroyed. A collective discipline was interrupted twice over, once by the dismantling of local networks and then by placing living spaces up in the air. The draughty landings and blurrily lit corridors of a tower block did not encourage unanimity or the control of children. 'No pubs, corner shops and no meeting points', featured in Cantril Farm life as they had been back towards the city centre, one resident said in another council report. In the midst of all the problems, changes and subsequent pressures, the collective discipline and solidarity of the old working-class areas was lost.

Peter Hooton began his job as a youth worker in 1980. He had a post-graduate teaching certificate but did not like the idea of working in a structured education system. His responsibility was on the street: encouraging young people into youth clubs, trying to help them discover a focus. His base was not an office but an estate, outside the Bow and Arrow pub in Cantril Farm. 'The level of social deprivation was stark,' Hooton recalled. 'But even in 1980 we didn't foresee the ravages of Thatcher's Britain. In 1981, 1982 it had really kicked in.'

By 1982, unemployment in Cantril Farm and nearby Dovecot had passed fifty per-cent. A report about the state of housing in Cantril Farm emphasised the importance of the docks and how many of the other manufacturing industries in the city relied on them. Sugar, for example, would arrive in the port then be taken over the road to the Tate and Lyle grain silo before being transported inland to jam factories. As dock activity declined, so did Tate and Lyle and when that refinery shut in 1981, costing an initial 1,800 jobs, it had a domino effect because another 5-6,000 were lost in the supporting brewing, sweets and confectionery, and cake and biscuit industries.

In Cantril Farm, Hooton witnessed, 'a complete lack of energy – people became apathetic because there was no work available, they had no money. There was a desperation, a hopelessness.' This was before the arrival of a new plague, 'that nobody had ever heard of, called smack'.

Into this stasis came heroin, a drug that initially seemed exotic and exciting. Officers inside Merseyside Police believed in the post Toxteth riot years, criminals – particularly drug dealers – were able to operate with greater autonomy because of the decline of a police presence. There were those theories about the authorities assessing the climate in Liverpool's south end, concluding that a doped-up community is easier to police than an angry and resistant one. It was also suggested that Liverpool's port was losing its relevance and therefore it simply become easier than ever for drugs to enter the city.

Hooton, who would emerge as another of those musicians like Pete Wylie touched by the influence of John Peel, could vividly remember the sight of an attractive-looking barmaid in the Bow and Arrow enjoying a 'toot' of smack on her break. 'You'd see all sorts of people heating it up in the pub,' he said. 'Smack was like a Saatchi & Saatchi campaign by the dealers. Whoever came up with the name would have won a business awards if it wasn't illegal. I was saying to users, "That's heroin, you know?"

"Nah, it's smack – it's different, you don't get addicted to this; you have it at the weekend then leave it," I'd get told. This was because they weren't injecting. There was a real ignorance about the drug and what it could do. The very fact it was called smack meant it did not have the association with heroin. It swept council estates and became a massive problem. It took everyone by surprise. It was like an avalanche.'

There was an epidemic in Liverpool which swept from Cantril Farm in the south of the city, up towards Croxteth, laying waste to every estate before Bootle – where the dealers operated on Marsh Lane – and then Waterloo.

'There was no epidemic in the middle-class areas,' Hooton stressed. 'It was down to the fact there was mass unemployment, people had time on their hands; there is always a certain escapism attached to drug abuse. People can't afford it but when they become addicted, they take risks to ensure they have it and this leads to an increase in criminality. If people had nine till five jobs, the majority wouldn't have even contemplated taking heroin. Instead, they were in bedsits listening to Pink Floyd with nothing else to do, going: "Here we go, try this; it'll make the music sound better..."' The authorities were overwhelmed. The warrens of Cantril Farm and the lay out of the estate made it easier to run for dealers, easier to hide for users and fundamentally more difficult for the police to intervene. From a 1963 council report which detailed Liverpool's problems only two pages across 579 concerned drugs – concluding that opium was only used then amongst the older residents of Chinatown for stomach complaints. In 1970, Merseyside Police had one dog trained to find cannabis. By the late 1980s, twenty-four were sniffing out heroin and cocaine. Jim Fitzsimmons later became a specialist in drug enforcement and he did not give the impression that he had ever been an officer who partook in the business of exaggeration.

'Heroin was everywhere,' he said. 'It takes control not just of the person but the family. It picked up such a pace and led to devastation beyond anyone's real understanding. If you were caught with heroin you were a criminal. There was no help anywhere. The mothers would come to me and ask: "What can I do – how can I help my son?" That used to break my heart because I didn't have any answers. I'd say, "If you can handcuff him in, I'll come around every single day to check he's there..." Reactions were ad-hoc. It put massive pressure on the police. It led to an escalation in crime, violent crime and crime from family to family. An addict will take from wherever they can get it. They don't care. They're not thinking realistically or logically. They only think about what they need to either stop themselves from getting a hiding because they owe money or to get their next fix. Families were having to hide valuables. Heroin became the biggest heartache.'

WHEN A PAKISTANI SHIP CARRYING HEROIN WITH A STREET VALUE
of £1million was seized in Ellesmere Port, customs officers admitted to reporters
they were losing control. It was April 1983, roughly around the time Brendan
Wyatt went back to a Birkenhead flat following a night out in Liverpool. He was
accompanied by a friend and two girls. What happened next surprised him. One
of the girls reached into her purse and brought out some foil. 'Then the smack...
it was dead casual, as if they were just smoking a spliff,' he remembered, through
the fug. 'Don't worry, it's just smack – you don't get addicted to it...'

Wyatt returned to his side of the Mersey without having tried 'this new drug'
but within a few years, it had taken him – just as it had already gripped Birkenhead
by that point, where nine per-cent of 16- to 24 year-olds were users. Research in
the 1980s found that if you lived on the Wirral estates, particularly in the Noctorum
area – which like those in Liverpool, were hastily built in the post-war years –
you were sixteen times more likely than the average person to die.

Wyatt marked the scourge of smack as a 'pandemic'. In 1981 the *Observer*
magazine published a feature called 'The Writing on the Wall' and it featured
fifteen children from Noctorum's Ford Estate, two of whom had won literary
prizes for poetry which detailed the anguish of their upbringing. Twenty-three
years later, when the *Guardian* went back to Ford, it discovered that only three of
the children who were originally photographed lying casually on a grassy verge in
front of a row of council houses one summer's evening were not using drugs. Four
people from the photo had passed away. Ford had the Buccaneer pub at its centre
and it had fighting, 'They were always fighting,' said David Thompson, a footballer
known for his own ferociousness while playing for Liverpool in the late 1990s.

Ford had always been the toughest part of the Wirral peninsula, with tough
people – though people who worked. By the mid-1980s, however, Ford was also far
and away at the top of Wirral Council's Multiple Deprivation Index. Frank Field
became Birkenhead's MP for Labour in 1979, a position he would hold for 29 years,
and his assessment of the plunge in living standards was rooted in grassroots
social leadership. 'Drugs would spread because the natural leaders on the estate
were either leaving for work in other areas of the country due to unemployment
levels,' he thought initially. 'Or they were being sent to prison where they were
corrupted into drug taking themselves and from there became drug suppliers.

When they came out of prison, they brought the habit with them back to their home estate.'

While Liverpool offered dock work, Birkenhead was a ship-building town, separate from Liverpool by the river and with its own identity but nevertheless coexisting in the same geo-political and economic space. Cruise liners like the *Mauretania* and *Windsor Castle* had been amongst the famous vessels to slide down its great slipways as well as the aircraft carrier, *Ark Royal*. It is still believed a secret clause in a deal between the British government and the European Commission in the 1980s reduced British shipbuilding capacity in return for £140 million, helping to sink the yard and employment levels.

Field had witnessed in a very short period of time Birkenhead's transition from a town where young men leaving school had a choice of firms in the docks to work for, to one where there were limited options if any at all. 'We had 26,000 dockers and that was knocked down to under 400,' Field recalled. 'Birkenhead's docks went from a place that had made an awful lot of people feel important to one where there was desperation; one where wages would provide for a family to one where the alternatives were the benefit system or in many cases criminality.'

There was one theory that smack penetrated Birkenhead's estates just before Liverpool's because Liverpool's gangsters wanted to use it as a testing ground – nobody was quite sure of heroin's capabilities. It had been around London's bohemian community in Soho for almost a century, but researchers believed its availability only began to spread after 1979 when revolution in Iran led to a refugee crisis across Europe. In Liverpool, smugglers marketed it as a non-addictive smokeable high but uncut and 90 per-cent pure, it would leave users like Brendan Wyatt 'off your head for hours – rather than withdrawing quickly'. It would feed off boredom, alienation and desperation.

Howard Parker, whose 1985 book *Living with Heroin*, dealt with case studies from the Ford Estate, believed that what happened in Liverpool and Birkenhead was a part of a cycle that began in the US in the 1960s, explaining that epidemics like these have lifespans of ten to fifteen years before the demand retreats because the next generation 'won't go near it – they've seen the impact'. Smack, therefore, only became 'dirty' and the drug of 'losers' when the lower orders in big numbers were hooked.

Wyatt was one of them. He had grown up amongst the terraced streets of Kirkdale, a fiercely strong-willed district and working class to its core. He had a vivid memory of his childhood and could envisage being in a classroom in 1979. 'Thatcher was elected in May 1979 and I remember the morning after clearly: a twelve-year-old devastated by politics – can you imagine?' He had learned about the realities of life early, after his mother died when he was just four. By the time Thatcher got in, his father had already been made redundant from his job on the docks because of containerisation. 'You're suddenly finding yourself on free school dinners, which was a label to carry. I'd rather not eat than have the stigma.'

He left school in 1982 and went straight into one of the dreaded Youth Training Schemes, promoted by the Tories – earning just £23.50 a week as a painter and a plumber. There had been just eleven apprenticeships and more than 3,000 applicants. 'We were bread to be thrown on the scrap heap,' he believed. 'I went to a secondary modern school and there was never any discussion whatsoever about university options. I thought university was what you saw on University Challenge. The expectation for decades before was you'd follow your dad into the docks but when that came to a stop, there was nothing else.'

Wyatt's father died in 1984 and it turned his life upside down. He started taking heroin because of the dulling effect of the hit and his naivety to the consequences. 'There were no skeletons walking around or people sleeping in doorways because the long-term impact wasn't visible. It was still early days with heroin. You'd see big, strong, well-dressed lads in pub corners smoking it. It's hard to explain how it makes you feel. It's not a high like Charlie, it sends you the other way quickly. It separates you from the world's problems and your own problems; it numbs any pain. Then comes the rebound where you feel worse than you did before you took it.'

Wyatt did not really stand a chance. No mother, no father, entering adulthood living in a city overwhelmed by unemployment and a drug epidemic. He was exactly the wrong age at exactly the wrong time – or the right time if you were a drug dealer. He was not the only target in this market. He and an entire generation would grow up with an ingrained drug culture – a black economy that sustained the city more than any government initiative.

'For a while, the routine is great: you're chasing the dragon and riding a wave. You've got all the jewellery, you've got a car and a lovely looking girlfriend. Anyone looking at me would have thought I was smashing it. It takes eight or nine months for it to unravel. You wake up one day and you're skint. You think you've got the flu and you haven't. You need gear to make yourself feel normal. The jewellery starts getting pawned, the car goes – you can't afford the MOT. The girlfriend goes and then your friends go. I lost all of my friends. Not because of anything I did but because you alienate yourself. You become very selfish and all you're interested in is that next fix. There are weddings, christenings – there's funerals to go to. You stop going. You pull away from society. It gets around then that you're on the gear. I'd get people coming up to me saying how disgusted they were because before, I'd been a good lad. By 1988, it was really noticeable. People started swerving me completely and rightly so. I'm a mad Liverpool fan and I've been to 35 countries to watch them. But I can't remember Liverpool winning the league in 1990. I didn't give a fuck about anything else by then. That's how much it depletes your interest in anything. The FA Cup final after Hillsborough was my last game until 1996.'

Wyatt returned from Sheffield after the Hillsborough disaster and headed to the State nightclub to try and find out information about what had happened.

'Everyone was crying and hugging but I didn't cry for three weeks,' he admitted. 'The only solution for me was to self-medicate. I went right on the rollercoaster. All sorts of drugs came into play. My only memories from the early 1990s was the Sunday mornings because it was harder to get gear then. The drug dealers had their day off – just like the dockers used to on a Sunday. I was out at nine o'clock trying to score with the street dealers. I'd look at fellas walking their dogs and I'd think, "What I'd do just to be like him."'

The symptoms of Liverpool's heroin epidemic came before a diagnosis was made. Officers like Jim Fitzsimmons saw an anti-social problem at first, where small gangs would gather in the communal hallways of blocks of flats and upon running away the police would find discarded baggage and vomit. Glue sniffing had been a problem before but not on the same level. 'It went from more-or-less nobody on the street being found with drugs to everyone being found with at least something inside eighteen-or-so months.' An explosion in crime rates across Merseyside followed. In 1981, crime went up 25 per-cent, in 1982, another 15 per-cent and in 1983, 12 per-cent – the year burglaries went up 20 per-cent in the first three months of the year and the use of firearm robberies almost doubled. 'Morality flies out of the window – when you're hooked, you get whatever you can to feed the addiction,' admitted Wyatt, who served three prison sentences in foreign countries, two in Germany, another in Switzerland – each time for shoplifting, 'to feed what I needed', which also led to him getting nicked in Liverpool several times. On one occasion, he was eligible for bail but only if he paid a long-standing £18 parking fine. 'When I told the copper I was skint, he said, "You must have someone who can pay it…" But I didn't have a person in the world who could pay that fine. So, I had to do two days in Walton. The copper was saying, "I'd pay it myself, but I can't." That's how isolated I'd made myself. I'd outrun all of my favours.'

Wyatt suffered a heart attack and needed chemotherapy to treat liver damage related to his addiction. Twenty-five years clean, he told me his story quietly in the back of the shop he now owns in Liverpool's city centre where he sells deadstock Adidas training shoes. The name, Transalpino, refers to the sleeper he took across France, Switzerland and Italy to the 1984 European Cup final in Rome, just before heroin really came into his life. He took 'absolute' responsibility for all of his actions as a drug user but wondered whether it would have been different for him had conditions in Liverpool been better. Wyatt, known more commonly as 'Jockey', estimated that more than one hundred friends had died because of smack – 'if you became an adult in the 1980s and you were from working-class Liverpool, I'd imagine you have at least one family member who is still addicted, in treatment or in recovery.'

'I'm one of Maggie's children,' he concluded. 'Smack made a lot of fellas my age desensitised and it has impacted the generations after us. Kids were brought up in crack dens and because of that, there's a lot of sociopaths knocking about today. Nobody has shown them any respect so why should they show respect back?'

4
Red Rising

IN 1983 UNEMPLOYMENT IN LIVERPOOL WAS ALMOST FOUR TIMES the national average. The following year would mark a record across Britain, with nearly 3.4million out of work. Paul Malone was one of those who stood in the dole queue as it snaked around the corner of Prescot Road in Old Swan. He was almost 30 years old with a wife and two young boys. He'd done more than a decade on the docks where his father and grandfather had 'slogged themselves to death' – and both of them had passed away in the wintertime after long days using their creaking limbs to carry cargo around.

Malone had wondered whether that would be his fate as well until he was told one afternoon that there was no point coming in the following morning. He'd felt the moment coming because Liverpool's decline had been evident since the mid-70s. Yet confirmation didn't stop fear setting in. 'How was I going to put food on the table?'

He had done 'alright' at school and in another world – another time – there would have been opportunities. Not now, though – not in the mid-1980s, when it felt like 'the world was caving in and there was no one to trust'. He wondered whether he might have felt differently had he been younger – had he not been married, no kids. 'I'd imagine it would have been different for lads in their late teens and early 20s with no responsibilities.' For some of them, at least, it would have been possible to be free-spirited – to live a hedonistic sort of lifestyle with few commitments. But for slightly older men like Paul, this was not an option. 'It felt like a fight for survival.'

He was long-term unemployed, more than six years. He filled the gaps through crime, 'moving drugs around, selling stolen goods'. He was caught once and spent a couple of months in prison. 'The shame of that,' he thought. 'My dad would have been rolling in his grave – but when there are no options, you still have to find solutions. You can't feel sorry for yourself. That isn't going to feed anyone.'

The pressure led to a separation with his wife and he only saw his children at weekends but he still had to find ways of supporting them financially. 'Unemployment killed loads of families,' Malone thought. It also led to more discussion about politics than there was before, a yearning for alternatives.

'There had to be another option surely... then Derek came along...'

IT WAS EARLY MORNING AND THE LIGHTS WERE SWITCHED ON AT the Vernon Arms. The new working day was a few hours away but the last one had not really finished. Drinks in the saloon had preceded a meeting upstairs where Derek Hatton, Tony Mulhearn and Tony Byrne were attempting to design the future. Liverpool faced an economic and social crisis: docks closing, mass unemployment, housing issues and a heroin epidemic. Meanwhile, Toxteth remained segregated and racial tensions simmered.

More decisions were made in the Vernon Arms than in any council chamber. It was the pub on Dale Street where the politburo of Militant, which controlled the council, gathered to discuss their plans. News of Militant's achievements in Liverpool was spreading and by 1984, when Margaret Thatcher arrived in Bandung, a Javan city in Indonesia set 12,000 miles away amongst volcanoes and tea plantations, she was greeted by demonstrating students shouting, 'Liverpool, Liverpool, Liverpool!' For the Prime Minister, this must surely have acted as a warning. Liverpool presented a problem for her, no matter how much some of her advisors tried to argue oppositely, long after the battle had been decided. Patrick Minford swatted his hand dismissively as if the resistance in Liverpool was a mere inconvenience to her and yet Militant was screaming about Liverpool's problems and Liverpool was not the only city in Britain with these problems. Militant were offering solutions and delivering on some promises, particularly relating to the key issue of housing. If Militant's message was being heard in Indonesia, surely it could be heard and related to in the working-class cities of Manchester, Sheffield or Birmingham. It would have been complacent of Thatcher's administration to ignore the threat. Unemployed dock workers like Paul Malone now had something to believe in.

There is no straight line in Liverpool's relationship with politics and this may have played into Thatcher's thoughts. Liverpool has not always been left thinking as it is now, with Labour's control of Merseyside in the 2017 general election almost absolute. A reflection of this change is in Bootle. Impoverished and one of the safest Labour seats in the country, it had been incredibly wealthy; the suburb where many of the sea captains moved to when Liverpool was the greatest maritime city in the world. Andrew Bonar-Law was born in Canada but he would learn about the mechanics of politics in Bootle, becoming the leader of the Conservative Party as the MP for its constituency in 1911 before emerging as Prime Minister eleven years later.

While other great northern municipalities like Manchester voted Labour, the swing to the left took much longer in Liverpool, where the workforce – unlike in Manchester – had been casual and therefore more difficult to organise and therefore politicise. Religion can also explain why Liverpool was slow to turn left, with sectarian divisions impacting on the unity of the working class. The Irish Nationalists nearly always had a Liverpool MP and it was they rather than Labour that had been the strongest opposition to the Conservatives and Liberals. The Nationalists could count on the Roman Catholic vote but when Ireland was partitioned in 1921, the group withered, and it was not until 1955 that Labour gained full control of the town hall for the first time. There were more Protestants living in Liverpool than Catholics, many of them working class, and a significant number backed the Working Men's Conservative Association instead. A religious argument cut through the class issues that existed in Liverpool, resulting in a unique political culture. Rather than inheriting the 'democratic non-conformist tradition of the Liberal Party in England', as Tony Lane put it, 'Liverpool acquired the conspiratorialism of Irish politics.'

Nowhere more in Liverpool was the sectarian divide more tangible than in the Catholic dominated Scotland Road and neighbouring Everton, the Protestant bastion. Tony Mulhearn, a Catholic, was born in 1939. By the time he had reached adulthood, religion had become less of a separator in Liverpool after the clearance of the slums which meant thousands of residents from both Scotland Road and Everton inter-married, having dispersed into the satellite estates such as those in Cantril Farm, Speke and Croxteth.

Mulhearn joined Labour because he identified them as the more compassionate party having witnessed his father go to war and spend the post-war years unemployed, which led to mental health problems and little support from the governments that followed. Mulhearn looked towards James Larkin for inspiration, the leader of the Irish Labour movement. He would carry Larkin's values in his political career, which led to him becoming the president of the District Labour Party in Liverpool. As one of Militant Tendency's leaders, it allowed him to influence the policies of Liverpool City Council when it was won by Labour in 1983, only a month after Thatcher had guaranteed her second term in office. While Derek Hatton was received as the flamboyant front of Militant, Mulhearn was the ideologue, respected for his steadiness.

'My dad was in the construction industry before the war,' said Mulhearn, a formidable looking man with a granite jaw. 'He went ashore at Normandy and came back a wreck. I wasn't politically conscious but I soon recognised the injustices in the world. My dad struggled for the rest of his life. Instinctively, I thought "This is ridiculous – why is no one helping him?"'

Mulhearn's first job was as a trainee tailor. He then baked in a café. When he went for an interview with the Blue Funnel shipping line at the India Buildings, he was told that he started the following Monday. He trained as a cabinet maker before sitting the entrance exam to enter the printing industry where he worked as a compositor and first became active in the youth wing of the union. In 1959, Mulhearn was involved in his first strike. He was 20 years old and already he'd accrued a lot of experience.

'The strike brought a significant change in my consciousness,' he stressed. 'Whereas before I had this resentment of the way society was organised, I was now understanding of the nature of capitalism which said we had no choice to accept things as the way they were. I recognised then it was important to be organised not only industrially but politically.'

A return to sea with Canadian Pacific followed. He married on his return ashore and then became active within in the Labour Party, covering Liverpool's Central Ward.

'There I came across a group that called themselves Trotskyists and began to recognise the shortcomings of the Labour leadership. They talked well until they got power when they couldn't carry out their promises. These Trotskyists had the correct ideas. They eventually became Militant. I began to read the great socialist writers: Trotsky, Jack London, George Orwell, Upton Sinclair. It was like a biblical

103

transformation. The scales fell from my eyes. I realised the nature of society where you've got this constant struggle between capitalism and labour. The purpose of capitalism is to maximise profit. The purpose of the working class is to defend and try and improve its working conditions.

HIDDEN BEHIND THE TOWERING GRAVESTONES OF WALTON PARK Cemetery and opposite the formidable walls of the district's prison is Noonan Close. It was February 2019 and a crowd of 600 or so had gathered to mark the 110th anniversary since the death of the Irish-born socialist writer, Robert Tressell – whose surname at birth had been Noonan. With their trade union banners and brass band from St Helens, the crowd would march to Tressell's resting place, a pauper's grave where a dozen or so other people are also buried. Thirty-four years after his death Tressell's book, *The Ragged-Trousered Philanthropists,* was credited with having a major bearing on the result in the 1945 general election, which saw Labour sweep to power. The novel was an account of the working lives of a group of house painters and decorators in a fictional town called Mugsborough. The story had been drawn from Tressell's experiences of poverty as an immigrant living in Liverpool, in Walton.

Walton has never had an era like Bootle – the area two miles closer to the Mersey, where the rich sea captains used to live. From this inner-city borough, Jimmy Deane emerged, whom Tony Mulhearn described as the 'real founding father of Militant in Liverpool'.

Until 1993, written material relating to the life of Deane lay hidden on the first floor of the All Saints library at Manchester Metropolitan University. Michael Crick described the setting in his book, *The March of Militant*, as somewhere students would hardly notice – next to the shelves holding politics material; a small windowless room containing a desk, a chair, a typewriter, a wooden cabinet and three metal shelves containing 104 green box files. A collection of letters, notes, minutes and financial documents, according to Crick, provided the 'most interesting and conclusive documentary evidence every discovered about the origins of Militant'.

Crick's research spanned 1983 and 1985 – peak Militant years – and so, it might not be coincidental that his access to the Deane files was difficult, as if someone somewhere in authority did not want anyone learning about the foundations of a group which troubled right-wing control of the country. Crick recalled his task accessing a closed section, which only bona fide academic researchers could use, but only after permission had been granted by the polytechnic lecturer who supervised the collection. Crick did not confirm whether he saw all of the Deane files (journalists were forbidden from looking at them), but he knew enough to reveal that in the four years since arriving in Manchester, only four outsiders had requests accepted and amongst the documents he did see, Tony Mulhearn's name appeared in several.

Liverpool's march to Militancy had been through capitalism and its failings. 'The docks and warehouses [in Liverpool] seemed as monumental as the pyramids,' wrote PJ Waller. The labour which built these modern pyramids and worked them came from the wave of immigrants, primarily Irish but also Welsh and Scots. This would later explain the rise of the Liverpool revolutionaries, according to Mulhearn, who together with Peter Taaffe, in *A City that Dared to Fight*, wrote, 'It is the rapid transformation of the living conditions of the masses which provides the fertile soil in which radical and revolutionary ideas take root.' Mulhearn rationalised that the resettling of a rural population to the towns amidst the turbulence of industry yielded the base for the growth of revolutionary Chartism in the early labour movement. 'Mostly driven from the land by hunger, the Irish immigrants transferred their hatred of the English landlords to the Liverpool capitalists,' Mulhearn added.

Chartism called for universal suffrage for men, equal electoral districts, voting by secret ballot, the abolition of property qualifications for MPs, and annual general elections. It did not grow in Liverpool as fast as it did elsewhere. While Chartist meetings in other manufacturing towns across the north gathered crowds of 300,000, one meeting at Liverpool's Queens Square in June 1839 attracted fewer than 15,000. One of the leading Chartists, however, was a native of Liverpool, William Jones who was amongst the Chartists to call Liverpool a 'seat of corruption' following the general election in 1830, when it was alleged that votes in the city were being sold for £5, with more than £10,000 spent on electoral fraud. The Conservatives won locally and were the largest party nationally, but divisions amongst them allowed the Whig leader, Earl Gray, to form an effective government.

Hostility towards the English shipping magnates in Liverpool was carried from generation to generation. 'This undoubtedly was a factor in fashioning the fiery temperament of the Liverpool labour movement,' Mulhearn said. He believed that the Liverpool capitalists adopted the classic divide and rule method already tested in Ireland and this was a weapon used in the city for the next century until 'the fumes of sectarian poison' dissipated after 1945. The slums, according to one commentator, bred a 'congenital urge to fight', which usually took on the form of a battle between green and orange rather than against the capitalists. The casual nature of the dock work made it more difficult for trade unions to manage themselves. And so, the capitalists were able to play one working class group off another and Labour as a movement would suffer.

For a few capitalists to make huge amounts of money, it required a huge workforce on low wages, which meant the majority lived in grime; the worst of the poverty being close to the docks. Though the interests of the trade unions were separated and this impacted upon efficiency, the increasing numbers involved in union activity outlined the threat to Liverpool's capitalists. By 1891 the Liverpool Trades Council had 121 delegates representing 47 trades and 46,000 members, which made it the largest trades council outside London. Arthur Forwood, the Conservative Lord Mayor of Liverpool, warned that 'dangerous doctrines were being preached by the new school of trade unionists'. In identifying leaders of those unions as 'demagogues', Forwood was acknowledging the threat of socialism – staining leaders as individuals and therefore disrupting a fundamental component of the ideology.

Jimmy Deane was born in 1921. His grandfather, Charles Carrick, had been one of the first Labour councillors in Liverpool, while mother Gertie was a committed Trotskyist. The shadow of revolution hung over Britain and this was an era of strikes: the dock strike, the railway strike, the police strike of 1919, where in Bootle 69 out of 70 officers walked out – the highest percentage of any force in the country. A general strike in 1926 followed and in 1929, a Conservative councillor from Liverpool called Margaret Beavan acknowledged Labour's success in recruiting the strikers. 'Labour's commitment in Liverpool was akin to that of the Crusaders,' she said. 'They are willing to make any sacrifice – week in, week out – for socialism.' When, in 1932, riots in Birkenhead broke out because of high unemployment, it did not take long for the disturbances to spread across the River Mersey and into Liverpool.

Deane was eighteen years old when, in 1939, he started his own branch of the Workers' International League in Liverpool. Five years later, when British

Trotskyists united the Revolutionary Communist Party, Deane became an editor of *Socialist Appeal* under the guidance of Ted Grant, a Trotskyist whose father had settled in South Africa after fleeing Tsarist Russia in the nineteenth century.

Walton remained the only certified left-wing area of Liverpool when Deane returned after the war to work as an electrician. He started a Marxist magazine called *Rally!* which amalgamated with London-based *Rebel*. A journal called *Young Guard* was followed by *Youth for Socialism*, which lasted four issues. It was Deane's idea in 1964 to disband another national magazine, *Social Fight*, and start a weekly newspaper in its place. That newspaper's name was *Militant*.

SHORTLY AFTER MICHAEL FOOT CAME TO LIVERPOOL IN 1934 AS A young graduate to work as a shipping clerk he attended a football match in Walton – at Goodison Park, where Everton beat Sunderland 6-4 in an FA Cup replay. Unusually, Everton's greatest centre forward Dixie Dean did not score in a game that moved Foot – a Plymouth Argyle fan – so much, that he wrote a poem which he sent to the *Daily Post*.

'The gates of paradise are opened wide,' is how he described his entry into Goodison, which perhaps contrasted with what he witnessed outside, where he 'saw for the first-time what poverty meant... I saw mass unemployment as the most fearful curse which could befall our people.' Foot's experiences in Liverpool pushed him towards socialism, and to join the Labour Party. Fifty years later, unemployment in the same city was driving young idealists to join Militant.

Religion was no longer dividing the working class. This was reflected in Liverpool City Council's key figures. While Tony Mulhearn was a Catholic from Scotland Road, Derek Hatton, the deputy, was a Protestant from Childwall and Tony Byrne, the finance specialist from Smithdown Road had planned to become a Jesuit priest. Of the three, Byrne – the quietest – was arguably the savviest of the socialists. Ted Grant had said: 'If you take over the economy, it's entirely possible to control society.' Byrne's specialism was the same as Patrick Minford's, only his language was politically opposite. He was described by Hatton as 'an unlikely figure for a politician'. Hatton was known for his snappy suits and smart appearance but, 'Tony is just as well known for his sweatshirts, bomber jackets and trainers. He's a quietly spoken, lean, bustling man and with his bristly beard and balding head looks more like an ageing student than a politician.'

Despite religious alignment becoming less of an issue, politics in Liverpool had stagnated and this contributed to the city's production as well as its attraction for new investors. In the aftermath of the riots in Toxteth, Michael LeRoy gave an impartial view that the city was 'administered by a bewildering array of local government bodies which operate a complex pattern of schemes and polices'. It was challenging to get anything moving in Liverpool because of this, with fiefdoms reigning and a lack of true leadership and accountability. In addition to the metropolitan authorities of Liverpool City Council and Merseyside County Council there was an Inner City Partnership scheme to co-ordinate their activities. In 1981, the Merseyside Development Corporation was added to the scene with the specific responsibility of redeveloping 865 acres of unused dockland in Liverpool, Bootle and Birkenhead. After Toxteth, another body was formed in 1981 – the Merseyside Task Force, under the direct control of the Minister of State for the Environment, Michael Heseltine.

The 1970s had seen a succession of hung councils, in which no party held sufficient strength to pursue its policies without serious compromise. In this climate, the decisive and radical policies which needed to happen foundered. Added to this, there was a crossover of interest between Labour, the Conservatives and the Liberals over the three-tiered structure of government and this meant 'it rarely proved possible to get two oranges in a row, let alone three', as LeRoy put it. Should it really be a surprise that amidst a climate of contradiction, a more strident version of local politics proved attractive and gained a foothold?

For Mulhearn, no Labour government has ever been truly a socialist one or ever really *that* affective. The opportunities had been there in the inter-war years to prove what socialism stood for but to Mulhearn's mind, Philip Snowden, the Chancellor of the Exchequer in those Labour governments, was a rigid old fashioned liberal, whose primary allegiance was to free trade and retrenchment. Mulhearn and Winston Churchill would share similar beliefs on this particular issue: 'The Treasury mind and the Snowden mind,' wrote Churchill, 'embraced each other with the fervour of two long-separated kindred lizards.' On that basis, perhaps it was unsurprising that the 1929-31 Labour government took no socialist measures or any other steps to reduce spiralling unemployment. Subsequently, Clement Atlee's post-war government's highly publicised commitment to planning did not translate into a single plan and Harold Wilson's two terms were underpinned initially by his unwillingness to devalue before embarking on a hybrid rather than an interventionist socialist policy a decade later. Wilson's successor James Callaghan then proclaimed in a Minfordesque speech written by his monetarist son-in-law, Peter Jay, that Britain could not spend its way out of a recession.

In Liverpool, Sir Trevor Jones had been the dominant Liberal party leader for decades. Though he was born in North Wales, he was brought up in Bootle and in the aftermath of the riots in 1981 was knighted for his services to local government where he was fearless amongst other councillors and quite different from most Liberals nationally. When Derek Hatton once shouted, 'I'll dance on your grave,' Jones replied: 'That's fine by me – I'm going to be buried at sea.'

Jones had worked with Michael Heseltine in the years before Toxteth, as Heseltine wielded the axe against local government spending. Assessments of the impact of Heseltine's achievements in Liverpool can be boiled down to whether you believe in capitalism or not. Liverpool had been expected by Heseltine to make 'savings' of £12.7million in 1980 and Liverpool's Liberal-Conservative coalition colluded. Three months after the Liberals took effective control, they had slashed spending and in an interview with the *Sunday Times*, Jones boasted, 'We did this even before Michael Heseltine's letter arrived.'

A massive 34 per-cent rent rise followed and that led to Richard Kemp, the Chair of Housing, resigning as a 'personal protest' for being 'compelled' to act as Heseltine's 'butcher'. Kemp, though, was soon back in position and in March 1981, reflected just how the controlling powers had given up on Liverpool's working classes by telling *The Times*, 'Really, we ought to be building houses for rich people. What Liverpool needs above all is more wealthy inhabitants. The dominance of council tenants only fosters the ghetto mentality.'

The government's plan to abolish county councils and heave control to the centre was supported by Jones, who believed Heseltine was moving along the right lines. 'His ideas support our view that the Merseyside County Council is a disaster and the sooner it is demolished the better,' Jones added. The result proved to be a 50 per-cent increase in fares and a catastrophic deterioration of public transport across the region.

The Liberals would flail. Before their demise, Jones declared: 'We are proud that we have reduced jobs in the city council... we think we can reduce more.' On his way out from office, Richard Kemp admitted: 'We are not ashamed that 4,500 jobs have gone from the city council.' Reg Flude, the Tory leader later defeated by Derek Hatton in his constituency, remarked: 'We don't need the majority on the city council – the Liberal Party are carrying out our policies.' The Tories even tried to present themselves as being left of the Liberals: 'The Liberals are more reactionary than the Tory Party,' claimed John Lee, a leading Conservative, whose financial autobiography was called *How to Make a Million – Slowly*.

To get Liverpool going again, Heseltine offered companies relaxed planning requirements, exemption from rates for non-domestic buildings, and 100 per-cent capital allowances for industrial and commercial properties. 'A tremendous bargain,' assessed Liverpool's development officer, though those who really benefitted were out of town contractors with their own specialised labour. 'So who really benefited from Heseltine's measures?' Mulhearn asked. 'What was given with one hand was taken away with the other...'

It is fair to say that Mulhearn and Heseltine did not share an ounce of political belief but both acknowledged that the Conservatives were the most successful political party in British history. While Heseltine described them as the smartest, Mulhearn preferred to say they were cunning.

'Between '79 and '83, Thatcherism could have been smashed,' Mulhearn believed. 'Prior to the '83 election she was the most unpopular ruler since Ethelred the Unready. Then came the Falklands War and the establishment of the SDP under people like David Owen, Roy Jenkins, Shirley Williams and Bill Rodgers – crypto-Tories in effect, who split the Labour Party as well as the Labour vote. Thatcher on the basis of jingoism and bellicosity attracted some working-class votes. It meant she was able to retrieve her position.'

'The Tories have always been very far-sighted,' Mulhearn admitted. 'They opposed the formation of trade unions but eventually succumbed to the pressure. Very craftily, they drew the trade union leaders into their own embrace. They advocated very high wages for trade union delegates; gave them places in the House of Lords. When the Labour Party was formed they did the same thing. Ramsay MacDonald – the great traitor – he was drawn into their ranks. They treated him like royalty at their country homes. It reached its nadir with Blair and Mandelson, who quite clearly entered the Labour party on a mission to rid it of any radicalism. Thatcher said her greatest achievement was Blair and New Labour. The British capitalist class is the most cunning. It appreciates the power of the working class and knows if it corrupts the leaders, the working class is an amorphous body. That's where we came in. We gave leadership to this abandoned movement.'

While in 1983 Thatcher was elected with a landslide elsewhere across Britain, Liverpool Labour earned one of the highest votes ever recorded, a remarkable feat considering the city's population had dropped from 700,000 to around 300,000 since 1945. All of the Labour MPs were then re-elected, and the Liverpool socialist council was also re-elected.

'Our programme was very clear: to emasculate the power of local authority despite the objections of Thatcher, who was carrying out enormous cuts. She had arrived in power claiming to be a great de-centraliser but she proved to be one of the most centralising prime ministers in history. She was clawing all of the power back to Westminster and demanding that the city councils all over the country carry out cuts.'

Of the Militant leaders in Liverpool, Mulhearn was the most convincing as well as the most consistent. His views were fortified by what he saw as the 'endless class struggle'.

'Everything that has happened has confirmed my suspicions about the capitalist system,' he said. 'The driving down of living standards, the attacks on the NHS, Labour councils implementing the cuts demanded by the government, libraries closing, facilities for elderly patients being shut down, so called "bed blockers" in hospital being condemned when they have nowhere to go, parks being built on, land being given for virtually free to developers – people like Heseltine being given the freedom of the city. All of this confirms what I, Militant and Trotskyists have always maintained. This is the future under capitalism and the only way it will change is if we move from capitalism to socialism.'

IF TONY MULHEARN IS CHINA: DEEP, MYSTERIOUS, UNCONQUERABLE; then Derek Hatton is Shanghai: loud, frenetic, neon. Mulhearn described Hatton as 'a man of immediate achievement', and despite wider doubts about him, Hatton 'was a great advocate of socialism and a great tribune – when he spoke, people took notice'. Hatton was more of a marked man than Mulhearn: 'They wanted to destroy him, no matter what; drive him into the ground,' Mulhearn said. 'Derek,' he emphasised, 'had no choice to do what he did,' referring to the 1990s, where he embraced capitalism and became a millionaire. 'He had to make something of it himself in order to defy the establishment. His instincts are always very good. But he expresses himself in ways that appeals to the base he moves in, though he never betrayed us. He never stabbed us in the back. Unlike a lot of them.'

Hatton looked wonderful for his age. A month before meeting him in his Liverpool city centre offices, where he ran a scheme that that encouraged adults to ride bikes to work, he had turned 70. This scheme and other schemes before had generated wealth. His status was visible: the sun tan, the immaculate teeth, the ironed shirt, the pin stripe suit pants, the shiny cufflinks, the huge watch on his wrist. But then, this had always been Hatton. Maybe nothing had really changed. Maybe the only nod towards change was the cardigan and its three fastened buttons.

Hatton lamented – and maybe he had a point – that any analysis of his appearance amounted to 'typical Tory hypocrisy', considering the criticism that came Michael Foot's way when he turned up to mourn fallen soldiers at the Cenotaph in 1981 wearing a donkey jacket. It was a jacket Mulhearn told me, having established through a conversation with Foot, that had actually been bought for him for him as a birthday present by his wife, Jill.

Hatton had written in his 1988 autobiography, 'I was not the unimaginative, sackcloth-and-ashes socialist they would have preferred,' and this was a message he would repeat to me. 'I did not conform to many people's notion of what left wing politics should be. I was too close for comfort to my critics because I liked a lot of the things they liked: parties, cars, nightclubs. I was not cast in the Militant mould the media wanted.'

Hatton insisted he acted and dressed according to his consciousness, while also conceding his appearance was partly a tool: a message that attempted to say socialism works – even for those who like nice things. 'Why should a socialist not be allowed to drink Champagne?' he asked.

Hatton and I sat on leather sofas opposite one another. To the left of us was an office table and on that table, lay a computer where he had just finished filing his column to the *Liverpool Echo* by email, the newspaper which he believed during the 1980s was part of right-wing plot to sully his name and therefore discredit the socialist revolution that was happening in Liverpool, ensuring it did not spread beyond the boundaries of Merseyside.

Upon his entry to the town hall in the summer of 1983, the *Echo* had introduced

THE LONG DECADE: 1979-1993

Hatton as 'the firebrand leader of the extreme left', even though he'd in fact been nominated as deputy of the city council behind John Hamilton who Hatton had described as 'a nowhere man'. Hatton, it is fair to say, wasn't afraid to judge the sort of clothes Hamilton wore: 'V-necked pullovers, an overcoat, a trilby and spectacles: every inch the retired schoolmaster that he is. He often reminded me of Mr Magoo, the cartoon character, bumbling his way through life like a genial uncle.' Hatton and the rest of the Militant leadership wanted Hamilton gone because he 'resented the fact Militant was really shaping policy', and that led to Hamilton being isolated. He was not a part of the Vernon Arms politburo.

Hatton, indeed, was someone who had made a 'dramatic impact' since his election as a representative for Netherley in 1979. 'Councillor Hatton is a distinctive Labour figure,' a profile read in the *Liverpool Echo*. 'While most of his Labour colleagues appear in old jeans, T-shirt and trainers, he is perhaps the best dressed member of the city council, with his athletic frame clad in the most up-to-date light weight suits.' According to the *Echo* it was his style of political interaction which had contributed the most towards him becoming 'such a controversial figure'. The profile continued: 'His aggressive vocal manner in the committee and council chamber alarms the milder mannered opposition members and words like 'scab', 'balloon-head', 'parasite' and 'fascist' are heaped on officers and councillors alike.'

I wondered whether he recognised the person being described thirty-five years later. He smiled, nodding acceptingly, though certainly not apologetically. He sunk back into the couch. The leather squeaked. And then he placed both palms behind his head. Hatton was now in the psychiatrist chair.

'Ali Machray is the editor of the *Echo* and he is the first one I haven't wanted to strangle,' Hatton fired off. 'It wasn't just the *Echo*, it was the entire media. The reality is, you have a situation where five billionaires own 99 per-cent of the newspaper industry and they're never going to be on our side. None of them were born on our street. If you take a stand like we did in the 1980s you're always going to come up against the media barons. That's inevitable.'

It was clear Hatton had not lost any of his zest. His voice was sharp and rising naturally. It was only the first question and the finger pointing had already begun. The K-word soon followed.

'Kinnock...' he rasped. '... took Thatcher's side rather than ours. Some of the papers tried to be a little bit friendly but when the chips were down and it really was a case of it being a direct conflict with the Thatcher government, you knew which way they were going to go… particularly when Kinnock helped Thatcher by denouncing us. That changed everything. Then you got the *Guardian* and the *Mirror* who were desperate to have a go at us anyway, having a real go because they had a reason to. Kinnock was against us. Kinnock… he was the worst Labour leader in history.'

The audience cheered when Neil Kinnock denounced Hatton and the 'grotesque chaos' of a Liverpool Council, accusing it of 'hiring taxis to scuttle around the city while handing out redundancy notices' at the Labour Party Conference in 1985. Hatton, with his sleeves rolled up, responded by shouting 'liar' at the Welsh Labour leader, who was only six years senior to Hatton but looked so much older with this thinning ginger hair and spectacles.

Like Kinnock, Ken Livingstone and Arthur Scargill, Hatton was amongst other left-wing socialist leaders propelled into high office in the early 1980s. Hatton was treasured by broadcasters because of his ability to summarise his feelings on issues succinctly. He was anything but a drone. 'His good looks, his instant availability, and his cultivation of relations with local journalists quickly made him the second most familiar government leader of all time – after Ken Livingstone,' Michael Crick wrote. Hatton's ascendency belied the fact he was not the Labour leader in Liverpool. And yet, Hatton came to represent Labour politics in the city, if not Militant's reputation across the country.

THE COVER OF DEREK HATTON'S AUTOBIOGRAPHY, PUBLISHED IN 1988, is garishly designed. The background is a newsprint of all the headlines he made, coloured in red and yellow. Above the title *Inside Left* is a blurred image of Hatton in an expensive looking suit that Reggie Kray might wear, accompanied by a zig-zagged patterned tie. Its sub-title, 'The story so far…' suggests there is more to come from Hatton and that would imply there was more to come from Militant.

Considering the number of column inches devoted to Hatton, 174 pages seemed an unusually short reply, yet Hatton would argue that was him – 'able to get to the nub of the point quickly'. Elsewhere, there are photographs of his expensive car and personalised *Deg5y* number plate. Each chapter begin with a faded print of Hatton wearing what appears to be a leather jacket. He is laughing and his hair is slicked back.

The first line of the prologue quotes Karl Marx, who before he died in 1883, said: 'Last words are for fools who haven't said enough.' Hatton promised the publication would not be his political obituary. He proceeded to describe himself in the third person. 'There are a million more things for Derek Hatton to do,' he wrote, insisting that his role in the three and a half years before 1988 would 'never be forgotten in the political history books'. It was his belief that with his life, 'I will have done more than most people have with theirs.'

He was right about that. In any political book written about the 1980s, the names Militant and Derek Hatton tend to be there, 'alongside Kinnock and Thatcher', he said, as if Kinnock and Thatcher – using only their surnames – were the same species. 'If they think Militant is defeated they have seriously miscalculated,' he warned. 'He [Kinnock] called us maggots, gnawing at the core of the Labour Party. He will discover that we are the core.'

Hatton reasoned that his emergence was only possible because of his background from a city where there is '... a natural spirit of competition, coupled with a belief that you're not simply as good as anyone else, you're better. It's that Liverpudlian arrogance which people found difficult to accept but without it you can't win.'

Yet Hatton was not an ordinary Liverpudlian. Unusually for a Liverpool family, Hatton was an only child and he grew up close to one of Liverpool's wealthiest suburbs, Childwall. In his own words, though, he grew up 'on the wrong side of the track' beside a disused railway line which ran from Bowring Park Road. As a politician, he was regularly accused of being a showman, someone who loved the limelight. He 'loathed and detested' school and ended up in a production of *The Merchant of Venice* in order to skip lessons, given the chance to tour Germany with the National Youth Theatre. At the Liverpool Institute, one of the city's best schools, he claims to have shared detention with Paul McCartney. Hatton developed a dress sense by working on Saturday mornings as a teenager at Jackson's, the tailors on London Road in Liverpool city centre. Upon leaving school at fifteen, his mother persuaded him to enrol as an apprentice telephone technician, but he'd soon follow his father into the fire brigade.

'I've been asked a million times and I haven't got a clue,' he would say when asked what made him turn to the left politically. 'There are certain things I can remember, but whether they are factors I'm not sure. I went to a chimney fire at a house in Bedford Street North in Toxteth when they were multi-occupancy. There was big room and fifteen Irish people were living there. In one corner, there was a mound of cinders from the fire and in the other corner there was a mound of shit. From baby to grandma people were living like this and I thought, "Hang on, this isn't right." Although I came from a council area, I'd never seen anything as bad as that.

'I started to get involved in the trade union movement in the fire brigade. Initially, I just went along to meetings to see what was going on. Terry Fields became the MP for Broadgreen and he was a bit older than me and guided me along. I said certain things at these meetings, I was only eighteen or nineteen, and when I said them people seemed to listen. I thought, "Oooh, I like this." So, there was a bit of an ego thing as well...'

Hatton studied at Goldsmiths, taking on a course in social work while working for campaigns like *Squatter*. A football fanatic and an Evertonian, Hatton was banned for life from the Essex League after thumping a referee who did not award his team a penalty. He turned his back on London after two years because 'some of the people, especially at the college, were academics who tended to see life from an armchair'. He had made enough of an impression for one of those academics, however, to predict he 'was bound to make his mark on community'. Aged 23 and now a Labour Party member, Hatton moved to Sheffield from Liverpool to work as a community worker where, by his own admission, he was unpopular amongst Labour's councillors which he believed to be right wing, particularly David Blunkett and Roy Hattersley's mother, Enid. Back in Liverpool, Hatton joined Knowsley Council as a community development officer where he again he faced opposition from old guard Labour right-wingers. When Hatton could not get things moving the way he wanted he set up his own community organisation and the *Echo* reported that two community centres banned him from their premises, while a public meeting was also held to complain about his activities.

An introduction to Tony Mulhearn had been an awakening for him, immediately identifying with the sort of politics he believed in. 'Tony is a powerful man in every sense of the word,' Hatton told me. Mulhearn was nine years older than him and he took Hatton seriously. The academia of London had been suffocating; being an outsider in Sheffield had not helped. With Mulhearn well connected, Hatton was in his home city and being heard.

'I've got a picture somewhere at home of the demonstration at the end of 1983 when 100,000 people turned up,' Hatton said, proudly. 'There are twenty or so people on the front row and out of those twenty people there's only me and Tony Mul still alive. Sometimes you look at it and you realise, shit – how young was I to be in that position of responsibility? I'd always been the youngest in everything I did. I liked being the new kid on the block.'

FOLLOWING THE RIOTS OF 1981 AND THE LINKS TO UNEMPLOYMENT, especially amongst the youth of Liverpool, Militant's message carried more weight. A twenty-minute Thames Television documentary focused on the newspaper's popularity and Militant's rise, immediately hitting the viewer with a stark warning from Terry McDonald, the Labour party constituency chairman in Kirkdale and a former Militant supporter. 'If they gain power parliamentary democracy will disappear,' he warned. 'They may gain power through parliamentary democracy by using the constitution. Once they gain power, we'll have a one-party state.'

Ted Grant, the founder of Militant and the editor of the weekly newspaper, spoke next. 'We stand for a peaceful transformation of society,' he reasoned. 'We stand for a Labour party getting a majority in parliament. Then on the basis of that majority, abolishing the monarchy, abolishing the House of Lords by an enabling act then taking over the 200 monopolies. We stand for complete democracy.'

McDonald proceeded to outline how Militant recruited its 5,000 active supporters and sixty staff, many of whom were political novices. An interest in trade unionism and a prior involvement in demonstration helped. Tony Mulhearn, also quizzed, was quick to address the issue of language. He dismissed the way the interviewer used the term 'target' as if Militant were doing something inherently wrong, reminding that any successful political organisation understands the landscape in which it operates and attempts to advance its programme accordingly.

Upon registration, Militant would assign a new member as a guide, someone who'd provide Marxist literature and back-copies of the *Militant* newspaper in expectation of a future discussion about the issues impacting on society. Each Militant member was expected to contribute at least a few pounds a week, which maintained the newspaper and through it, the expression of their viewpoint. Terry McDonald described Militant as a 'well-organised party' which had four or five officers operating in Liverpool. Militant's 'centre' was in East London, where the newspaper was edited by the Birkenhead-born Peter Taaffe, a figure Derek Hatton described as 'legendary'.

'To this day there is no single individual whose political brain has so impressed me,' Hatton said. 'I am convinced that he is the greatest political thinker I have ever met and has no equal where political strategies are concerned.'

Liverpool's council was run by a Conservative-Liberal alliance but the biggest single group was Labour, which had fallen under the control of Militant through the process of entryism. Ahead of Labour council meetings, Militant would meet separately and discuss how to approach debates and votes. There was nothing undemocratic about this but Militant's enemies implied there was. By patiently canvassing in a number of Liverpool wards and taking them from other parties, Militant's strategy would mean they eventually had enough councillors to take control of the District Labour Party and from there, they could direct party policy across the whole city. Appropriately, Tony Mulhearn – the ideologue – became the chairman of the DLP.

'Liverpool's Labour party had taken its constituents for granted but Militant did not,' Hatton insisted. 'Our determination to change the way things were inspired hope for those desperate for change but amongst those in the way and the Labour politicians that had not done enough – or had failed to make the right decisions on behalf of Liverpool's working class in the previous decades – Militant's enthusiasm and organisation brought fear.'

It was claimed Militant was a party within a party, that Militant was using democracy as a tactic. 'If Militant was voted out of government would it accept being out of office?' Terry McDonald asked. He would advocate the expulsion of Militant from Labour even when it was put to him that his suggestion sounded like the sort of witch-hunt he'd expect Militant to carry out if they ever took control. 'If you've got a diseased hand, you cut it off and you don't allow it to take over your whole body,' he argued.

Derek Hatton has his own way of describing the landscape in 1983, the year Labour finally took control of Liverpool's council.

'The Liberals emerged in Liverpool during the 1970s because the Labour Party didn't give a fuck,' he thundered. 'It got to the stage in an awful lot of wards in Liverpool where you could put a donkey there with a Labour rosette around its neck and it would get in. They never bothered doing any work for the people in the area, they just assumed they got the vote. A few clever Liberals in the late-60s got involved with Trevor Jones and managed to get a degree of control. But once that was done, they went away and came back with a few piques. Now, you could have Liberal group meetings in a telephone box.'

'The city was falling to bits,' Hatton recalled. 'In terms of jobs and economy and everything that went with it, there was just nothing there. When I was a kid my dad was a fireman and occasionally he'd be stationed on the docks. I used to sometimes go and see him after school and get the bus back with him. This was in the 60s when dockers were like ants. It felt like there were millions of them; they were everywhere, scuttling around – total activity. You look at the 80s and all of a sudden that had gone. You can't take an industry like that out of a city like Liverpool and not expect it to have a massive impact or a reaction.'

'I do think what was happening in Liverpool and was worse than anywhere else in the country,' he continued. 'We relied so much on ships and I mean, so much. Everything came from that. For that reason, we were in a different position. If you look somewhere like Manchester, they had lots of other industries and so did Birmingham. If they lost one they had something else to fall back on. We lost the docks, we had nothing else. Something had to be done. Though it wouldn't be achieved overnight, our strategy was focused on uniting the city and getting some money back off the government. In real terms, it was probably going to be a shortish-term solution because the government was never going to bow time and again. Unless the rest of the country – and that means all of the other councils – decided to follow our lead.'

The Thatcher administration had cut local council spending and Liverpool was suffering. By 1981, it was calculated that the city would end the year in the red if it did not meet the government's spending limits. By 1982, the Liberals were considering rate rises of up to 30 per-cent to solve the crisis. Meanwhile, the drip of Liverpool's population to new towns on the urban fringe and much further afield in search of employment due to the decline in industry had eroded Liverpool's base for rate revenue and grants. Michael Crick described what happened next as 'the most dramatic confrontation ever between a local authority and a British government'.

When Britain recorded a swing of 3.9 per-cent from Labour to Conservative during the general election of 1983, Liverpool swung 2.4 per-cent from Conservative to Labour. For the first time in its history, Liverpool had no Conservative MPs. Voting in local elections five weeks later followed the same pattern. While the Conservatives made small gains in town halls elsewhere in the country, Liverpool elected a Labour Council for the first time in a decade. Liverpool had stood against the Tory tide.

Hatton would be a symbol of that change. A different voice. A different age. A different approach. Not traditional Labour. When Hatton stood in Tuebrook only to lose by 91 votes in 1978, he reacted by releasing a volley of verbal abuse at the Conservative victor. He was elected as a local councillor on the same day as Margaret Thatcher became prime minister in 1979 and within four years had surged from novice councillor to deputy of the city council underneath John Hamilton, who was not a Militant member.

His rise had been underpinned by quite simply according to Hatton, 'a lot of campaigning and a lot of grafting', recognising also that it helped he was 'only at the end of the line to any media guy that wanted to ask me a question'. Hatton was so familiar with broadcasters at Radio City that he would often turn up unexpectedly with a story for them. He became known as 'Hatton-the-Mouth.'

In 1983, he was hugely confident, stating: 'I thought to myself, "Not only are we going to change Liverpool, we are also going to prove what Militant is all about. The revolution starts here." He can remember vividly the moment it was announced that Labour had taken Liverpool from the Liberal-Tory alliance and defied what was happening elsewhere in the country.

'Our lad standing in Warbreck called was Jimmy Hackett. His brother Johnny was a well-known comedian. In Warbreck, there was an old Tory councillor called Reg Flude. He was a Cockney and had a carpet warehouse. He was one of these cockney lads who I always got on great with because he was working class. But I always told him, "I'll come for you." There was no similarity at all [when it came to politics]. He was an old reactionary. Reg had this great backing in Warbreck, where everyone knew him and he was known as an affable sort of chap. We'd been to Netherley and we were driving across the fly-over. The radio was on and the presenter says, "We've got a result in Warbreck... and it's a Labour gain." Well, I nearly drove the car over the side of the road. I'd have died there and then. You knew at that moment we'd taken control; you knew we had the majority. You couldn't win Warbreck and not take the rest of Liverpool.'

TWO MONTHS AFTER LABOUR WON CONTROL OF LIVERPOOL

Council, the Conservative government was told that further cuts would not be happening in the city. A campaign called 'Merseyside in Crisis' was organised to build support. One hundred and eighty thousand leaflets entitled *Not the Echo* were distributed because it was believed by Labour that the *Echo* had acted as a megaphone for the Liberals and the Conservatives. It was Labour's conviction that the private sector – or capitalism – had abandoned the city and the only way it could recover was through public sector investment. Instead of making more than a thousand workers redundant, they followed through on their vow to create 600 new jobs.

When Hatton and other Labour councillors met the Tory environment secretary Patrick Jenkin to discuss central funding for Liverpool, Jenkin claimed that the council had intensified the city's problem and therefore should instead raise rates by seventy per-cent and slash services. Jenkin said that Liverpool Council was 'proposing to go outside the rules and spend money it hasn't got and is asking us to go outside the rules to make it up'.

Hatton told Jenkin that the government had stolen £30million from Liverpool, warning him that if he did not return the money, demonstrations outside his London home could not be ruled out. Jenkin was quoted calling the Liverpool councillors 'a nasty lot', and Tony Byrne was a 'hard Trot'. The following day, the right-wing *Daily Express* called the meeting 'one of the most chilling insights ever into the violent nature of left-wing extremism'. Hatton reacted to that, reasoning 'none of us spoke to him in threatening terms... there will obviously be a time when young people react.'

When Hatton and the other councillors met Neil Kinnock in parliament, the Labour leader suggested it was wiser to comply with the government's suggestions rather than be thrown out of office for breaking the law. John Hamilton reminded that the government had found some resources for Liverpool after the 1981 riots, asking why they couldn't now. Did Liverpool have to reach another crisis point if it was not a crisis already? Militant's view was outlined in their pamphlet – 'Liverpool fights the Tories' – where it encouraged industrial action and mass protest against the government who wanted Liverpool's Labour council to provide funding so 'big businesses and the banks can go on collecting their rent, interest and profit from the people of Liverpool'. Though the council was unable to set a budget, its popularity increased and in the 1984 local elections the turnout was 20 per-cent higher than the previous year, with Labour increasing its majority.

Only now did the local press coverage begin to change, with the *Echo* beginning a 'Save our City' campaign, where it outlined its new stance, writing: 'The inner-city deprivation which all Northern cities suffer from is more widespread in Liverpool – and the blame for that cannot be laid at this council's door.' Liberal leader Trevor Jones admitted Labour in Liverpool had 'raised the consciousness of the people' while Kinnock invited new discussions about funding.

When Jenkin visited Liverpool in 1981 to inspect the Garden Festival site flanked by Michael Heseltine, he claimed he did not have the time to see the rest of the city. His next trip from London would come four years later and only then did he witness, smell and taste the desperation of the housing situation. 'I have seen families living in conditions the like I have never seen before, they are very grim indeed,' he admitted.

Though Hatton had suggested £30million was needed for Liverpool's problems, at a subsequent meeting in London, Jenkin agreed a settlement of £20million though for the money to be processed he expected the deal to be kept quiet until it was authorised by the full council as well as the government, enabling both sides to claim a sort of victory. Instead, Liverpool's councillors returned home triumphant, with Hatton, having already said that the Tories had sustained a bloody nose, then claiming, 'there is no way Thatcher can take on the might of the working class of this city. And this is just the start'.

'We had to get the information out quickly to back them into a corner,' Hatton reasoned. 'They'd said yes, they knew they'd said yes but they didn't want us to tell people. You have to ask, why? We couldn't have done that. That wasn't the way we worked. It never seemed to me like he was concerned about Liverpool or its people but he was concerned about what would happen if they did nothing – there would be another Toxteth Riots.

'You've got to remember that prior to us in politics everyone played the same game,' Hatton began to whisper. '"We'll give you a bit of money but don't say anything and everyone will be happy – we'll stay in power and you'll stay in power." We weren't like that, we couldn't have been like that. We'd gone down there [to London] and there were thousands back here [in Liverpool] waiting to see how we'd got on. How the fuck could we go, "We've done our best and as soon as we know, we'll let you know; as far as we're concerned it's going splendidly!" Fucking 'ell, we couldn't do that! We discussed what to do on the train and when it was suggested that we should let everyone know the truth, not one person objected.'

Jenkin accused Liverpool's council of 'dancing on his political grave' and the government vowed not to be outmanoeuvred again. The revelation of a Conservative retreat was untimely for them because of the battle running concurrently with the mineworkers' union. Hatton recalled being warned by Teddy Taylor, the Tory MP for Southend, that Jenkin had been ordered to make concessions on this occasion for Liverpool because the focus of the government had been with Arthur Scargill, the leader of the NUM. 'We want Scargill, he's our priority,' was the message. 'We'll come for you later.'

History would not reflect well on Militant's decision to reveal their gain. Had it been a tactical display of strength to encourage other councils to follow them, none of them did. Some non-Militant Labour councillors have said that Hatton got carried away, while others believe that he and the rest of Militant failed to capitalise on an opportunity to work with government members who were sympathetic towards Liverpool, though Hatton denied there were any. The anti-Militant Malcolm Kennedy fell into that category, saying: 'You had to oppose what the Conservatives were doing, you had to demonstrate, you had to make your point of view, but you also had to negotiate. It's like being on the ground in a boxing match and coming out arms flailing. You have to do a bit of dodging as well as swinging the fists.' And yet, a more practical response was dismissed by Tony Mulhearn as being an 'arid concept of history'.

Within six months, Patrick Jenkin was sacked by Thatcher, the doors of the government were shut firmly on Liverpool and soon Neil Kinnock was denouncing Militant at the Labour Party Conference in Bournemouth.

IN OUTMANOEUVRING A GOVERNMENT THAT DID NOT WANT TO give, Militant had nevertheless achieved a sensational heist. Much of the money gained would be invested in new housing on the fringes of Liverpool's city centre, housing that more than thirty years later remained in good condition – still earning steady income for the local authorities. However, the manner of the victory meant Thatcher had lost a propaganda war and when the government branded what was happening in Liverpool as 'Municipal Stalinism', other socialist councils across the country did not have the courage or organisation to follow Militant's beat in Liverpool.

Neil Kinnock did not agree with the ideology behind Militant and nor did he like its methods. Derek Hatton saw an enormous gulf between the pressures facing his city and those elsewhere, as well as a gulf between the working-class councillors of Liverpool fighting for their constituents and those more middle-class leftists in other areas like Islington, which he branded as the centre of the 'looney-left'. These were, according to him, politicians who spent 'more time in those meetings in London behaving like middle class intellectuals – they appeared more concerned that we called the chairman the chairperson or a manhole cover a personhole cover than they were over what he thought were real issues'.

When Hatton met Thatcher in October 1984, he and the other Liverpool councillors did not stand upon her arrival and shake hands, forcing her to stoop down. 'This really annoyed her,' Hatton smiled. 'At the end of the meeting, when I asked whether she was going to help 37 Cammell Laird dockers who had been jailed because of her policies, she turned around and said: "Any respect I've ever had for you Mr Hatton has just gone, and by the way I never had any anyway."'

The government would no longer negotiate at a time where one of its own reports confirmed that 32,000 more jobs in Liverpool were threatened. Mulhearn suggested this report proved that private enterprise was failing and the *Liverpool Echo* predicted that by 1990, Liverpool would have no industrial base at all. This was a city which had once been the main port of the British empire.

Tony Byrne responded by securing a £30 million loan from a French bank in order to build more homes and generate more income through rates. Liverpool, though, was back where it was twelve months before and Hatton believed a second year of begging and borrowing with solutions being found was not met with the same sense of appetite amongst Liverpool residents and some anti-Militant marches followed.

When, in March 1985, Liverpool council remained £43million short of what it needed to stay afloat and said it was 'impossible to set a rate' or a deficit budget the following month, the District Auditor warned councillors that the city was moving into the realms of illegality and this made bankruptcy a possibility as well as disqualification. In May, the Heysel Stadium disaster witnessed the deaths of 39 Juventus fans and more than 600 fans injured, further isolating Liverpool because – according to the press – it was entirely the responsibility of the Liverpool supporters. Across different columns in the week that followed, Liverpool as a city was labelled 'feral', 'barbaric', 'Neanderthal' and 'murderous.'

Militant did not want to be accused of hypocrisy, having confronted the Liberal-Conservative council in 1980 for falling in line with national Tory cuts. This resulted in another warning from the District Auditor who said that by September the council must cut spending, use the courts to set a balanced rate or sack its 32,000 employees. Hatton and the rest of the Militant hierarchy insisted that they never planned on sacking anyone but tried to call the government's bluff by issuing redundancy notices to all workers with a covering note explaining that it was a tactic to buy the council another three months to find a way forward.

'No, I don't look back at it as a mistake,' Hatton reflected. 'Maybe the way we communicated it was a mistake. Having said that, we had meetings everywhere. There wasn't a single work force in this city that didn't have a meeting with us, where either me, Tony Mul, Tony Byrne or John Hamilton didn't go and address them saying, "It's a load of crap, it's a tactic; you're not getting made redundant – no one's losing their job, more will come." There's always going to be people who panic, of course there is. I thought at the time we did everything that we could to explain it.'

In *Militant Liverpool*, Diane Frost and Peter North reminded: 'Sometimes the way things are done can matter more than what is done.' Some of the redundancy notices were infamously delivered in taxis and this gave all of Militant's opponents an excuse to kick them, including Kinnock at the Labour Party Conference.

'Kinnock's speech changed everything,' Hatton rasped, though he believed that voters in Liverpool still backed the council. Depending on how reliable you consider a poll conducted by *Channel 4 News*, the results suggests the support – though still a majority – was not as convincing as it had been before. While 47 per-cent blamed the government in this particular stand-off, and 33 per-cent blamed the council. Fifty-one per-cent said they would still backing Labour in the next council elections.

'I think Kinnock did more to aid and abet Thatcher than any other person around – any member of Thatcher's cabinet,' Hatton continued. 'I was on a television show with an old aggressive Scottish Tory MP called Terry Taylor. He came over and told me, "You know what, Margaret couldn't believe what Kinnock has done. She was actually preparing the plans to take on Liverpool and she realised then she didn't have to."

'Thatcher was the absolute worst – I despised her,' Hatton continued. 'But the reality is, I understood where she came from and who she was. She was a reactionary Tory, a right winger; she said that and did it. You accept that, even if you don't like it. Kinnock was the complete opposite. He was supposed to be a socialist in the Labour movement and all he did was ensure that everything related to us, the miners – whoever – were defeated by Thatcher.'

Having not visited since Militant's rise, Kinnock finally made it to Liverpool three weeks after reviling Hatton in Bournemouth. Hatton claimed in his autobiography in 1988 that Kinnock recognised Liverpool's problems and would have given the city some backing, though the Labour leader denied this when it was made public. It prompted Hatton to write an open letter where he finished with the observation, 'you seem more intent on launching into a vitriolic and venomous attack on the city council. Our impression is that your concern is more with spearheading a witch-hunt than in attempting to solve the problems and its people.'

In October 1985, the church turned against Militant with both of Liverpool's bishops writing a letter to *The Times* condemning their tactics. By the end of November 1985, Kinnock had announced at the Labour Party's National Executive Committee that the Liverpool District Labour Party, including Derek Hatton and Tony Mulhearn and 45 others, was being suspended pending investigation, writing in an infamous statement: 'It is generally recognised that Militant Tendency is the maggot in the body of the Labour Party.'

Liverpool Labour, with Militant at its core, had won two council elections and Militant's leadership had attracted higher votes than in any election since World War Two. This explained why support was forthcoming, because policies had tallied with the wishes and desires of many people in the city. The legacy of the socialist led council was undeniable and still visible for all to see in Liverpool. Yet many choose to ignore boring stuff like homes and leisure centres because of the way it all ended for Militant: with expulsion from the Labour Party. 'Kinnock had been,' Hatton reflected on the leader at the time, 'more undemocratic than even Thatcher.'

BEHIND PETER KILFOYLE IN THE LIVING ROOM OF HIS FAMILY HOME in the West Derby area of Liverpool was a book case where the shelves were filled with titles that reflected his political beliefs. There were memoirs written by Tony Blair, Cherie Blair, Alastair Campbell, Kofi Annan and Bill Clinton. He kept the story of Francisco Franco because he thought 'it better to know how the worst ones think'. The thickest of the autobiographies was Harold Wilson's.

'I thought he was exceptional, I really did,' Kilfoyle beamed. 'The Labour Party is a coalition of interests and Harold was very good at managing people and personalities and getting them to pull in the same direction. It was often said he had 'Big Beasts' in the cabinet but he was able to keep them under control.

'He also had a common touch. I remember the general election of 1974. On successive days, I saw Tony Benn and Harold Wilson campaigning. Tony Benn was outside what was then a bingo hall on Sheil Road in Kensington. Some women were coming out and he was talking to them about unilateral nuclear disarmament. You could see that were looking at him as though he was from the Planet Zonk. It was way over their heads, they didn't understand it.

'I then saw Harold at what was then a Safeway supermarket on Wavertree Road. He was talking to a group of women, asking them, "How much is that butter, love? I hear it's gone up a penny..." He was talking about everyday things that people appreciate. He was a very clever man but he was able to relate to ordinary people.'

Kilfoyle would say he was more of a centrist Labour man. In the eyes of Derek Hatton and Tony Mulhearn, that made him right wing.

Mulhearn: 'On the face of it, he [Kilfoyle] fancies himself as a bit of a scholar, an intellectual. He quotes Shakespeare and various erudite authoritative figures. But then, he was also a Stalin-type. Very thick-skinned. A brutal element. The type of mentality that was required to do the business in Liverpool. He was given unlimited power. In terms of his actions, he carried out a one-sided civil war against the party of Liverpool.'

Hatton: "Oh, he [Kilfoyle] was just a useless lump o'lard. He did Kinnock's work for him but only because he had Kinnock's backing. He had nothing about himself. He totally contributed towards the dismantling of Militant but anyone could have done that with Kinnock's backing, along with the entire media. You didn't have to be the brightest person in the world to come and do it, you know what I mean?"

'I am a social conservative – with a small C obviously, but I'm a policy radical,' Kilfoyle explained. 'I'm not someone for great change. I think of family as being very important. I see things in what some would say is an old-fashioned, idealised way. I've always seen social policy in a simple and straightforward manner.

When it comes to foreign policy, the more I've travelled and the more I've seen, the more radical I've felt about the injustices of the world and the way we allow bigotry to ride roughshod over what I consider to be moral imperatives.'

Kilfoyle enjoyed being listened to and was proud of his oratory skills, as well as his ability to form his opinions in written blogs which he publicised on social media. One of his posts related to the suggestion that Liverpool is now a left-wing city and will be forever, but he thought differently.

'The way I see things, I don't accept left and right; I only accept right and wrong,' he said. 'There are always people who want to tell you how left wing they are. A good friend of mine was a docks official. I was with him and a couple of other dockers. They were going on about the dockers support for the oppressed blacks of South Africa. I said, "Hang on, you're the official for the docks, Jimmy; you've been through those periods when there were up to 28,000 workers on the docks. You tell me, how many black guys did you have in that work force?" He could think of two. And yet you had all of Liverpool 8, which is effectively a ghetto for black people, running alongside the southern docks when they were operative. You can't truly be a socialist if you say you support the end of Apartheid in South Africa but you don't put your own house in order.'

'When you say, "Labour forever" there's no such thing as forever,' he continued. 'If you go back to the early 1970s there was a huge controversy around the new inner-city Liverpool ring road [the one which led to the decline and demolition of Gerard Gardens]. There was one Liberal councillor then, Cyril Carr. In no time, the Liberals had pushed Labour out of the way taken over the council from the Tories. It was a big reaction to self-satisfied do-nothing Labour councillors, not so much a vote for the party. Things can always change if you don't do it your job properly. Liverpudlians are smart.'

He did not think much of Joe Anderson, the current mayor, comparing his time at city hall to that of what he called, 'the Hattonista period' when a younger version of himself was deployed by Neil Kinnock to bring Liverpool Council back into line with national policy. Kilfoyle was a formidable looking character, able to stand the full-blast of a central heating system that remained throughout a bleak mid-winter's afternoon. His enormous frame was attached to an armchair, and he coughed and spluttered through the interview because of a chest infection. He suffered from chest infections terribly following a quadruple heart bypass. But he was determined to get his words out and have his say – particularly about Hatton.

We raced through his childhood. He was one of fourteen children, ten boys and four girls. His father had been a labourer and his mother worked as a cleaner at Alder Hey Hospital. His interest in politics came when he was just 'eight or nine', helping a neighbour hand out Labour party leaflets, though he did not know what they stood for at the very beginning. He was bright and passed the exams to study at Durham University, but only after his mother had borrowed £20 from the parish priest to pay for the train fare. Surrounded by public school boys, he 'couldn't hack it', so he returned home and married, spending the 1960s on building sites. In the 1970s, he witnessed a political shift. 'People in Liverpool became radicalised and espousing visions which hadn't really had much of a hearing before. I'm talking about Trotskyites. This was a different view, even for those on the left of politics as I was. We'd gone from a combined Labour Party and trades council, with political and industrial interests inter-mixed, to a separation. The Labour Council and the trades council were no longer attempting to achieve the same aims. For many people, trade unionism was far more important and meaningful than Labour party politics. I never felt quite like that and I stayed on the side of the Labour Party.'

Kilfoyle admits that the manner of his departure from one job left 'a sour taste' in relation to the union, who 'when it came to it, looked after its own interest rather than one of its workers'. His sacking, particularly as it supposedly stemmed from his own union activity where he 'used the rule book to try and improve conditions', acted as a 'wake-up call to the realities of powerful organisations no matter who they stand for'. By his own admission, it left him suspicious of authority and disillusioned by the direction of Britain, which explained why at the start of the 1970s, he moved to Australia for work. Militant members would later gossip about this gap in his life and rumours would spread.

'I remember a banner outside one of the council meetings appearing. It read: "Kilfoyle Go Back to Australia." They'd done a background check on me and a Peter Kilfoyle of the Australian SAS came up. So, they put it about that I was brought in by Kinnock to deal with them because of my supposed SAS background to do a secretive job on Militant. It was fantasy. I'm not sure whether they all believed it or not but some of them certainly did.'

Kilfoyle was primarily known by his enemies in Militant as 'the chief witch-finder'. As Hatton and his colleagues took a defiant stand against both the Conservative government over local authority budgets and the Labour leadership,

Kilfoyle was sent back to the city by Kinnock to 'clean it up'.

'Neil was a really decent guy. He meant well. He wanted to do the right thing for Labour across the country. He wanted the right thing for Labour in Liverpool. And by and large, he backed me all the way. I had my differences with him. I can remember being at one National Executive meeting and Neil was upset because I was arguing over a couple of parliamentary selections. As Neil left, he stopped with his hand on the door and came over to me. He said, "Peter, you were making a powerful case. But you have to realise that sometimes there are things I've got to do as leader of the party that won't please everyone." I said, "I know, Neil." And I did. That was the measure of the guy, you could have a difference of opinion and argue but he wouldn't necessarily hold it against you if he knew that your motives were the right ones.'

From afar, Kilfoyle had developed a dim view of Militant.

'By the mid-80s they had become well organised and co-ordinated and they dominated what passed for the Labour Party in Liverpool. There was no real discussion, no real consideration of options. It's was far more tribal: you back your own people. You back Labour. You back your neighbourhood. The idea that you should argue, debate and work out a productive or logical way forward was not part of the thinking. You are either with or against them.

'I believe in freedom of speech, exchange of ideas, argument and debate. What I objected to was a party within a party. If they wanted to have an entirely separate programme to the Labour Party – which they did – they ought to stand alone and win support for their cause. I don't believe it was right from them to feed off the Labour Party and pretend to be Labour when, in fact, they weren't Labour at all. They were an entirely separate political party. The party ought to be what it says it is, and that counts for the Conservatives too who have previously tolerated fascists. No party should harbour a creature within. It's a bit like the Alien movie in a political sense, waiting to burst forth in all of its horrors. That's how I saw Militant.'

Kilfoyle spoke succinctly about Hatton: 'I found him loathsome, I still do. I have absolutely no time for the man. Stands for nothing but himself.'

On Mulhearn: 'He was of a different order because at least I could say with Mulhearn that he was consistent, he appears to believe in what he believed in. I disagreed with him, totally. But you see, he was one of those [Militant].'

Kilfoyle had some admiration for the initial stealth with which Militant used entryism to dominate the Labour party in Liverpool. Hatton and Mulhearn could be aggressive in meetings but both reasoned this was because of who they were and where they were from: the council was not used to working-class figures having a say. Kilfoyle saw Militant as bullies. 'They'd shout people down, hurl abuse. Again, this was not my idea of what a left-wing group was about.' Kilfoyle spoke about the physical intimidation that came his way when he was sent in by Kinnock to realign Labour in Liverpool in a casual sort of manner, as if to suggest it didn't bother him. 'If you're born and raised in this city, with a certain background and certain experiences, you can handle that kind of stuff. But you have to bear in mind there's an awful lot of people who cannot. They won't put up with it and it turns them off. We alienated huge numbers of people from the Labour cause because of the way Militant behaved in meetings. It was dreadful. It was water off a duck's back for me, but others were totally threatened by the atmosphere they created.'

According to Mulhearn, one person who 'really hated' Kilfoyle was Eric Heffer, the Labour MP for Walton who lost the party's leadership contest to Neil Kinnock in 1983. Heffer was one of the chief defenders of the left-wing Liverpool Council. It was believed that Walton was an impregnable Militant area but when Heffer died in 1991, it gave Kinnock the opportunity to purge Labour of Militant once and for all. Instead of Lesley Mahmood, the preferred candidate of the left, Kilfoyle stood for Labour in Walton and there were accusations of rigging. 'It would have horrified Eric to think Kilfoyle came in after him,' Mulhearn said, knowing that Heffer's replacement was more than eleven per-cent down on his own result in the previous general election. 'As far as I was concerned, Walton no longer had a person representing them who really reflected the interests of the people.'

THIRTY-YEARS HAD PASSED SINCE MILITANT'S EMERGENCE WHEN, IN 2013, Derek Hatton went into the BBC studios in Salford for an interview with Roger Johnson, the *North West Tonight* presenter. A two-minute clip showed archive video footage of Liverpool as a city in the 1980s, reflecting the rise of Militant as well as its fall, but not really anything Militant got right – or why their fight mattered. It implied that society has not suffered, that Margaret Thatcher was right because no other council followed Liverpool's lead in challenging her.

Hatton, with his legs crossed and his left arm leaning casually on the back of the red couch, could not hide his fury. When Johnson led with a question, 'Do you feel a bit ashamed?' Hatton was waiting. 'You had a wonderful opportunity to start to show what was really going on at that time,' he began.

'Don't forget, you had a city where one in four people were unemployed, where £20million had actually been robbed by the Thatcher government in terms of housing allocation for the city while the Liberal and Tory alliance in Liverpool just stood by and watched it. You had a situation where people started to feel a little bit angry. We got elected with a massive majority...'

Johnson would try to intervene but Hatton was on his way. 'We made a lot of gains in 1984 as a result of people saying, "That's what we want to vote for." Hatton described what he'd just witnessed as 'one of the worst pieces of journalism I've ever seen, it's absolutely disgraceful. It's naïve and lazy. My grandkids could have gone and Googled and picked up that same stuff.'

From there, Johnson had lost the thread of the interview, yet what was happening live on air left an indelible impression of the person at the centre of it. Hatton accused the reporting of being unbalanced and he had a point. Five out of the six people interviewed about Militant were indeed, figures that had helped engineer its downfall: Neil Kinnock, Jane Kennedy and Peter Kilfoyle amongst them. Johnson and Hatton was no longer an interview and rather an argument. 'Why didn't you go and interview some of those that got jobs, houses?' Hatton asked, his pupils narrowing, the whites of his eyes becoming more prominent. 'We succeeded with the jobs, we succeeded with houses, we kept getting elected – eventually it was the House of Lords that removed us and I tell you what Rog,' he concluded, pointing his finger. 'Not many people in Liverpool voted for the House of Lords.'

5

Possessed With
A Particularly
Violent Nature

THE STATE WAS A FORMER BALLROOM THAT STARTED LIFE AS A restaurant in 1905, attracting diners with its old world elegance which included Grecian columns, marble floors, wall carvings and magnificent limestone toilets. When Littlewoods bought the venue in 1949 as a social centre for its staff, it slipped into becoming one of the world's most luxurious storage spaces but in the early 1980s, having been reopened as a nightclub, it helped launch the careers of Liverpool artists like Jegsy Dodd, whose first gig as a performance poet involved supporting The Farm and the Manchester band, A Certain Ratio.

Dodd was from Wirral but Liverpool's social field was magnetic, drawing him in every weekend to the pubs and clubs which thrived in spite of the political struggle and economic plight of the city. Dodd realised that the decade will have felt differently for families – those fathers and mothers looking for jobs. If, like Dodd, however, you were in your twenties, a sense of nihilism existed and the more Militant fought back – the more they generated headlines – the more exciting Liverpool became, and the more he was drawn to its dimly lit streets, its hidden entrances and its epicurean nightlife.

On stage at The State, Dodd had been 'ranting on – offering the crowd fights', when John Peel came over and said: "'You've gotta come to London and do that…" I was like, "Yeah, yeah, yeah…" But three days later he was on the phone selling the idea. I needed a backing group. All of my mates wanted to be in it. It felt like being God, deciding who was allowed in. The rest of the 80s was filled with touring; Germany, Holland and Belgium.'

Jegsy Dodd & The Sons of Harry Cross, as they became, recorded the album *Winebars & Werewolves* in 1985, albeit at their own expense. Then twenty years would pass between hitting number 19 in the UK Indie Charts and Dodd's next release, *Wake Up and Smell the Offy*, which was then followed by *Loquacious, Loquacious, Loquacious.*

Listening to him while sat at a table looking out towards the Irish Sea in a Wallasey pub, there was a feeling that football and journeys involving the fortunes of Liverpool FC had always been his priority and it 'sort of got in the way of everything else', though he insisted he wouldn't have done it any differently. In his writing, he'd described Anfield and Liverpool as 'his drug of choice, a lifelong addiction of which there is no known cure'.

On his mobile phone, Dodd had a photograph of his younger self, back when he was 15 years old in 1973, standing between Bill Shankly, the Liverpool manager, and Tommy Smith. Moments earlier, Liverpool's captain had been presented on the pitch at Anfield with the team's first league winners' crown in seven seasons. Shankly, who proclaimed Liverpool as the 'club of the people' when he arrived fourteen years before with the team rooted in the Second Division, had transformed the club into the best in the country through his mix of charisma and socialist zeal. In front of the Spion Kop stand, which had become the largest roofed terrace in European football, Shankly would thrust the trophy using one hand into the air, surrounded not so much by the players he'd signed but by the children of the boys' pen and the lifeblood of Liverpool's febrile support. Dodd, wearing a distinctive red and yellow bobble hat and tartan jacket, was one of them. 'Getting that close to Shankly,' Dodd reflected, 'was like an audience with the pope.'

Football, however, had become a particularly violent environment. Dodd's first game was away at Stoke when he was thirteen, taking the train with a group of mates from Lime Street. A year later, he was chased by Leeds fans, all the way from Elland Road on the edge of the city to the train station in the centre. 'I never wanted to go back after that day,' he admitted. 'But soon, it would become really exciting.'

Following Liverpool all over the country was intoxicating. 'You soon reach the situation where you can't not be there, simply because you don't want to miss out on any of the madness and the tales.' From Lime Street to Euston, there were two early trains that took supporters to games in London, one at half six in the morning and the other at ten to seven. This would avoid the police but not the welcoming committees of hooligans from Chelsea, Arsenal or Tottenham. Dodd, nevertheless, thought football supporters were treated with impunity. He recalled a school friend with who got fined £500 for flicking a peanut at a Birmingham City supporter across a terrace. 'He could have flicked a thousand peanuts and there wouldn't have been any damage.'

Football, he recalled, was not consumed by the middle classes. Now, it is a theatre with goodies, baddies – a staged sort of drama. Then, it was a working mans' game watched in the stadium and rarely on television. 'It's a different cross-section of people who go to the game now,' he rued. 'The middle class have their opinions and air them on Facebook.' Football, for him, was a release. He says he was not the same person at a football ground as he was elsewhere. Emotionally, it allowed him to unload his frustrations from other parts of his life. It also allowed him to make friends from other parts of Liverpool and those friends have remained close to him for forty years. An ex-girlfriend used to half joke with him that he'd spent more nights in the same bedroom with Ally, a mate from Anfield. He considered what had kept him going for so long and realised that if the community spirit in football that brought people together was no longer a feature of a Saturday afternoon or a Wednesday night, he would stop altogether.

Football hooliganism was on the rise. Segregation was introduced at all football grounds in England after events in 1974, when a young Blackpool fan was stabbed to death by a Bolton Wanderers supporter and later that year, Manchester United's Red Army hooligan firm caused mayhem at grounds up and down the country following the club's surprise relegation from the First Division. Leeds United were later banned from European football for four years after their supporters rioted in Paris in the aftermath of a European Cup final defeat to Bayern Munich. Then, in 1977, Manchester United were also banned but later reinstated into the Cup Winners' Cup and made to play the second leg of a tie with Saint-Étienne in Plymouth following crowd violence in France.

'Segregation created a divide, an us-and-them mentality: "We must abuse them and they must abuse us,"' said Dodd, an 'Annie Road ender' – which meant that rather than stand in the Kop as he got older, he watched from the Anfield Road end of the ground, where skirmishes with visiting hooligans in their section of the terrace known as 'Compost Corner' was a regular feature of any match-day. He would explain the phenomenon of hooliganism not through any form of economic or social hardship but as the purest form of tribalism.

'If you live in a valley in Wales, you don't like the next valley,' he reasoned. 'If you're competing at a rural Lakeland show, you're desperate to beat the next village at tug of war. Nobody likes their neighbours. Roads don't like the next roads. Countries don't like bordering countries. Liverpool and Manchester don't like each other, but the media have always wanted to have their cake and eat it. They widen the division sometimes even further than it actually is. They will call Liverpool and United the biggest rivalry ever to sell newspapers or increase viewing figures but when there's trouble on the terraces or on the pitch, they all frown.'

Youth culture was changing rapidly. In the 1950s, 21-year-olds would dress modestly like their fathers and follow them into the docks. By the 1980s, lads from Liverpool were wearing straight-legged jeans, training shoes, cagouls and floppy fringes like Bryan Ferry. The scally, though, was a difficult person to pin down, as Peter Hooton explained: 'As soon as someone – usually a smart arse in the media – tried to define exactly what a scally was, it was time to change because in Liverpool the real scallies didn't know they were true scallies and nobody wanted to admit they were a scal anyway.'

A casual culture emerged. Clothes were acquired following Liverpool Football Club across the continent but they were also acquired in other parts of Europe because of the search for work with the docks in decline.

In the summer months, Jegsy Dodd translated menus in Ibiza, worked on building sites in Jersey, picked tomatoes on the Greek Island of Ios, and when he whitewashed walls in Perpignan, southern France, he was once so hungry that he waited for tourists to finish their meals and eat what was left behind before a waiter took the plates way.

'Scousers did get on their bikes, as Norman Tebbit asked,' Dodd insisted. 'We got off our arses and were prepared to go to other cities and countries in pursuit of work, though we were often met by hostility because of our determination to make our mark and do well.'

He wondered whether the willingness to travel stemmed from the merchant navy having a history in many families like his. 'Everybody knew someone whose been to sea. It's in the blood of the city. The river means things were always coming in, they were always going out. If you had tales from your granddad when he went to New York, it raised your level of consciousness and made you want to travel as well.'

Liverpool's progression into the most successful football team in Europe ensured that Dodd would always return home, though conversely the achievements of the club he loved fed his desire to travel. There had been adults who'd never been to London and yet, when Dodd was still a teenager he'd been there twenty-odd times and knew which tube stations to use. Football would allow him to visit nearly every major town or city in England, whereas non-football people had barely left wherever they came from. Between 1977 and 1984, Liverpool won the European Cup four times and Dodd was at each of the finals and many of the games en route, having learned how to doctor train tickets that would mean rather than spending money he did not really have on a return to Sofia, he'd only pay as far as Paris.

Rome in 1977 was Liverpool's first European Cup final. Bill Shankly had retired to everyone's surprise in 1974 and his successor, Bob Paisley, created a championship winning team that was more sophisticated and ultimately more relentlessly successful than any of those delivered by Shankly. Yet without the foundations being laid before Paisley was appointed to a role he did not even want – only accepting it because he thought he was preserving the jobs of the famous Boot Room staff – it seems implausible that he would have been able to achieve the same feats, becoming the most decorated English manager ever in European competitions.

Whereas Shankly, a granite-jawed Ayreshireman, was rapier-witted and led by his passion, Paisley shunned the limelight and was less communicative, with players not understanding his mumbled messages most of the time. His tactical judgement, however, was unparalleled and he was able to take Liverpool's supporters to places they'd never previously been. Dodd was one of thirty thousand Liverpudlians in Rome, where the opponents were German champions Borussia Mönchengladbach. He thinks many of them had never been abroad before. Many carried with them temporary one-year passports bought from local post offices.

'People didn't travel in such volume,' he thought. 'When Nottingham Forest won against Malmö in the final held in Munich two years later, they took just 10,000 and Munich is a lot closer to Nottingham than Rome is to Liverpool. It took two and a half days to get there and two and a half days back by train with no running water. 'We were travelling through countries where we didn't even have the currency. I remember returning to Lime Street on the Friday around tea time, the train limping in with three or four hundred supporters aboard. We were applauded off by the rail staff and shoppers. It was like heroes coming back from war.'

Liverpool's 3-1 victory was by followed more success twelve months later, this time over Club Brugge at Wembley. In 1981, just before Toxteth smouldered, Real Madrid were defeated in Paris and Liverpool became three-time champions. Liverpool's dominance underpinned an almost absolutely English control of the competition across eight seasons, where Nottingham Forest (twice) and Aston Villa would also become champions, though it could have been different for Villa in 1982 when their semi-final with Anderlecht saw crowd disturbances which led to 20 injuries and 27 arrests. Anderlecht would appeal to UEFA, suggesting that Villa should be kicked out, but instead an eight-man committee merely fined the Midlands club £14,500 and ordered them to play their next European home match behind closed doors.

By 1984, the number of Liverpool supporters either willing or able to get to Rome for their next European Cup final had halved compared to seven years previously. Dodd, again, was one of them, believing that the drop in numbers was explained by the reduced income levels across Merseyside during the 1980s as well as the threat of violence. Liverpool's opponents would be AS Roma in their home ground – their first European Cup final. This had only happened before in the formative years of the European Cup when fans travelled less and has never happened since. There was no consideration by UEFA to host the match at a different location on safety grounds or on the basis of neutrality.

Dodd was unemployed but he was never going to miss this moment, finding enough money for a week-long trip which began in Rimini, the northern seaside resort, by selling much of his record collection. There, he and his mates were chased by men on scooters wearing balaclavas and a fight ensued, giving warning to what was waiting in Rome and the start of 'the maddest twenty-four hours of my life', which began with him being pelted with bananas and apples as he passed through the doors of Rome's Termini station where there were riot police carrying machine guns and CS gas canisters. 'This was at 7.30 in the morning,' he emphasised.

The train back to Rimini was scheduled after midnight and this meant Dodd and the rest of his gang did not have the sanctuary of a hotel. 'We were hunted like packs of animals,' he recalled. Others had travelled on official trips organised by travel companies in conjunction with the club. From their arrival at the airport, a cavalcade of scooters pursued the buses and bottles were thrown dangerously underneath the tyres of the moving targets.

At the Olympic Stadium later that night, Dodd would see flares and fireworks used inside a football ground for the first time, as well as banners that covered entire terraces. It was meant to be a neutral venue, but Liverpool were very much visitors on rival territory and their supporters were subjected to a hailstorm of lira.

'When it went to penalties I remember saying, "If we win here, we're dead." Liverpool did win but the glow of victory in spite of the odds being against them subsided quickly. 'We had the Italians trying to kill us and the police next to them beating us with truncheons. I was in my prime and I could sort of deal with it, you can take a few knocks, but you felt sorry for the families and the kids – the good Liverpool fans who were mixed up in it. It was horrible.'

Tragically, Roma's defeat on their home turf would result with the death of their captain, Agostino Di Bartolomei, who took his own life on 30 May 1994 – ten years to the day after the final, shooting himself through the heart on the balcony of his villa with a .38 Smith and Wesson pistol. Only a note in his pocket, which had been torn into 32 pieces, gave indication of di Bartolomei's torment. Financially, there had been problems, but he had also struggled to find space 'in the world of football', following retirement. But for Miguel Munoz, Real Madrid's captain in 1957, he could have been the only captain to have lifted the European Cup in his own city, describing the final with Liverpool as 'the game of my life'. Most Liverpool supporters would remember the final for the wobbly legs of Bruce Grobbelaar, who managed to unnerve two of Roma's penalty takers in the shootout, but Dodd could not wait to leave the city which had offered what he called, the 'smoke, tear gas, and flare final'.

The reaction to the disturbances the following morning in Italy was immense embarrassment. *La Repubblica* headlined, 'Manhunt against the English,' *Corriere dello Sport* reported, 'The aftermath of the match brought a night of vile, blind violence that disappointment cannot justify,' and *Il Tiempo* said, 'This could have been an occasion to demonstrate civility. Instead, the usual group of fans with knives, bottles and sticks went on an odious manhunt.'

On a press bus, one Radio City journalist helped a bleeding fan who had been stabbed, and yet the violence was barely given any coverage in the English media.

As he looked out across Wallasey's beach recounting the escapades of his youth in far foreign lands, Dodd described the overwhelming sense of relief as he returned to Merseyside in one piece, though he did warn friends of his concerns about the prospect of Liverpool ever meeting another Italian team in a final at a neutral venue. His worst fears would be realised twelve months later.

DEREK HATTON RECALLED HIS *QUESTION TIME* APPEARANCE WITH Robin Day in November 1984 with a giddy excitement. A couple of nights earlier, he'd been drinking in Huyton with Peter Reid and Adrian Heath, the Everton footballers. They were talking about politics and Heath's father issued Hatton with a challenge. 'Mention our Adrian on *Question Time*,' he said. 'Why's he not playing for England? It's a matter of national debate,' and with that, a £100 wager was raised. Heath's father said Hatton would not do it. Hatton said he would and he'd forgotten about the bet as he strode into the studio in combat mode, anticipating that *Question Time's* host and the other three guests on the panel would have a very different interpretation on matters relating to the politics of the day because by then, as Hatton put it, 'Liverpool as a city was cut adrift from the rest of the country'. He fought his way through the questions. Then right at the end, Hatton and the rest of the panel were invited to reveal which person they would like to grill having been grilled themselves. 'It would have be to Bobby Robson, the England manager,' Hatton said in a flash, his thoughts returning to the pub talk days earlier. 'Why on earth aren't you picking Adrian Heath? He's one of the best players at the best team in England!'

Suddenly, Liverpool had a new domestic rival. Everton were top of the league, and Liverpool were in tenth, trailing their neighbours by nine points. An injury to Heath sustained in a game against Sheffield Wednesday would mean that he missed the final months of a campaign where Liverpool recovered to second, but Everton would still clinch their first league title in fourteen years.

In one of the last league games of that glorious season, against Liverpool at Goodison Park, the Everton captain, Kevin Ratcliffe, wrote in his programme notes about how amazing it was that the two best teams in the country came from a struggling provincial city. While Everton had already been crowned as Cup

Winners' Cup champions having qualified for Europe by lifting the FA Cup twelve months before, Liverpool still had a European Cup final left to play in six days' time against Juventus at the Heysel Stadium in Brussels.

'There was a lot of anger within the city and the success of the two football clubs seemed to take a lot of that anger away, along with music,' Ratcliffe reflected when I met him at a busy hotel lobby not far from his home in Connah's Quay in north Wales. 'It was a dark period off the pitch. If you took away football, if you took away the music scene, you wonder what might have happened in Liverpool. What would have been left to enjoy? The city took a lot of confidence from football because the two teams were doing so well. It meant the majority of people were a lot happier than they would have been if one was doing well and the other wasn't – or, like it was in the 1990s when the trophies dried up for both clubs.'

'Look at the gates,' Ratcliffe continued. 'In some games, the teams were poorly supported despite how successful we were. This was mainly because of money. People couldn't afford to go, even though it was a lot cheaper to get in than it is now. There was also concerns about hooliganism, of course. Even in the derbies, you wouldn't always get a full house. At the start of the 1980s it would be 60,000 but by the late 1980s it was down to 57,000. The only other big gates would be whenever Man United and Leeds and came to Goodison – over 40,000. The clubs in Liverpool were well supported and the passion remained in the city but not in terms of attendances.'

It was interesting to listen to Ratcliffe about his own awareness, and whether as a focused footballer trying to forge his own career he really noticed at the time what was happening in the place which offered him employment but not thousands of its own residents. He had made a profound statement in his programme column because the only city in Britain to since have two teams competing against one another at the top end of the league has been in Manchester, though United and City were fuelled by enormous wealth pouring in from overseas.

Ratcliffe's impression was that of an outsider albeit with inside access. His journey from Wales by car every day to Everton's training ground at Bellefield in West Derby involved a route through the Wallasey tunnel, taking him along Scotland Road. He would see crumbling tenement blocks and groups of young men huddled in the streets with nothing else to do but try to escape the vile winds. He would also read the headlines in the newspapers, but not necessarily the stories. The football supporters of Liverpool and Everton liked to think their players thought like them and suffered like them but in reality, they did not. Paul Jewell, a teenager at Liverpool, later reflected that he was the only socialist in the Liverpool squad, though Michael Robinson – also a committed socialist, and someone who would play in the European Cup final of 1984 in Rome – reasoned that he never discussed politics with teammates, revealing that he was considered odd for reading the *Guardian* while others on the bus to training rifled through the pages of the tabloids. It was rumoured that Kenny Dalglish and Graeme Souness were Tories, though this could have stemmed from Dalglish's supposed reluctance when it came to buying rounds of drinks, as well as Souness's renowned flamboyance and nickname of Champagne Charlie. Ratcliffe, who was 25 when he captained Everton to the title, admitted that really, he was politically unconscious.

'Young men are quite selfish in sport and are quite selfish by nature partly because of the demands for focus in the industry,' he reasoned. 'You're on a ride and all you think about is your own careers and the success of the team. It's not until you look back, you realise how hard it was for other people. If all the players thought about what was going on, it would have added pressure. You look back now and think, "Jesus – how did Liverpool as a city reach such a point?"' The Welsh coastline that runs parallel to the River Dee and towards Chester was also affected by the political and economic measures of the Conservative government. Ratcliffe's grandparents had worked in the steelworks and they had shut down. A paper mill had also closed. This impacted on the social clubs, of which 'there were more of than pubs in Flintshire at one point... but the 1980s brought that collective culture to an end'.

At Everton, there were youth team players on amateur contracts who were not being paid and this forced them to sign on at the dole office. One of them was Steve McMahon, a Scouse midfielder, a boyhood Evertonian and a one-time ball boy at Goodison Park; someone Ratcliffe described in training as being 'like a bottle of pop – he could have gone off at any minute'. The movements in McMahon's career would reflect the unlikeliness in Everton's rise because he would become one of the first-team's best players, before leaving for Aston Villa, then fortifying an already great Liverpool team by making the controversial decision to sign for them. Ratcliffe had lived in digs and spent a lot of time at McMahon's, where his mother made sandwiches in between training sessions. Everton's manager was Howard Kendall, a former player who had formed one part of the Holy Trinity midfield beside Alan Ball and Colin Harvey when Harry Catterick's team last won the title in 1970. 'It's fair to say Howard knew a thing or two about midfielders,' Ratcliffe appreciated. 'It was clear he rated Steve but I think Steve wanted a small pay rise of something like £20 that reflected his status in the team and Howard wouldn't give it to him because he thought that if he gave in to him, he'd have to give in to everyone else.' McMahon had been linked with a move to Liverpool but that was only realised after two seasons at Villa. 'I don't think he could have ever gone straight from Everton to Liverpool. I think he had the chance to do that but he turned it down because Everton were still in his heart at the time.' Ratcliffe wondered whether McMahon, despite becoming a serial winner at Anfield, wishes that success could have instead been at Everton and he blamed Kendall for not ensuring that it was. 'Sometimes managers don't like players,' Ratcliffe said. 'All they see about them is the negative things, not the positive things. There's absolutely no doubt that Steve should have been a big part of our history.'

Without McMahon, Everton would win the FA Cup, the Cup Winners' Cup and the league title in the space of two seasons. For Ratcliffe, it was only when Kendall got the balance of the midfield right in McMahon's absence that the possibilities increased at Everton.

In 1983, pressure had mounted through the autumn, with 'Kendall Out' painted on the garage doors of the manager's Formby home after Everton had lost 3-0 at Anfield, a result which put Liverpool top of a league they had won in seven of the previous ten seasons. Meanwhile, Everton – without any trophy whatsoever in thirteen years – languished in seventeenth place. Suddenly a crucial sequence of positives happened and, for Ratcliffe personally, the most important was the first: the promotion of Colin Harvey – a midfield partner of Kendall's the last time Everton won the title – to first-team coach before a game against Coventry City in the League Cup. 'It was massive for me,' Ratcliffe said. 'I'd been with Colin from the age of sixteen right through the reserve team and he was such a good coach and an inspiration.' Coventry proved to be 'the night everything started'. In front of just 9,080 spectators at Goodison, Everton came back to win 2-1 with late goals by Adrian Heath and Graeme Sharp, though Ratcliffe points to Peter Reid's second-half introduction in midfield as a key moment. 'Reidy came on as a sub and he changed it.'

'It had been a horrible period,' he reflected. 'You could hear the shouts from the terraces. In fact, not only could you hear what people were saying you could see who was having a go at you as well. Cushions would get hurled from the main stand. Howard tried everything. He used to get in early and turn all the lights on to make sure the place was brightened up rather than dark. We used to train on the pitch at Goodison to try and make us feel more comfortable. Once a week there would be drills of crossing and finishing: the sort of stuff that gives you a bit more confidence, making the place feel like home. The relationship with Goodison had to improve.'

Anfield is a mile's walk from Goodison Park. When the best team in the country lives on your doorstep and has been so dominant for so long, as Liverpool had been (along with the seven league titles since Everton's last trophy, there had also been three European Cups, two UEFA Cups, three League Cups and an FA Cup), the task of overhauling them is amplified. There was a sense of Liverpool being an immovable object. 'The gap was enormous,' Ratcliffe emphasised. 'It was probably bigger then than it is now (when Liverpool have won everything there is to win bar the league since Everton's last trophy in 1995). It felt like they were always laughing at us.'

When Liverpool crushed Everton 5-0 at Goodison in November 1982, four of the goals were scored by Ian Rush, the Welsh centre-forward Ratcliffe had escorted to the game because of a driving ban. For Ratcliffe, Rush made that Liverpool side formidable because of his movement and work-rate, which set the entire team on the front foot. Rush's endeavour would enable him to become the club's all-time leading goalscorer. A record of 346 in total is unlikely to be beaten. Frustratingly, Rush – like Ratcliffe – was a boyhood Evertonian, a club he scored 26 times against, and he never lost in any of those games in which he scored.

'He'd come from all sorts of angles. He was a very clever player, much cleverer than people assume,' Ratcliffe said. 'He was always thinking how he could hurt you. He knew how to take you as a defender into positions where he could put you in trouble. He was lightening quick as well. For us to win a derby, we had to make sure that he didn't get a sniff and that was hard because of the quality behind him.'

In 1970, Everton's average attendance was greater than Liverpool's and they had spent the previous decade spending lavishly on players, earning their tag as the 'Mersey Millionaires.' Ratcliffe thought that Liverpool had simply recruited better than Everton since: replacing good players with better players. Everton were able to do it in certain positions but not all of them. 'Brian Labone and John Hurst were the central defenders in 1970, which became my position. I'm not sure that combination was fixed until the 1980s. Clubs have to understand that it doesn't become easier to be successful when you win, it becomes harder. Why did they let Joe Royle go so early? He was 25 when he left Everton. To some extent, I think Everton began resting on their laurels whereas Liverpool took nothing for granted, never praised the players, and became more and more ruthless in replacing them.'

In 1983, Everton's key signing was Andy Gray. The Scottish forward had won the PFA Young Player and Players' Player of the Year awards in 1977 but six years later appeared weakened by knee injuries, which meant Everton paid £250,000 for a someone who had cost Wolverhampton Wanderers £1.5m. Ratcliffe said that Gray brought an extra confidence to Bellefield and his personality allowed other personalities to emerge. Gray was determined to prove that he was not finished as a footballer and Ratcliffe was taken by surprise by his enthusiasm, even though he did not train all the time and earned the nickname 'Ice Man' because of the regular treatment he requited on his knee. 'When he did train, it was as though the world was ending the next day,' remembered Ratcliffe, who was appointed captain despite his clashes with Kendall, which could have led to him signing for Stoke City or Ipswich Town. Ratcliffe had wanted to play more often and felt as though Kendall was holding him back but, on reflection, he looked back at this period as a crucial stage of development because it made him more resilient. Come January 1984, Kendall would slide over to Ratcliffe and tell him that it was the Chinese New Year of the Rat. 'Do you know what that means?' Kendall asked. 'This is the year.'

Ratcliffe would lift the FA Cup that May in Everton's defeat of Watford. Kendall, he thought, knew about Chinese calendars because he spent so much time in Chinese restaurants. The social scene at Everton would become a crucial feature of the club's fabric, but especially after bad results, when Kendall would insist players met at Chow's House on Nelson Street in Chinatown on a Monday afternoon. These were exercises designed to air out any differences before they became problems, though Ratcliffe stressed that like at Liverpool, players never complimented one another anyway in order to keep everyone grounded. Ratcliffe recalled a game against Manchester United when on the coach he threw a pillow at Kevin Sheedy, telling him he might as well use it if he didn't get involved from the isolation of his position on the wing. 'Fuck me, he was the best player on the pitch by miles that day,' Ratcliffe smiled. 'But you've got to be thick-skinned. I found it difficult early on in my career with some of the stick that came my way. It does affect you as a player. You can't hide. It takes a certain breed to survive if you play for a Merseyside club. I've seen players come in and fold quickly. It's riding a storm and getting through it. Goodison is a big place when things aren't going right. The main stand hangs over you, as if it's about to topple. Players from smaller clubs would arrive at Everton not used to getting stick if they had a bad result. At other clubs, it'd be okay if you won one in three. At Everton, you had to win all of the time, even if that wasn't always realistic.'

It started to become realistic, however. A 2-1 win at Tottenham Hotspur, with Andy Gray scoring the first, sent Everton clear at the top of the table in March 1985. What separated this team from those now chasing them, Ratcliffe believed, was the standard of the goalkeeper Neville Southall, whose save from Mark Falco defied scientific probabilities. Ratcliffe described Southall, who had worked as a binman and a hod carrier before joining Everton having been recommended to Kendall by a friend who ran a pub in Llandudno, as 'an underrated mathematician' because of the way he appreciated the space between him and the defenders. Southall was, according to Ratcliffe, 'the best player I've ever played with, easily'. Everton could have won a treble but lost the FA Cup final against Manchester United at Wembley just three days after Rapid Vienna were beaten 3-1 in Rotterdam at the final of the Cup Winners' Cup where amidst a culture of hooliganism, Evertonians were credited for their behaviour, described by *The Times* as being 'impeccable from sunrise to sunset and a credit to Briton' after the Dutch police – with good humour and astute diplomacy – zealously took part in impromptu football matches organised in the market square by Everton and Rapid supporters. Ratcliffe's face would glow when talking about those weeks, when Merseyside – despite its enormous economic and social problems – felt like the centre of the football world. For that confirmation to be realised, all Liverpool needed to do was beat the Italian champions Juventus at Heysel, an athletics stadium in Belgium.

PETER ROBINSON WAS UNHAPPY AND NERVOUS. HE HAD BEEN ONE of the most respected administrators in football since the 1960s, when Bill Shankly was Liverpool's manager. In February 1985, his secretary at Anfield took a call from the Belgian Football Association, requesting an urgent meeting. UEFA had chosen Heysel in Brussels as the venue for the European Cup final and Liverpool as reigning champions were expected to feature, with a possibility that Juventus, the Italian champions aiming to win the competition for the first time just like Roma a year before, would join them.

When that tie was confirmed, Robinson flew to Belgium to inspect the stadium and pick up tickets for the game. Liverpool and Juventus had been given 14,500 each but he was immediately concerned that a supposed neutral area was next to the Liverpool area. UEFA had never used a 'neutral' area in any final before and they did not explain why it should be implemented this time. Controversially, the 'neutral' area would be at the expense of tickets to Liverpool supporters, who had their terrace behind one of the goals halved.

Robinson expressed concern that if those tickets fell into the hands of Juventus supporters, it would be a recipe for problems. He would ask why Liverpool could not simply take over the entire end and move the neutral pen elsewhere in the ground, but he was told the outlined system was the only way the authorities could comply with UEFA regulations in a stadium built for athletics events.

In Rome twelve months earlier, each of the participating clubs had an input over ticketing. With Liverpool, Robinson had been to four finals and he had a decent understanding of what needed to happen to ensure everything ran smoothly. Safety was at the forefront of his mind. Though the British media and the British authorities did not stop for long to consider the impact of the brutality experienced by lots of Liverpool supporters in Rome, including families, the memories from that night for Robinson were still fresh.

It was a wet, blowy afternoon and the UEFA officials seemed more interested in showing Robinson around the dressing rooms and executive areas of Heysel. When he looked at the terraces, he realised that the dividing line between the Liverpool pen and the neutral pen was little more than a chicken wire fence. He was told that the Belgian police were used to handling large crowds but was unconvinced when it was claimed that tickets for the neutral area were totally being controlled in Belgium, especially as a sizeable Italian community lived there. He considered where they might end up but when Robinson proposed that Liverpool switched ends with Juventus to avoid any potential conflict, his request was rejected, though he was reassured by the general secretary and his assistant at the Belgian FA that on the day of the final the sale of alcohol would be stopped around the ground.

Back on Merseyside, it became clear that there was a problem around black market tickets. When Liverpool FC were offered them in big numbers by agents,

Robinson arranged for all of the tickets sold by Liverpool to be stamped, so if someone had one without it stewards would know it wasn't genuine.

Instead of turnstiles, checkpoints would be used to enter an athletics stadium built for spectators, who 'observe and applaud', as Kevin Sampson, the author and Liverpool season ticket holder, wrote. 'Fans roar, bounce, roar, sway, jump and fall... could the Heysel Stadium be up to that? UEFA thought so.'

Two days before the game, Robinson expressed his grave concerns to John Smith, Liverpool's chairman. He then spoke to Neil McDonald, the government sports minister who arranged for a Telex to be sent to the FAs of Belgium and England expressing Liverpool's concerns about counterfeit tickets. But nobody from the Belgian FA ever replied. And nor did the English.

IN 1985, TERRY WILSON WAS 18 YEARS OLD. HE WORKED AT A FRUIT and veg stall in St John's market and all of his money went towards his three passions: smoking weed, listening to Groundpig play live at The State, and travelling to away games with Liverpool. A trip to Brussels would be his first outside of Britain. 'I wanted to see the team win the thing for the fifth time having grown up with everyone else's stories about the European Cup,' he explained enthusiastically. 'I was expecting a pure party atmosphere.'

Wilson described himself as a 'low-grade' football hooligan, meaning that he was not a part of an organised group. 'If it went off, it went off and sometimes I'd join in,' he admitted. 'More than anything, it was being a part of something; boys will be boys n' all that. There was a camaraderie and I liked it. There didn't seem to be any harm until the proper hooligans from other clubs and places started using blades. That's when I questioned whether it was going too far. A few years earlier, it was more about fighting with your fists and in the most aggressive scenario, throwing a bottle. But it was shifting from that and I didn't like it.'

At the start of the 1984/85 season, he had gone to Stockport on a Monday night for a League Cup first round first leg tie. He would witness a 0-0 draw and a fan 'getting stabbed in the arse'. This resulted in the victim not being able to sit down properly for months. At Aston Villa, someone else had been slashed across the nose, creating a scar that stayed with him for life. When Tottenham came to Anfield, he could remember a police officer 'literally holding another lad's back together' following another knifing. 'That's when I started to pull away,' he said. 'It was getting really sinister.'

He would take the train from Lime Street to Euston and then get a ferry from Felixstowe to Ostend. The weather was fantastic and the trip was living up to his expectations: 'A bevy, a spliff, a party... in Brussels, everyone was buzzing. I was involved in a game of footy with Juventus fans in the middle of the town square and the ball landed in the fountain. Everyone cheered.'

There had been no signs of trouble until later in the afternoon as the day wore on and the strong Belgian lager began to take effect. By then, Wilson had exchanged bobble hats with a Juventus fan. He did not have a ticket for the game but was able to buy one from a tout at face value in the neutral zone of block Z. 'The security was so flimsy, we could have easily bunked in,' he thought, as he passed the only checkpoint. 'The whole place was falling apart. Even after a few ales and spliffs, it was clear to me that this was not really a football ground capable of hosting an important final.'

It was still a couple of hours before kick-off. 'The mood in Block Z was a bit weird – it was meant to be a mixed area but the Juventus supporters way outnumbered the Liverpool supporters. A chicken wire fence separated the block from the Liverpool supporters to our left. The bizzies didn't check our tickets but they removed the poles from our flags. When we got in, we noticed that quite a few of the Juventus fans still had their poles.'

This unnerved Wilson as well as the 'group of scallies' he was with. They were young but experienced enough to know when trouble lay around the corner. 'Some of the Juventus fans were flicking blades, trying to see if they could get a reaction so a few of us went down to the bottom of the terrace to speak to the *gendarmerie* in crap French, telling him that we wanted to move into the Liverpool section. The bizzies, give them their due, pulled us out.'

Wilson joined the 'brilliant atmosphere' of the Liverpool section, but he was positioned right by the fence and could see what was developing on the other side of it. For him, the context did not excuse what then happened – no amount of context ever could. But he did believe it might explain and increase understanding. Thousands of people will have different stories about the events from here, but this was Wilson's: 'You're looking over and you can see Juventus fans kicking off on Liverpool fans. The majority of Liverpool fans that I saw left in there were dads and lads or lads with their birds, not lads into fighting. A young lad wearing a shirt and a scarf started getting attacked and this is when the bottles started getting thrown backwards and forwards. For us, it was like, "We've done everything we can to swerve this and they're still booting off..." From our point of view, it was like, "Let's get over there and help our fans..."

'The only way for us to get over was to remove this chicken wire fence, which was no problem. The fence comes down and Liverpool fans go over, including me. There were scuffles here, there and everywhere. Initially, it wasn't particularly unusual. It had happened loads of times at different matches: people running around, fists flying, some kicks. But it did escalate.'

Temporarily, according to Wilson, there was a break in the violence. Not many Juventus fans had engaged in the scuffles; in fact, the majority had retreated into the corner of the terrace, down by a perimeter wall. Wilson believed that the critical moment was the sudden arrival of the police, who, rather than form a cordon as they would have done in English football grounds, batoned the Liverpool supporters because more of them had spilled into the open terrace in Block Z having been packed into their reduced space at that end of the ground.

There was talk of a flare being fired from the Liverpool section into the Juventus section, which sent more supporters caught on the fringes of the fighting retreating into the corner of the terrace. But Wilson's focus by then was with the police. 'A lot of Liverpool fans turned around and started fighting back,' he admitted. 'All I can assume is that all the Juventus fans then thought we were coming back, causing them to run in the opposite direction. Our issue was with the police by that point, though.'

Wilson appreciated that he was surmising about an incident that happened in a rush more than thirty years before. He could not escape the idea that had the police stood in a line, a second wave of violence would not have happened. 'When the Juventus supporters saw us coming towards them again, especially the ones who had no part in any of this, they must have been petrified. They must have thought, "Let's get out of here." But the only way to avoid getting hurt in a moment's thought would have been to mix with the crowd that had built up in the corner. The police made everything a lot worse.'

There had been a feeling of frustration amongst Liverpudlians that 12,000 football supporters had been squeezed into a terrace designed for 6,000 athletics fans. Next to them had been a much quieter pen of mainly Juventus fans, now almost empty; many of them trapped in the far corner but nobody getting out and from a distance, nobody would be able to understand why. There was now an opportunity to reclaim that terrace and in theory, this would mean those Juventus fans left would be escorted around the running track to their end of the ground. What happened in Rome twelve months earlier was surely in the minds of some Liverpool supporters in Brussels. Yet there will have been those not necessarily interested in fighting but determined to take back a section of the ground that they believed should have been theirs anyway.

When Liverpool supporters in their allocated terrace tried to get a look at what was going on, this resulted in a crush barrier collapsing under the weight of pressure, prompting even more movement into Block Z and most likely, fears of a third wave of attack. Suddenly, there was the quiet cry of steel as more crush barriers at the far end of Block Z began to contort under the strain of the numbers that had gathered there. As they fell one by one, Juventus supporters and some neutrals were trampled on and that is when the masonry began to disintegrate. With a tremendous crack, a wall collapsed, sending a puff of smoke into the warm air of this putrid evening.

TERRY WILSON WAS A BEARDED HIPPY-TYPE WHO SOLD POT TO THE La's and did LSD before discovering Christianity, later becoming a lifeguard. You could not imagine his violent former self, the sort of man whose actions would contribute towards a crush which caused 39 deaths and serious injuries to more than 600 people.

Impossibly, the final went ahead, with Liverpool losing to a penalty kick from the French midfielder Michel Platini, who celebrated the moment in front of an abandoned terrace which possessed the appearance of catastrophe.

'We did not know anyone had died as the game was going on either,' Wilson maintained, saying he had not even seen the Juventus fans being carried away on makeshift stretchers far away to his right when he returned the Liverpool section of the stadium. 'Nothing anywhere near that scale had happened at a football match before.'

There was a drip of information. Reality would hit at a train station in Brussels, where a Liverpool supporter came running down the platform with news that Wilson did not believe. In the food galley on the ferry back to Felixstowe, he remembers arcing his neck at a small television screen and seeing bodies covered up at temporary open-air morgue beside the terrace where the battle happened. "'Oh no,' I said, "what the fuck has happened?'"

The wording of the question reflected how Wilson felt at the time. Though he was involved in the fighting, he did not immediately feel responsible for the dreadful outcome. Returning to Liverpool, he and a mate, Steve McDonald, spoke to a reporter from the *Sunday People* but in their teenage attempt to explain the morbid dynamics of a terrible event, ended up saying enough to publish the headline: 'We led soccer death charge.' On reflection, Wilson thought the photograph which accompanied the article, where McDonald – who was never charged – clenched a fist and was pictured smiling, was more insensitive than anything he really said.

'I was still angry that I'd tried to get away from Block Z in the first instance,' Wilson disputed. 'I said something along the lines of "Who knows what could have happened to our fans if we'd not gone over there and tried to help them out." To the reporter, this was food and drink and I became a gloating yob. Nobody else was stupid enough to talk but we did, and the interview came to represent a collective view of Liverpool when the rest of the world was looking for answers.'

He was operating a forklift truck piling potatoes onto a crate when the police came to take him into custody. Even then, Wilson was shocked that it had come to this and his initial reaction to the arrest, he admitted, may have made him sound unremorseful. 'They said, "We are arresting you for the manslaughter of Mario Ronchi and 38 others." I tried to go back to work. "You're having a laugh, aren't you? They were attacking us…"'

It had not been the national newspaper interview that had led the police towards him, rather the television camera footage which made him identifiable because of his Juventus bobble hat and mop of blond hair. It still puzzled Wilson why only supporters of Liverpool and not Juventus were put on trial for Heysel because, as he argued: 'I've seen footage where their fans are running across the terraces with weapons; punching and kicking our fans as well.' In his conclusion, he rationalised: 'It was easier to make Liverpool fans the guilty ones because of how the terrace was segregated, and how it ended rather than how it started or even played out.'

He would come to understand the meaning of manslaughter, spending a year in a Belgian jail, but any suggestion that he had initially gone to the country intent on causing trouble still annoyed him. 'This word "premeditated" kept getting used,' he explained. 'Reactions may have been based on past experiences and someone somewhere might have had a grudge because of what happened in Rome, but that wasn't a part of any conversations that I heard before we went to the stadium that day.'

In 2005, before Liverpool faced Juventus for the first time in a competitive match since the disaster, he would travel to Italy and meet one of the victim's family as part of a feature for the French football magazine, *L'Equipe*. Though he would shake the hand of a son whose father had died at Heysel, he had trouble convincing them that he was anything but 'another English animal', and this told him that the reputation of the country had gone before Liverpool's.

Of the 26 men who were charged with manslaughter, however, the majority of them were indeed from Liverpool. Peter Robinson suggested the National Front had a role in the violence after encountering supposed Liverpool supporters with southern accents who had bought their tickets on the black market, but wouldn't show them to him in the uncertain corridor of time when the game was delayed and nobody knew whether it was going to go ahead. It did in the end, because UEFA believed a postponement would lead to more violence.

There had been so many rumours, like the one Wilson heard about a Liverpool supporter hanging from a tree because of Italian retaliation in the streets around the stadium. Robinson found it unusual that they would aggressively shout, 'Shankly! Shankly! Shankly!' in his face even though Bill Shankly had not managed Liverpool for eleven years, concluding that they were trying too hard to prove their allegiance. Meanwhile, Bruce Grobbelaar, the eccentric Liverpool goalkeeper, still insists that somewhere at his mother's home in Zimbabwe is a leaflet that she picked up on the ferry over to Belgium declaring that hooligans from London would 'get Liverpool kicked out of Europe'.

The findings of an inquiry held by Marina Coppieters across eighteen months came too late for a sense of balance to be present amongst the historical discussions around Heysel. It was found that the police and the authorities, in addition to Liverpool supporters, should face charges. Jacques Georges, the UEFA president, and Hans Bangerter, his general secretary, were threatened with imprisonment but eventually given conditional discharges. Albert Roosens, the former secretary-general of the Belgian Football Union was given a six-month suspended prison sentence for 'regrettable negligence' over ticketing arrangements. So was gendarme captain Johan Mahieu, who was in charge of the policing the stands at

Heysel. 'He made fundamental errors,' Pierre Verlynde, the judge, said. 'He was far too passive. I find his negligence extraordinary.'

Though the report of the deputy chief of the London Fire Brigade was never included in the inquiry, his findings on behalf of the British Government concluded that the deaths at Heysel were, 'attributable very, very largely to the appalling state of that stadium' due to the crush barriers being almost 50 years old and not being able to contain the weight of the crowd and the fact that the collapsed wall's piers had been built the wrong way around. For Heysel, the consequence was demolition.

All of the blame in those days, weeks and months after the disaster, however, was placed on the Liverpool supporters. There were abundant falsehoods led by bias in the official reactions and in the media coverage, particularly those from authorities with something to lose, or maybe something to gain. From a summit in Mexico City, Margaret Thatcher announced that she wanted to see some of the football correspondents 'who saw what happened with their own eyes', and one of those correspondents was Jeff Powell, a reporter from the right-wing *Daily Mail* who later claimed the British Prime Minister was 'the woman who saved Britain'. Meanwhile, the UEFA observer at Heysel, Gunter Schneider, said that 'Only the English fans were responsible.' Given the unprecedented scale of the tragedy, there was little that convincingly could be argued aloud in Liverpool's defence. Quiet sympathy in respect of the dead was the only right way to react.

'You can't ignore 39 people dying, you have to do something; it couldn't go on like this,' Jegsy Dodd acknowledged, though the subsequent theme of supporters from other English clubs moralising over the idea that Liverpool fans and Liverpool fans alone had got everyone thrown out of Europe bothered him. 'If they were getting pelted, they'd have done exactly the same thing,' he said. 'The pattern of behaviour before reveals that.'

Though the wider focus fell on English football with all clubs collectively punished, but for immediately withdrawing from the following season's UEFA Cup in disgrace, the tragedy was one Liverpool tried to avoid and this bred long-term resentment from other places.

Within hours, the Football Association were under pressure from the government to announce that no English club would play in Europe during the 1985/86 season and this would mean that Everton would be denied their chance of winning the European Cup, while Norwich City would not feature in their first ever European campaign. Two days later, UEFA announced an indefinite ban on

English clubs, which was reduced to five years with Liverpool serving an additional three years as extra punishment for what happened at Heysel, though that was later reduced to one. Elsewhere, though charges were never brought against any Juventus supporters, they were made to play two home games behind closed doors and Belgium was banned from staging a final of a European competition for ten years.

Back in Flintshire, Kevin Ratcliffe's immediate concerns were around the safety of friends and their families. Melwood and Bellefield were less than half a mile apart and he, of course shared lifts with Ian Rush to work. The wives and families of both footballers knew each other well. Phil Neal was Liverpool's captain and was filmed telling fans to calm down across a public address system. Ratcliffe wondered what it would like to be in that position and then having to go and play. 'There were so many thoughts filled with dread that night,' said Ratcliffe, who did not stop to consider that Everton would be punished for the actions of another club's supporters and a wider culture that existed. Peter Reid, the Everton midfielder, compared banning Everton and every other club to the banning of the entire Canadian athletics team because Ben Johnson had been caught cheating, describing the punishment as unfair. 'There were no attempts to find an alternative punishment, despite Liverpool's decision to withdraw from European competition,' Reid wrote in his autobiography. 'Margaret Thatcher wanted us all to suffer because that suited both her dogma and the class warfare that she was waging.'

'Football was bad PR for Thatcher because it reflected the frustrations in the society she'd contributed massively towards,' Ratcliffe thought. 'If you suppress football and limit what people can do, those frustrations aren't quite as visible. Of course, she needed private companies to come and invest in the UK and football showed the UK as a sort of lawless place, so why should they come? Meanwhile, English clubs had been dominant in the European Cup and you wonder what UEFA made of that.'

Ratcliffe reminded that football supporters tended to be Labour voters rather than Conservative. He also appreciated that Heysel had the potential to fracture the sense of community and political spirit that existed in Liverpool, a city with two successful football teams where the allegiances tended to cut through family bloodlines for no particular reason at all. Derek Hatton, of course, was an Everton supporter, who sometimes travelled to European games on the team plane. 'The whole political thing was a bit above most of our heads at the time but its only now you think back and realise how things may have been,' pondered Ratcliffe, who with Phil Neal became one of the speakers involved in the Merseyside Unites campaign in the months after Heysel which aimed to bring both Merseyside clubs closer together – including their supporters. It seemed impossible to him that Thatcher and her advisors did not realise the social implications of the ban involving a city whose council, led by Hatton, had been a thorn in her side. Heysel was an opportunity to present Liverpool as being the lowest of the low, identifying it as the root of any problems that existed in the country and that it should not be followed in any situation.

It would transpire over the next five seasons that supporters of Manchester United, Tottenham Hotspur, Southampton, West Ham United, Sheffield Wednesday, Oxford United, Coventry City, Arsenal, Nottingham Forest, Wimbledon, Luton Town and Derby County would miss out on European football because of Liverpool, thus intensifying resentment towards a club and a city. It was a city which might have even turned on itself considering Everton would win the First Division title again in 1987, only to miss out on another European Cup appearance.

Listening to Ratcliffe, there was more than a lingering sense that he'd have relished the chance to prove himself at the very highest level and take Everton to where they had never been before and have got nowhere near since.

'I was gutted,' he admitted. 'We were proven to be not just a good side but a great side. We'd been voted as the best European team of 1985, even better than the champions of the European Cup. You've worked hard to get there and then you have opportunities taken away. Is that against European rights? Should we be able to fight against loss of earnings? You could never have suggested that then – or maybe even now – because the families in Turin are still grieving. We all seem to have taken it on the chin and got on with it, but we do realise that this was the starting point of the decline for Everton Football Club. Even though we won the league again two years later, I don't think that title involved quite as good a team as the one in 1985.'

Having secured that second title, Howard Kendall decided to leave for Athletic Bilbao in Spain. He had been approached twelve months earlier by Barcelona but decided to stay at Goodison Park before realising that he was enjoying management less because of the restrictions placed on his club. 'I'm quite confident that had it [Heysel] never happened Everton would have asserted their domestic dominance on the European stage and I would never have had itchy feet,' he said. Ironically, Peter Robinson had suggested his name after an approach for Kenny Dalglish, the Liverpool manager, was rejected. In passing on his responsibilities to Colin Harvey – 'unanimously considered the right choice as manager' according to Kendall – there was an assumption that he would continue the success he had already been such an important part of, just as Bob Paisley and Joe Fagan had after Bill Shankly at Anfield.

Like Kendall, however, players wanted to experience European football as well and Everton would lose Gary Stevens (aged just 25), Adrian Heath (27) and Trevor Steven (26) in the space of the next eighteen months to the Scottish champions, Rangers and Espanyol from Spain. For Ratcliffe, the replacements were just not good enough and he felt Everton's decline also lay in the sort of complacency that permeated the 1970s when 'those in charge didn't seem to realise it actually became harder when you're top of the tree. From 1986 onwards, there was less quality coming in. It was a slow decline. By 1990, you were looking at a club not competing, while other teams were getting stronger.'

The same could be said of Liverpool, who may have lifted another three European Cups had it not been for the ban. Like Everton, though, Liverpool would gradually fall away from title conversations after 1990 and a feeling of bitterness filled the space in discussions that in the past would have been taken up by boasts of success.

Ratcliffe thought that this could have been avoided had Everton been permitted entry back into the European Cup five years after Heysel, but it was never a consideration amongst the authorities. That he remained the last Everton captain to win the league mattered more as time moved on from an era where hundreds if not thousands of Evertonians would stand on Anfield's Kop stand come derby day and be able to taunt Bruce Grobbelaar for being a clown, an era where likewise, Liverpudlians would get away with teasing Neville Southall for his weight from their positions on the terraces of the Gwladys Street end at Goodison Park.

A younger Everton fanbase frustrated by their team's shortcomings would search for answers and arrive at the actions of some supporters from their closest rivals. Meanwhile Liverpudlians were no longer able to *laugh at themselves* in quite the same way, not only because of the reality of their team's fall but also because of what followed at the scene of another disaster.

The year was 1989.

6

Truth And Lies

IT WOULD TAKE 30 YEARS FOR ANYONE TO STAND TRIAL FOR WHAT happened at Hillsborough, where 96 Liverpool supporters were crushed to death. From his position in the well of the courtroom in Preston, Graham Mackrell looked straight on when the verdict was read out, that he – as Sheffield Wednesday's safety officer – had failed to ensure there were enough turnstiles to prevent a build-up of large crowds outside the football ground he was responsible for.

The prosecution claimed, indeed, Mackrell had 'effectively shrugged off all responsibility for these important aspects of the role he had taken on as safety officer'. He had 'committed a criminal offence by the failure to agree with police the number of turnstiles to admit Liverpool supporters to the Leppings Lane end'.

Presented before the jury at the very beginning of the case was the Green Guide for safety at sports venues, a warning to football clubs of previous disasters at Ibrox and Bradford and of the 'potential scale of death and injury at a crowded sporting event'. It was, according to the guide, 'essential for ground management to take such steps as are necessary to ensure reasonable safety at their grounds'.

Footage was played from another FA Cup semi final between Tottenham Hotspur and Wolverhampton Wanderers in 1981 when crushing on the Leppings Lane terraces at Hillsborough led to police allowing Spurs fans out, sitting them on the side of the pitch as the match was being played.

Though this led to the terrace being divided up, Sheffield Wednesday did not initially change the turnstile arrangements outside to ensure people entered into specific pens, which by 1989 had fences at the front and the sides leading to the 'obvious risk of overcrowding', if supporters were allowed in 'uncontrolled', with 'a serious risk of death'.

The capacity for the terraces at the Leppings Lane end had been overstated considerably and this 'meant the scene was almost literally set...' for subsequent failures. An expert assessed that following the stand's division into pens, the maximum capacity was 5,246 and though the safety certificate permitted 7,200, nearly 3,000 more tickets were sold to Liverpool supporters attending the club's FA Cup semi-final with Nottingham Forest on 15 April 1989.

Mackrell, previously secretary at Bournemouth and Luton Town, was accused of failing to draw up contingency plans having 'effectively abdicated his responsibility as safety officer' by turning a 'blind eye' to his duties. David Moore, Sheffield city council senior environmental officer, had concerns about safety management at Hillsborough, describing Mackrell as 'flippant about the appointment of a safety officer', recalling 'a feeling of resistance' to the position.

The Green Guide had been updated in 1986 after the Bradford Fire a year earlier and Sheffield Council wrote to Wednesday, saying it was 'essential that management [of stadia] should be entirely familiar with it and follow its guidance.' In 1987, the council implored Wednesday to take 'immediate steps' to appoint a safety officer and Mackrell replied, confirming 'my duties encompass that of the safety officer'.

Moore had been 'looking for evidence of strong safety leadership' but he 'couldn't see evidence of that leadership'. When Moore asked whether he would carry out safety officer duties, particularly on matchdays, Mackrell 'told me he would be too busy entertaining corporate clients'.

It was established that in 1988, changes were made to the turnstile arrangements after all and the prosecution argued successfully that this contributed towards greater congestion at the Leppings Lane entrance where on average, 1,443 people had to pass through each of the seven turnstiles – almost double the recommended safe figure in the Green Guide. There was, however, 'no evidence' the police were notified of these changes which only created a 'further and more pronounced bottleneck' than before.

While there were 23 turnstiles in total for 24,000 Liverpool supporters to go through (an 'unsafe' total of 1,065 through each turnstile), there were 62 for Forest fans who used the Kop end of the ground, where a safe number of 468 passed through each turnstile.

Repeatedly played on the screens in Preston were the scenes which resulted in a catastrophic 'compacted crush'. While the jury at the end of the eleven-week trial was unable to reach a verdict over the role of match commander David Duckenfield, who denied the gross negligence manslaughter of 95 Liverpool fans, Mackrell was found guilty on health and safety charges for which he was fined £6,500 and ordered to pay £5,000 in legal costs. Outside court, Louise Brookes, whose brother Andrew died at Hillsborough, called the sentence 'shameful' and said the fine amounted to £67.70 per life lost.

'My weekly shopping costs more...'

NEIL HODGSON HAD BEEN FASCINATED BY THE NOISE AND MOVEMENT of football crowds for as long as he could remember. As a child, his mum would open the door to the back yard of his house in Kensington so he and his brother Carl could hear the roar of Anfield from two miles away. Each derby weekend, she would attach a red rosette to his chest. When Liverpool beat Newcastle to lift the FA Cup in 1974, the street celebrations seemed to go on and on – until Bill Shankly shocked the game by announcing his retirement six weeks later.

It made Neil sad when another announcement came. The Hodgsons were moving to Skelmersdale because of his dad's work, which had relocated from the manufacturing zone near Liverpool's docks. A return to the inner city two years later, though, brought him even closer to the place which fascinated him the most. In Anfield, the stadium was just a couple of hundred feet down the road and Liverpool, now being led by Bob Paisley, were just a few months away from becoming European champions for the first time.

He compared Saturday afternoons to the frenzy and filth of a religious pilgrimage. The reliable sight of thousands of people in red. The smell of beer and chip fat. The queues and the litter. Waste filled the space between the bay window of his terraced house and front wall like a bin. When police horses walked up and down, mums would follow their trail with brushes and scoops, mopping up the shit to use as fertiliser on flowers. It was close to Neil's birthday when Anfield staged a qualifying match for the 1978 World Cup between Scotland and Wales and he found a bike in the hallway. It was not a present – a supporter had cycled all the way from Wales to see his country play and had asked Neil's mum to mind it.

'It was then I realised how committed supporters were – it came on me like a fever.'

His older brother would proudly reveal one Friday that the following afternoon, he would make the progression from watching the crowds funnel into Anfield and follow them in himself. He was planning to enter the Kop, 'the scary place' – and this prompted Neil to snitch. 'Mum, Carl's going in the Kop...'

Neil, two years younger, needed to find the money to join him so he started to help his uncle, one of the few remaining chimney sweeps in Liverpool. They would clean the bigger houses in Crosby and Waterloo. Sometimes, his uncle stopped a wedding and kissed the bride – a tradition, which he'd get paid for. Near Toxteth, there was a café where they'd have a bacon buttie each Saturday morning before finishing the shift at one in the afternoon.

He'd make himself £3.50 and Neil's hands would be black. He'd scrub himself hard in the bath, though despite his best efforts he'd never be absolutely clean. It cost 75 pence to get in the Anfield Road end opposite the Kop. With two of his mates, he'd perch himself on one of the crush barriers. A sense of generosity existed. He recalled a much older supporter depositing a half pound bag of chocolate limes into the hood of his coat so Neil and his mates could reach in and eat their way through the match. There was an honesty too: Mars and Marathon bars would get thrown across terraces by food vendors, coins would get lobbed back. Above them, pigeons roosted in the rafters. 'You could see their bums, they looked like hot cross buns – and if they opened, you were like "woah!" Most football grounds were Victorian, but thanks to the determination and vision of Shankly, Anfield had been modernised since the 1950s – 'Anfield was the only place I ever wanted to be – it made me feel part of something and safe.'

Before, away fans had mixed in the Anfield Road, but segregation was being introduced because of crowd disturbances. Anfield was not immune from hooliganism but it certainly was not the worst place for it. Hooliganism was not organised like it was amongst the supporter bases of other clubs. Like Jegsy Dodd, Neil thought segregation invited an even greater sense of 'us and them – let's go and abuse them'. He asked: 'Was it really football's problem anyway – would lads be fighting if they had jobs to go to on a Monday morning?'

As the 1980s progressed and Margaret Thatcher went to war with the miners, Liverpool's rivalry with Nottingham Forest became more bitter – the club managed by Brian Clough to successive European Cup titles, perhaps at Liverpool's expense. It had been in Nottinghamshire where some miners had chosen to go back to work in spite of the strikes. Whenever Forest came to Anfield, they were accused of being scabs. 'I was still too young to really understand what it all meant but I thought, "Bloody 'ell, you've got to stick together."'

His first Liverpool away game was Aston Villa, 'where the police were never nice'. He came to prefer travelling by car rather than coach – in his mk2 Escort, which was gold in colour with a brown vinyl roof. His mates would call it the away mobile – it went everywhere: to Nottingham, to Newcastle and to London. He was never going to miss the FA Cup semi-final of 1989 with Forest at Hillsborough, though he nearly did when en-route to Sheffield the driver of a Nissan he was trying to pass on a single lane road near Hyde decided to speed up. Suddenly, a wagon was heading towards him – 'I thought it was going to be a full-on collision.' Swerving to avoid the wagon, he was forced to cut back across the Nissan and his car's back end caught the other car's front bumper. 'We could have been dead there and then,' he thought.

At the Silver Fox pub in Stocksbridge, where he and his friends had stopped to play pool – as they always did for games at Hillsborough – he pondered the consequence of a potential crash and where it may have left him; how he had reached this point and what he might have left behind. Like other interviewees in this book, Neil had left school in 1979, just after Thatcher's successful election campaign. Brought up a Protestant, he had studied at Anfield Comprehensive and his teenage years had been filled with anxiety: what if there was a nuclear war? Where will the IRA attack next? It reassured him that around the streets of Anfield, there were lots of Irish families. It made him wonder about how the British government felt about that – especially after Lord Mountbatten was murdered just after Thatcher came to power. Neil joined the Boys Brigade but never took it that seriously and he went to Sunday school as well, but religion wasn't taken particularly seriously either, though in the quieter moments during games at Anfield when the Kop chanted, 'Rangers, Celtic,' he always sang for Rangers.

The 1980s, in fact, had not been too bad for him. His father had worked as a lift engineer and understood electronics, an emerging technology. He joined a YTS scheme worth £25 a week – one of those pioneered by Thatcher. This led to a placement outside of the classroom, one based out of the docks where a schooner was being built called the Spirit of Merseyside. The opportunity gave him a sense of purpose that few his age were afforded. He considered himself, 'one of the lucky ones', having listened to the story of one of the instructors who'd worked in the docks for decades as a blacksmith. 'There was a vast old shed with work stations as far as the eye could see. The place was derelict, tools lying about everywhere. Liverpool, it felt, was closing down – leaving behind lots of people with trades and skills behind.'

Having gone to the job centre to try and find something more permanent he found an enormous queue before him, but he got lucky, eventually becoming a foreman at an electrical company. He was never out of employment during the 1980s. 'I was desperate not to be a statistic but know lots of people that were even though they tried not to be,' he reflected.

Across the moors and now approaching Sheffield, they dropped down into the city, parking on Harris Road before beginning the walk down Middlewood Road to Hillsborough at around 2.30pm.

The entry at Leppings Lane was like an hourglass, squeezing into a narrower point before opening up beyond the turnstiles.

'It was a boisterous and optimistic crowd rather than a rowdy one,' Neil remembered. 'It was really busy. I said to myself several times, "It just wasn't like this last year." It was around 2.45 now and I was also beginning to realise we weren't going to make kick off even though normally, arriving fifteen minutes before left you with plenty of time.

'The lack of checks further up the road as there would have been normally meant there was a bottleneck. People were beginning to climb on the walls to get out of the crowd. I was thinking, "Get down, dickhead..." Bunking in did happen sometimes. Little did I know, they were up there for a reason: they were getting crushed.'

Neil was accompanied by one of his friends at this point, Dave.

'I said to him, "Bloody 'ell Dave, this is getting scary." There were some railings and I was worried about breaking my leg on them because the pressure of the crowd was so intense. It was really, really frightening – we weren't going anywhere.

'Our tickets were in pen D. As I entered the pen, I immediately got spun around. I'd been to a lot of matches and I was used to dealing with big crowds, understanding how to use your body to keep your position without losing your feet. You almost become professional. In that pen at Hillsborough, you felt helpless.

'Rather than facing the pitch, I'd done a 360 degree turn and I was facing the Leppings Lane stand. I'm a big lad. That shows you how powerful the crushing was. I was facing Dave who was right up against the crush barrier. It almost felt like a comedy scene because I was asking him to tell me what was going on. Dave said, "We've just had a corner… but I'm struggling here, mate."

'Very, very quickly Dave's face was turning purple. His lips were going blue. He was whispering, "I can't breathe… push me off, push me off." I pushed, I pushed and I pushed and his chest started collapsing. His last words were, "I can't breathe…" and then the barrier snapped.'

Dave's trajectory sent him over the top of his friend and suddenly, Neil found himself on the floor of the terrace. For so many people who fell to the floor at Hillsborough there was no way back. Yet somehow Neil was uninjured.

He had been a Sunday league goalkeeper for his local pub, The Breckside, and this meant his hero was always Liverpool's number one. Before it had been Ray Clemence, now it was Bruce Grobbelaar.

'I always looked for him as soon I went into any ground. As I hit the floor, I thought straight away about the gate that was just by his goal. I'd seen it only a couple of minutes earlier and now, this was the only thing on my mind. I was on my hands and knees and I had to get to this gate. Outside the ground I'd got scared because I had time to think. I didn't now. It was pure instinct to try and get out.

'I couldn't get up because the crush was so bad. I crawled through people's legs. It was quite a way back in the pen but I made it to the front wall and then turned right. Mayhem was going on up above. The noises were terrible. Screaming, groaning; there was the smell of urine. It was a hell hole.'

Neil was one of the first Liverpool supporters onto the pitch. Grobbelaar had told stewards to open the gate behind him.

'My first thought was my mum. If she'd have seen me on the pitch, she'd have thought, "What are you doing?" I managed to get myself together. Loads more people were spilling out and Bruce was there, stood in the goalmouth. The game was still going on. I glanced to my left and Dave was being handled over the tops of peoples' heads, then over the spikey railings.

'I looked around and someone appeared with an advertising hoarding. Behind us, the pen was like a rice pan spewing. Only then I knew something was seriously, seriously wrong. Before lots of the signs had been there that something was wrong but my instinct was purely on survival, so I wasn't able to take in the magnitude of what was happening.

'Some fellas helped me carry Dave on the board away from the Leppings Lane. We ran up to the west stand in front of the Forest fans. He was shaking and rattling.

More and more injured followed. Fireman appeared, started trying to resuscitate some of the them. The Forest fans were shouting nasty things – they thought we'd invaded the pitch. I was screaming at them, "It's fucking not like that."

'Dave was in a bad way. A paramedic came – all of the ambulances were still outside. I told him I was okay but Dave wasn't. "He was crushed against the bar, mate – he was blue and purple." As they went to lift his Liverpool shirt and open his jeans, he started screaming. He'd been crushed that badly that the zip of his jeans had jammed into his body and amalgamated with his skin. As they pulled his jeans, his skin was coming with them.'

Dave was put on a stretcher and taken to Northern General Hospital. There, he saw vicars and priests standing on tables shouting out descriptions of people who had already died.

'You'd hear: "We've got someone with a denim jacket and a blue top on, brown adidas jogger shoes…"'

Though Dave was seriously injured, he was on a ward and receiving treatment. Neil returned to Harris Road where a family had taken care of his friends – as well as his brother, who'd been out searching bodies in the tunnel of the Leppings Lane.

Driving back to Merseyside, the number of dead steadily increased and everyone sat in silence. Rather than go home, Neil went to the pub, The Breckside, where he stayed until two in the morning trying to piece together what had happened. His dad, alone in the house because his mum was in hospital, greeted him with a thump when he finally came through the doors. 'He'd heard I was okay, but he'd sooner I'd come and told him myself.'

The following day, he decided with his friends to return to Sheffield to thank Craig and Fran, the couple from Harris Road who had helped them. Fran was pregnant. Another friend who wasn't there on the Saturday – an Evertonian – drove them. 'We gave Fran a bunch of flowers, a box of chocolates and a Liverpool shirt for the baby when it was born. Then we all agreed that we should go back to Hillsborough. I'm not sure why. Everything was mangled. I kept looking across at the other end of the stadium, thinking: "We should have been down there." It was so much bigger.'

*

WHEN LIVERPOOL RETURNED TO ACTION IN THE CLUB'S FIRST MATCH after the disaster, Celtic were the hosts in a friendly match. Travelling back from Glasgow, Neil would pass Blackburn on the M6 when the Escort suffered a rear end tyre blow-out. The car hit the barrier and flipped on to its roof. He was upside down in the fast lane on the other side of the motorway. When the emergency services arrived, an ambulanceman announced his surprise that nobody was seriously hurt or worse. 'He said, "I can't believe it, when we got the message in the control room, we put our gloves on and thought we'd be scraping you off the motorway. You Scousers survive everything…"'

Though Neil had come through three brushes with death, others had not. A cousin of his then wife died at Hillsborough. Meanwhile, since that day, he has not seen one of the friends he travelled to Sheffield with. 'He fled Liverpool and never came back – it was his way of dealing with what had happened.' Everyone in Liverpool seemed to know at least one person affected by the disaster and people who you wouldn't normally associate with came together. Neil, for example, is now close friends with Bruce Grobbelaar, the goalkeeper whose instruction may have saved him. When his first son was born, he would name him Sean Bruce.

BEHIND A COMFORTABLE MIDDLE-CLASS BACKGROUND WAS another rabid Thatcherite. Kelvin MacKenzie, originally from Thanet in Kent, had long-term ambitions in politics, announcing to colleagues that he would one day lead the Conservative Party. By 1989, he had edited the *Sun* newspaper for eight years and this position had given him a significant platform from where he could increase his profile and project his own views.

MacKenzie thought he understood the mind of the tabloid reader better than anyone else. 'He's the bloke you see in the pub, a right old fascist, wants to send the wogs back, buy his poxy council house,' he declared at an editorial meeting having been returned to the paper from the *Daily Express* in 1981.

According to a desker at the *Sun*, who I met while working on this book MacKenzie was 'afraid of the unions, afraid of the Russians, hates the queers and the weirdos and drug dealers. He doesn't want to hear about that stuff…'

That stuff was actually the stuff which influenced people's lives the most: the relatively dry subject of economics, the consequences of political dogma, how chicanery works when the interests of powerful institutions align; the favours traded by controlling authorities.

As a Conservative, it then suited MacKenzie for the focus of his work to fall instead on the individual or the collective but rarely the system: of greater interest to him was the hamster-eating comedian or the pop star with a secret; the country like Argentina during the Falklands War, or a city like Liverpool as it mourned in the days after the Hillsborough disaster. 'He did not believe in society,' a journalist who used to work for him told me. 'He was only out for himself.'

The *Sun* made Britain turn in on itself. When McKenzie thought the paper was 'getting boring' he had, apparently, turned to his feckless and all-too-keen to please brother Craig, asking him whether the rumours about Elton John and underage 'rent boys' were true. Craig, whose appointment at the paper was recognised by staff as blatant nepotism, was now on his own with the office floor listening and clearly feeling cornered: 'Well, yes,' he responded nervously. Amongst the revelations in the story that followed was the unfounded claim that John had the voice boxes of his dogs removed so they could no longer bark. This detail in particular, it transpired, was complete and utter make-believe.

MacKenzie took what may have seemed like risks to some but the *Sun's* status as the most popular paper in Britain generated the sort of wealth that meant when popstars like Elton John sued for the printing of stories without any basis whatsoever, a million pounds in damages didn't really matter. In 1989, its owner Rupert Murdoch was already a billionaire. His business, News Corp, had been built around tales of scandal and controversy. Murdoch thought of himself as an outsider and so did MacKenzie, who within weeks of entering a South London newsroom for the first time as a teenager, broadcast that aside from a couple of reporters, 'everyone else here is a wanker'. His career would take him to Birmingham and then to Fleet Street. After departing what appeared politically and socially as his natural habitat at the *Daily Express* for the *Sun*, whose readership lay further down the class system, he would tell his superiors, 'Fucking crap paper tonight.' There, his assumed South London accent suddenly became stronger, his manner more aggressive – his ambition more naked than ever. MacKenzie revelled in putting other people down and bragging loudly about his own abilities, even if achievements did not correlate with what he was saying about himself.

Murdoch, though, would take him to the *New York Post* before another spell at the *Sun* as well as a period back to the *Express*, a move which initially angered

Murdoch before seemingly making him realise what he was missing. Murdoch re-opened the door to his empire but it became messy and when the *Express* insisted MacKenzie saw out the remainder of his contract, Murdoch agreed to a job share. For a few weeks in 1981, MacKenzie was so highly thought of by Murdoch that while he night-edited the *Express*, he was also editing the *Sun*.

MacKenzie came to loathe the *Express* when it did not meet his purpose, he hated the *Daily Mirror* and the *Guardian* for their supposed sogginess and willingness to be introspective about the state of society – for aligning itself with 'the people' as he put it. Yet he feared the *Daily Star*, seeing it as the main threat to the *Sun's* domination of the tabloids. In wanting to drive this threat 'from the streets', MacKenzie had to come up with even more sensational headlines than those published by the editors before him.

The front page, MacKenzie believed, was his most important decision of each working day. He regarded the *Sun's* features department, where there was potential for more layers of detail and explanation, as a younger, less relevant brother in the family. 'Lightweight bollocks,' he would call investigations that had taken time or may have involved the sort of nuance that required considerate, thought around headlines.

In their 1990 book, *Stick It Up Your Punter!: The Uncut Story of the Sun Newspaper*, Peter Chippindale and Chris Horrie tell an incredible narrative about the paper under MacKenzie's fist, one which is so scandalous he would probably have serialised had it not been about him. MacKenzie never concerned himself about where the idea for stories came from. 'They could be lifted from the radio or television, overheard in a bus queue or hoicked out of another paper,' Horrie wrote. In meetings with old friends at the *Express* it was alleged he was known for staying sober long enough for journalists to reveal whatever they were working on. Breaking to the toilet, he then noted down 'new' ideas on a scrap of paper or on the inner cuffs of his shirt, presenting the lifted information the next day as his own at content meetings. Some might call this journalistic intuition because listening is a key part of the job. MacKenzie, though, rarely listened to anyone whose view did not complement or enhance his own. Fairness did not appear to matter to him. If a journalist refused to follow his lead, it was assumed he was against him.

'Many saw him as the ultimate playground bully, on his own, but always surrounded by eager acolytes willing to hold his jacket while he mentally worked over some weaker unfortunate.'

When Princess Diana became a royal, tabloid interest accelerated to the point where MacKenzie issued a policy of running a front page splash every Monday, traditionally the slowest day of the week because Sundays were usually so quiet in terms of news developments. When the Argentinian ship the General Belgrano was torpedoed in the Falklands War – a timely distraction for the Thatcher government just as the social unrest in her own country threatened to destabilise her own leadership – MacKenzie waded in, skipping to the jingoistic beat by printing the headline: 'GOTCHA'.

The moment would lead to a new rivalry which defined the media landscape for the remainder of the decade. When the *Mirror* questioned whether the war was really worth it, the *Sun* accused it of 'treason', a word even Thatcher would not use in public. The *Mirror* then called the *Sun* a 'coarse and demented newspaper', that was 'to journalism what Dr Joseph Goebbels was to the truth'. The *Sun* had swiftly been moulded into MacKenzie's newspaper. His messages were being received. In 1979, when Thatcher became Prime Minister, half of the readers thought it backed Labour but by 1983, BBC research suggested that 63 per-cent now recognised its support of the Conservatives. Meanwhile, the *Mirror*, edited by card-carrying members of the Labour party, began to change direction in 1984 after Robert Maxwell bought the paper from Reed International.

Pictures of scantily clad women began appearing on its pages and the *Sun* accused its rival of copying editorial practices. Maxwell had been driven by the whiplash of failure, having twice lost out to Murdoch when he bought the *Sun* and the *News of the World*. Maxwell was now obsessed with beating Murdoch and a tabloid war intensified between the press barons and with that, MacKenzie's appetite for the outrageous was exposed in an even more grotesque manner.

In 1988, 85 per-cent of Britain's readership bought tabloid newspapers. Four years earlier, Neil Kinnock – who did not like Maxwell – believing he was an autocrat – decided to support his buy-out because Labour did not have many allies left in the national media and ultimately, the *Mirror* remained hugely influential. Again, this arrangement left Liverpool stranded on the national stage. Though Militant got some things wrong, so long as Kinnock and Maxwell got along even the stuff they got right – particularly relating to housing – was never going to be presented fairly or presented at all. As MacKenzie had said, that sort of *stuff* didn't seem to matter anymore in a society driven and consumed by jealousy of the next person and a determination to see them fall.

At a café in Wapping, the area of London which replaced Fleet Street as the centre of the British newspaper industry, I would meet one of MacKenzie's former underlings at the *Sun*. He claimed that by the late 1980s, the paper's newsroom did not have a single Labour supporter. At the time of the Hillsborough disaster, no Liverpudlian was in a position of influence at the *Sun*.

'Liverpool,' he said, 'felt like a lost sort of place. Nobody outside of the city was really behind the causes that existed there and this made it easier to attack if and when it was ever in the news for whatever reason.'

Before MacKenzie became the *Sun's* editor, its Sunday paper *News of the World* had been behind two thirds in the number of libel cases facing News International but since 1981, the figures had switched. After Elton John successfully sued, MacKenzie's brother Craig would leave the company and get another job – perhaps unsurprisingly, at the *Express*. MacKenzie, meanwhile, was broiling, shutting down any office discussions about the story which had led to hours of private meetings with Murdoch, who nevertheless kept him on and this only led to a sense of empowerment. When Heysel happened, the *Sun* had gone further in its claims about the things Liverpool supporters had supposedly been up to earlier that day. A group of looters had, apparently, stolen £150,000 worth of gems from a Brussels jewellery store. Yet when claims like these are not backed up by proof, it means nobody is able to contest them. Perhaps MacKenzie remembered this after Hillsborough. How could the story be taken further? How could he avoid another embarrassment after the Elton John story? The answer was in the place of Liverpool itself. While the slurs he would print were indemonstrable, libelling all of the Liverpool supporters present at Hillsborough, MacKenzie remained protected legally as nobody in particular was identified.

Some Liverpool supporters had, according to the *Sun*, 'picked the pockets of victims'. Some had, according to the *Sun*, 'urinated on brave cops'. Some had, according to the *Sun*, 'beat up PC giving a kiss of life'. Other newspapers would follow the *Sun's* lead by repeating the allegations, but the *Sun* had gone first and no other paper had led with the headline which MacKenzie came up with: 'THE TRUTH.'

Liverpool was at the centre of a war between two major tabloid newspapers in Britain. The *Liverpool Echo* had quickly turned around a special 28-page issue and in leading with the headline 'OUR DAY OF TEARS,' had captured the feeling in the city without intruding on the excruciating details of a horrific event which had left family members not knowing whether their loved ones were missing, injured or dead.

The *Sun*, according to the McKenzie's former colleague, sent 'at least 25 reporters up to Liverpool' in the 36 hours between Saturday night and Monday morning. 'They had been told to get as much information by whatever means possible.'

Near Anfield, there are residents who can remember 'local' reporters knocking on doors, purporting to be from the *Echo* but speaking with southern accents. 'At least three came to my house but when I asked them to show ID, they tried to change the flow of the conversation,' one person said.

When the scale of the disaster was displayed in terrible detail through the development of photographs, the sense of competition between the tabloids intensified. On the pitch at Hillsborough, survivors can remember seeing some photographers turning over bodies with their feet so they could get clearer images. Deborah Routledge, who was by the fence and being crushed to the point where she could only take 'short gasping breaths', could recall someone holding on to one of her ankles for two minutes before the grip became looser and the hand let go. She would appear on many the front pages in the days that followed because of the photographer working away in front of her. 'I recalled thinking, "he's going to take a photo of me and I'm going to die,"' she told a courtroom thirty years later.

Before 'THE TRUTH' there was MacKenzie's 'GATES OF HELL' splash which included a dozen pages with images of people either being crushed or receiving treatment. The *Sun* wasn't the only paper that day to use similar images – the *Mirror*, in fact, printed them in colour, not knowing as well whether any of the people turning blue in the crush had actually survived. Initially, Liverpool's fury was directed at the *Mirror*, with lines to the Radio Merseyside Roger Phillips phone-in jammed with complaints.

When MacKenzie was warned about printing the unfounded allegations against Liverpool supporters, according to his former colleague he initially replied in dismissive fashion, 'Yeah, yeah...' His instinct was to use the headline, 'YOU SCUM,' but then he changed his mind – 'not something I'd ever seen him do'. Inside the tabloid press it was commonly believed that once an editor had second thoughts a story was already slipping away from him, but those watching MacKenzie as the afternoon wore into the evening weren't sure whether he was hesitating or concentrating. As MacKenzie worked on the layout of the page, the subeditors seemed to vanish from the room. 'We muttered amongst ourselves – it was clearly the wrong thing to do. But nobody had the guts – or the authority – to stand up to him.'

The story would begin like this: 'Drunken Liverpool fans viciously attacked rescue workers as they tried to revive victims of the Hillsborough soccer disaster.' The source had been the homophobic, apartheid supporting, death penalty advocate Irvine Patnick – a Conservative MP in Sheffield who five years later was knighted. Patnick said he he'd been supplied information by a 'high-ranking police officer'. This was a smear MacKenzie must have figured had no comebacks: Patnick was quoted repeating something he'd heard from someone who was never identified and the story was accusing nobody in particular. When Liverpool City Council discussed whether it could sue the paper, it realised it could not. 'Kelvin will have known there was no legal response to this, unlike some of the stories he'd been caught out on in the years before,' the reporter at the *Sun* thought. 'Because of this, I think he saw it as an opportunity to settle any lingering doubts about his judgement as well as his power.'

Despite the paper's coverage of Heysel, there was no sense in the newsroom that MacKenzie had particularly strong negative feelings about Liverpool, though he certainly wasn't knowledgeable about its history or dynamic.

MacKenzie would take a 'no smoke without fire,' attitude whenever Liverpool was in the news – believing anything negative as an absolute reflection of the way things were. He recognised Liverpool was a theme he could attack – readers were interested in the supposed scandal that came from the city. 'It was my view that he [MacKenzie] had a subconscious view about the way things supposedly were in Liverpool and being the individualist, he saw the story as an opportunity he could exploit.'

MacKenzie, though, had underestimated the social networks that existed in Liverpool as well as the ferocity of reactions and the strength of resolve. Liverpool's football supporters were experienced and well-travelled, they understood how crowds flowed, what those authorities with a duty of care standardly needed to do to ensure safe passage – and the accusations that came Liverpool's way rather than the direction of the authorities in the aftermath of Heysel heightened this appreciation. By speaking to one another and absorbing the otherwise accurate and non-sensational reporting of what had happened at Hillsborough, the community of Liverpool quickly established a true course of events.

The city would rid itself of Britain's biggest tabloid newspaper. Even though the *Sun* was printed in Kirkby, copies of the newspaper were spontaneously gathered from each newsagent across the town and piled high on a field in front of a council estate before being set alight – the first time newspapers had been burned on British streets since the 1930s when copies of the *Daily Mail* were torched in Jewish east London following a front-page endorsement of British fascist Oswald Mosley and his pro-Nazi Blackshirts.

Elsewhere across Merseyside, the paper was removed from the mess rooms in the manufacturing industries that remained and thrown in incinerators. Those seen carrying it on the street would have it snatched and ripped up in front of them. While the *Echo* challenged the London papers and Sheffield's police to 'PRODUCE YOUR EVIDENCE', Merseyside's Police described the allegations made by the federation in South Yorkshire as 'despicable'. Before the Hillsborough disaster the *Sun* had sold on average around 120,000 copies a day on Merseyside but within a just a few days, that figure had dropped to just over 30,000. 'We thought readers would drift back,' admitted the newsman at the paper. He would speak about the paper as though it was a serpent. You might cut its head off but there was a confidence that it would recover and continue to grow. Though suppliers continued to push shopkeepers to take the publication, fewer and fewer people were buying. Within a fortnight, 90 per-cent of copies on Merseyside remained unsold, meanwhile sales of the *Mirror* increased, which had raised more than £1million for the disaster fund by raising prices temporarily.

The *Sun* was unrepentant in its claims about Hillsborough. From inside the paper, though, MacKenzie was feeling the heat – 'but only because sales had fallen through the floor, not because of the nature of the story' – and this prompted him to call Kenny Dalglish, the Liverpool manager, asking him how he could improve relations. Dalglish recalled the conversation in his autobiography, telling him, 'You know that big headline, "THE TRUTH?" All you have to do is put "WE LIED" in the same size.' When MacKenzie said this was impossible, Dalglish replied, 'I cannot help you then.'

The subsequent boycott would become one of the longest and most successful in history, costing Murdoch's News International Empire hundreds of millions of pounds. In 2019, it was selling less than 2,000 copies a day in the region.

The struggle for justice was sustained by the boycott, helping campaigners believe they could achieve something. While MacKenzie – and many others – considered Liverpool to be 'self-pity city', the reality was quite the opposite because few were feeling sorry for themselves. They were actually trying to do something about it and would not go away despite all of the horrendous emotional setbacks.

In 2016, when the inquests about what happened at Hillsborough were finally heard, delivering a verdict of unlawful killing, MacKenzie finally apologised for his role in the reporting but even then, he implied that he, somehow, too was a victim: 'I feel desperate for the families and the people and I also feel that in some strange way I got caught up in it.' Twelve months later, he would leave the paper once and for all after comparing Ross Barkley, a Liverpool-born footballer with Nigerian grandfather, to a gorilla.

Back in Wapping, the one-time reporter at the *Sun* considered his own role in the aftermath of Hillsborough. Could he have done more to stop MacKenzie? 'Not really,' he said flatly. 'Everyone was too busy looking after themselves.'

'We were all hoping we would have some sort of closure today and we haven't,' said Margaret Aspinall on the steps of Preston Crown court almost 30 years to the day since her son James was crushed to death at Hillsborough.

IT WAS APRIL 2019 AND THERE HAD BEEN NO VERDICT IN THE TRIAL of police match commander David Duckenfield who was accused of gross negligence, causing the deaths of 95 people. It had taken the court clerk five minutes to read the names of the deceased at the start of the trial three months earlier.

Duckenfield's 'extraordinarily bad' failures, according to the prosecution amounted to manslaughter after he failed to try and 'avert tragedy' after Gate C in the Leppings Lane end of the ground was opened.

Duckenfield was charged with only 95 deaths because the 96th victim, Tony Bland, died four years later. Laws in 1989 said no crime causing death could be charged if the victim died more than a year and a day later, though that law was abolished in 1996.

There was 'no evidence the police were notified or consulted' of the layout changes at Leppings Lane that had taken place in 1988 which meant 10,100 people a year later had just seven turnstiles to enter the ground.

The prosecution outlined the crown's case: 'the risk of death was obvious, serious and present throughout the failings of David Duckenfield to show reasonable care in discharging his duty as match commander.' He had not monitored the 'desperate situation' outside the turnstiles and did not take action to relieve the pressure, including the option of delaying the kick off.

One of his officers, Robert Purdy, admitted: 'Something had gone wrong in terms of policing the approach to...Leppings Lane' and the crowd should have been stopped further up the road.

The pressure of the people in this 'bottleneck' was so severe that the securing spike for a large metal gate outside bent and the gates 'sprang open under the pressure,' though at that point a South Yorkshire police officer incorrectly said on police radio that Liverpool supporters had 'broken the gate down.'

Purdy believed the overcrowding at the Leppings Lane turnstiles remained so severe that 'people would die if the situation was not relieved' and this led to the opening of the exit at Gate C at which point Duckenfield 'failed to take any action himself...to prevent crushing to persons in pens three and four by the inevitable flow of spectators through the central tunnel.'

The prosecution: 'Duckenfield's failures continued, each was compounded by successive failures, each was contributed to by earlier failures; each...flowed from his own personal decision making and fell squarely within his persona; responsibility as match commander.'

Eighty five of the 96 people who died at Hillsborough were in pen three and 23 of them had come through Gate C when it was opened.

Duckenfield had given evidence in the inquests between 2014 and 2016 where he accepted some of his failings were 'grave and serious' and that his 'most serious failure' was not closing the tunnel before ordering Gate C to be opened.

In conclusion, the prosecution said: 'Ultimately [Duckenfield] failed in the most appalling manner to monitor what was happening in pens three and four and to...prevent...the...crushing the life out of so many people.'

While Duckenfield's defence case lasted just 74 minutes and consisted of read evidence from his deputy on the day, Bernard Murray, the jury deliberated for longer than 29 hours but was unable to agree whether the match commander was guilty or not guilty of manslaughter by gross negligence.

Steven Kelly, whose brother Michael died at Hillsborough, did not want to see a retrial after eleven weeks he did not want to 'go through again.' Barry Devonside, whose son Christopher was one of the victims, felt differently. He wanted a conclusion: 'an end so we can return, as a family, to some sort of normality.'

*In November 2019, two months after first publication of this book, Hillsborough match commander David Duckenfield was found not guilty of the gross negligence manslaughter of 95 Liverpool fans in the 1989 disaster.

Speaking at a press conference after the verdict was delivered, Margaret Aspinall, whose 18-year-old son James died in the disaster, said: 'The families know who is guilty. Our city knows who is guilty. He can walk around now and get on with his life with a not guilty verdict. To me that is a disgrace.'

The trial of two former police officers and a police solicitor accused of altering police statements after the disaster, originally scheduled for April 2020, was in February 2020 postponed for a further twelve months.

7
Let's Get A Kid Lost

JIM FITZSIMMONS WAS RECALLING SOME OF THE SCARIEST EPISODES in his career as a policeman in the Merseyside force, a region where self-governance sometimes made it slightly easier to do his job. There had once been a disturbance at the Jester Pub on Great Homer Street, the boulevard that runs parallel to Scotland Road and south from Everton valley towards the city centre. Liverpool had beaten Nottingham Forest earlier that day in a First Division match and just as the small screen in the corner of the main lounge started to beam the opening credits on *Match of the Day*, the licensee – an Evertonian – turned the volume down and told everyone to drink up and go home. When bottles were thrown, the landlady called 999 and Fitzsimmons headed towards the scene with a sergeant who was well-known within his division as a hot-head. His reputation made Fitzsimmons nervous and this led to him trying to take control of the situation in front of him.

'"Right, put your drinks down, finish up," I said. Then this big lad – and I mean a monster – gets up and goes, "Fuck off out you black bastards."

'I leaned towards the sergeant and said, "We can't let that ride, we're going to have to nick this fella; I'll do it…"

'As I walked towards him this other monster appears, standing up. Thwack, goes his fist. The first monster falls over. "Officer, my brother's out of order; he shouldn't be speaking to you like that…"

'Everyone was a bit angry because they missed *Match of the Day* but they went home without another punch being thrown. I think the story reflects that understanding of respect existed, of people appreciating what is fundamentally right and what is fundamentally wrong.'

On other occasions, Fitzsimmons was not so fortunate. Like the time when, as a junior officer, he entered another pub called the Arkles in Anfield – one of the closest pubs to the football ground – and was beaten over the head by thieves. The attack made the news and after being photographed in the *Liverpool Echo*, Phil Thompson and other former teammates at Liverpool – where Fitzsimmons had spent time as an apprentice footballer – visited him in hospital, fearing the worst, though the deep gash made the confrontation seem more dramatic than it actually was. It was just before Christmas and regulars in the Arkles organised a whip-round for Fitzsimmons, raising close to £500.

His path into the police had been unusual because of his family's background on the docks, Liverpool's base for employment – a place where workers did not like authority sticking their nose in. His dad was a docker and all of his uncles were dockers. They lived in Bootle and he was the eldest of six. When his dad went on strike in the 1960s there was no strike pay and all of the dockers needed the support of their families. The strike sufficiently disrupted the business, giving the unions more power, but his dad would not live to see the years when that power grew stronger, having died of lung cancer when Fitzsimmons was thirteen. In Fitzsimmons's words, 'the unions went too far', and he would not end up following his dad's path. Having passed the 11 plus, he qualified for grammar school at Salesian, the same institution attended by Peter Hooton, Jamie Carragher and the educator Sir Paul Grant. Football was his dream and at Liverpool, he learned a lot about leadership by watching the club's greatest managers.

'At the end of every training session, there would be a big game: the staff versus the kids,' he remembered. 'The staff would pick a couple of kids to play on their team. You were either on Bill Shankly's side or against him. But he was watching you. The game always went on until Shankly said it was over. And it was never over until Shankly's team was winning. Being selected for their team made you feel like they trusted you. But sometimes if you'd been struggling they'd pick you to see whether you were able to dig in.'

He joined the police after Liverpool let him go because of the growing influence of his father-in-law – a policeman. 'Dock work and police work were conflicting worlds,' he admitted. 'It wasn't something someone from my family would normally consider doing. But when I spoke to the police, they realised I played football and I realised I could play football for them, so it was an easy decision.'

The term for young troublemakers back then was bucks rather than scallies. Fitzsimmons did not see Liverpool as a place where an anti-establishment sentiment had deep roots. 'There's a desire for fairness and for people to be straight. When Liverpool sees authority not adhering to our expectations, it doesn't sit down and accept the status quo.'

'Liverpool's problems have always related to unemployment,' he continued. 'During the 1980s unemployment was rife and it had a major bearing on the way people in the city lived. When I joined the police, we were poorly paid. But Thatcher and the government realised they needed our support. There was a review of pay and conditions by Edmund Davies. We got a pay rise which took us from several levels below teachers into line with junior doctors. It was a breathtaking decision. On reflection, it was probably a bribe. Thatcher saw the social problems that were coming and she needed our help. Probably, the police were being used to try and fix something that was really badly broken.'

Kenneth Oxford, the chief constable during the Toxteth Riots, was typical of his era.

'We were a semi-disciplined organisation and he treated us as such. Oxford was ex-military, not sophisticated with the social aspects of what was required and more into the practical solutions. He was quite well-respected and fought for his men.'

He paused to think about Oxford's battles with Margaret Simey, who said of those local people in Toxteth involved in the confrontation with the police that 'they would be apathetic fools... if they didn't protest.'

'I understand her viewpoint a lot more now than I did then but we were biased,' Fitzsimmons admitted. 'It would be hard for us not to have a biased view because we had to believe that everything we did was for the right reasons, though on reflection I'm not sure whether it was all right.'

After witnessing the ravages of heroin in the 1980s, Fitzsimmons became a specialist in drug enforcement during the 1990s.

'Liverpool creates good music, good football teams, good comedians and prolific criminals,' he concluded. Liverpool's criminals were operating nationally and internationally before the criminals of London, Birmingham, Bristol, Glasgow and Manchester. 'They would make partnerships, get into other big cities; they understood how to run businesses,' Fitzsimmons added. 'The unemployment levels meant people were desperate for work and could be used. It's no different to a global organisation like Giro setting up its headquarters in Bootle. Where do all the employees come from?' And without waiting for an answer, he gave one: 'They come from Bootle.'

IT WAS EARLY ONE FRIDAY EVENING IN FEBRUARY 1993 AND JIM Fitzsimmons was driving in his Vauxhall Cavalier towards the police station on Marsh Lane in Bootle. Lapping through his mind were thoughts of his own childhood on nearby Partington Avenue and how he'd caused his mother anxiety the time he'd gone missing for twenty minutes after leaving her in Woolworths. He had once travelled all the way to Allerton by himself for no particular reason. Then there was the occasion when a photograph of the Liverpool team he loved was printed in the *Hornet*. He wanted it so much that he visited nearly every newsagent from Bootle to the other side of city centre and two and a half hours later, the police caught up with him – much to his mother's relief and fury. He was convinced that something similar had happened to James Bulger.

The previous Monday, Fitzsimmons had been promoted from detective sergeant to detective inspector. The previous years had gone well. A family pools win had made life easier and this helped him make the decision to study at the University of Liverpool and achieve a 2:1 BA Honours degree in Management and Policy, adding Spanish as an option – which meant he spent the summer months honing his new language in Salamanca.

Back with the police, he was expected to enrol at another management course in Preston the following Monday, but the case of this missing child would change those plans.

He had been at home in Blundellsands eating a sandwich when his pager beeped, telling him to head not to Copy Lane in Netherton where he was expected to go first but to Marsh Lane, close to where James Bulger had vanished from the The Strand Shopping Centre where he'd been with his mother Denise, along with a friend who was shopping for knickers.

'I wouldn't normally get involved in a missing child because most missing children get found very quickly,' said Fitzsimmons, whose new responsibilities meant working this particular Friday, covering the entire division for other detective inspectors from Bootle up to Southport. 'The usual routine would be an eight until eleven shift, popping home briefly for dinner before going back out and checking around the stations, seeing what was happening or doing some paperwork. But the circumstances around this missing case felt unusual. James had been missing for three hours and twenty minutes. I'd made it to the other side of Liverpool in two and a half hours as a kid. He could have been anywhere. But I was still confident we'd find him in the Strand.'

A known paedophile had been spotted earlier that day. Fitzsimmons's first instruction had been to tell a uniformed officer to find him. The Strand was shut by now. Fitzsimmons had five detectives at each of the three stations across Sefton doing late shifts. James's mum, Denise, had a terrified look on her face. Fitzsimmons was a dad. His son Daniel was twelve, Joe was ten and Louise was six.

'I remember saying to her something like, "It is odd and these things don't happen often but they do normally get found. We've got to be positive and think there's a possibility that it's a prank – maybe with some kids who he's been playing with. Maybe he's got lost."

'In the Strand, they had a list for every key holder of every shop. I asked for every key holder to be contacted and for them to open the shops. I called the Operational Support Division on St Anne Street and asked for every member of staff they had available. I didn't want the key holders searching through the shops but instead the officers, in case James was asleep somewhere. I also wanted someone going through the CCTV and a radio appeal.

'At around 9pm we received a statement off a woman who'd seen two small boys with a very small boy and they were walking down the path towards the canal behind The Strand. She didn't stop them. It was the first indication that they could be outside of the building where we hoped he still might be.'

Following the radio appeal, Merseyside Police was inundated with information. There was a taxi driver from Southport who'd dropped three kids off, one of them being a lot younger than the other two. There was a sighting in Chester near the train station. 'We were trying to make some sense out of the details coming through.'

At eleven o'clock, Fitzsimmons called Jack Leyland, the detective superintendent for the whole of the Merseyside force.

'I said, "Jack, I think you should come down." Normally, he'd only be involved if there was a murder. But I told him, "Jack, I'm just not happy with this." I wanted the HOLMES team out, which is the major investigation unit. It was a big call because it involves a lot of money. He said, "Okay, Jim…"

'Something just wasn't right. It was the fact that we'd done everything we were supposed to do and nothing solid was coming back. It was based on facts or rather the lack of facts or evidence. When I worked in France, the officers there would tap their nose as if they could smell something that was wrong, as if their intuition was telling them the right path to follow – particularly amongst officers that had never led an investigation. With me, it was always about the evidence in front of me.

'Peter Jones was a detective inspector that I worked with for a long time. At 1am he called me over to The Strand and showed me the first CCTV image. It was only then we knew for certain that James had been abducted. We then had to get the grainy stills ready for the papers in the morning. I told Denise about the development. We'd invited her to go home but she didn't want to. We now knew James had left The Strand with two boys and they looked like young boys. "This could be positive," I told her.

My instinct was to think that if James had been taken by an adult, it was for sinister motives. My instinct was also to think that they were two juveniles and they'd been messing around in a bombed-out house somewhere. What could they seriously do?'

The quality of the CCTV images were poor and they were sent to the RAF to be enhanced. Fitzsimmons thought the two boys with James must have been around fifteen-years-old, but nobody was able to identify them from the originals.

Saturday was agonising, juddering into Sunday when Jim Fitzsimmons took a couple of hours away from the investigation to see his son's football team play a match in Formby before going to visit his mum, who was in Walton Hospital with a chest infection. She'd been warned about her smoking, told that it would result in her leg being amputated if she carried on. But she was Catholic and believed that if God had decided that it was her time to go, then it was her time to go. The hospital was a mile and a half inland from Bootle so en-route, Fitzsimmons drove around the area hoping he might see James or even find clues as to where he might be. 'My mum had seen me on TV and was quite proud that I was leading the case,' he remembered.

Then the call he'd been dreading finally came. A body had been found on the railway line in Walton, a quarter of a mile away from the hospital.

'I still harboured the thought that something had gone completely and horribly wrong, that it was somehow a misadventure.'

From Marsh Lane, Fitzsimmons drove in silence to the tracks in the same car as his superiors, Albert Kirby and Geoff MacDonald.

'At the embankment, Walton Lane Police were there preserving the scene. There was a small bundle and soon, a small tent was put around the bundle. It was a really cloudy day and it was going dark. Visibility was poor. Nobody was saying a great deal. As we left Walton Lane, Denise was walking through the car park. She asked what we were doing. Geoff volunteered to go and tell her. I got home at about midnight. That's when it hit me and I cried with my wife.'

Fitzsimmons now had a huge team of detectives and leads coming through. Through witness statements, he was able to tell which route the two boys had taken James on and so, Fitzsimmons, Kirby and MacDonald went on a walk from The Strand, past Christ Church, and up towards Breeze Hill. As a child, he had roamed these streets near Derby Park and as a Catholic had considered the parishioners at protestant Christ Church as the enemy. Near a roundabout, another CCTV camera had caught an image of the three boys and he decided to measure their size against the wall behind them. 'I realised, "Christ, they're smaller and younger than I thought."'

When a father accused his son of being in The Strand on the Friday, the son was arrested but later released after it was established the father had got the wrong day. This failure placed enormous pressure on Fitzsimmons. It was late on Wednesday when a policeman he knew from his former station at Walton Lane approached him casually.

'He whispered, "A woman's come in. Her friend has got a son... she's saying it can't be him because he's only ten, but he was sagging school with somebody else and he's come home with paint on his jacket – but it can't be him..." The woman wouldn't make a statement but she did leave a phone number. So, I called her...

'It was nine o'clock at night and the other officers were having a drink at the bar. I asked one of them to go and take a statement from the woman because I thought there might be something in this. In the meantime, I found out what school this kid went to and I managed to get hold of the headmistress. I said, "Look, we know the kid was sagging... who was he sagging with?"'

✳

JAMES BULGER'S BODY WAS DISCOVERED ON VALENTINE'S DAY, 1993. Within a few hours, a shrine had been set up in his memory. As the days passed, more and more flowers appeared and the mourners began spilling out onto Walton Lane, sometimes disrupting the flow of the traffic. It was the half-term holidays and, on the Tuesday, Robert Thompson spent part of his afternoon looking at the shrine, dominated by white lilies. The following evening, Jim Fitzsimmons received the tip-off he could not ignore. On the Thursday, at 6am, Robert was arrested for James's murder along with his school friend, Jon Venables. They were ten years old.

While Jon was taken to a cell at Lower Lane Police Station a couple of miles away in Fazakerley, Robert was held at Walton Lane, the station next to the shrine, the one just around the corner from Robert's home where he lived with his seven brothers and his mum, Ann; the station, indeed, which overlooked the railway line where James was found.

Dominic Lloyd was appointed as Robert's solicitor on the Friday around mid-morning. Lloyd was around 6ft tall and when later standing at the spot where James was murdered, he was able to see over the brick wall which backed on to the station. Had someone been looking out of the window in the police station when the three boys were on the railway line, it is possible that the murder could have been stopped and James saved. But nobody knew that for certain. 'It was February and bare; there was nothing on the trees,' Lloyd remembered. 'You could see officers putting spoons of sugar in their coffee.'

Walton Lane was on shut down and all of the other prisoners had been removed. The same happened at Lower Lane, where Jon was. Not a lot of other police business was happening, if any. There was someone operating the front desk, taking calls. There were concerns about safety. Hundreds of young boys had been arrested in the hours and days after James went missing. The country was gripped by his disappearance. Locally, answers were demanded.

Lloyd recalled Walton Lane being incredibly busy but absolutely silent. 'There were a lot of policemen around,' he said. 'Robert was in a juvenile detention room, which is like a cell without a gated door. Instead, it had a wooden door with a wide glass, school-type window. There was no window at the back of the room but instead, heavy glass bricks so there was plenty of natural light in there. The sun was cutting through. A lot of officers were smoking and to my shame, I joined in. Someone from the youth justice organisation arrived and told us off. "He's ten years of age." There was a lot of nervous energy from the adults. This resulted in lots of black coffee as well.'

Robert was accompanied by his mum. She supported him up until the point where she could not anymore, when it became clear that he'd been present when something terrible had happened. In her place, an appropriate adult stepped in.

'When his mum was there Robert was self-contained. He wasn't effing and blinding. To me, he seemed too young to be involved. I've been castigated before for suggesting that he had a high-pitched voice, and this translated as me making it out to be an excuse for what he did, but I cannot deny how struck I was by how young this kid was. I'd seen plenty of young kids in custody but when I heard him speak for the first time I was like, *that's straight from primary school*. Kids in trouble were usually in secondary school. He wasn't a small lad, but his voice gave his age away.'

Lloyd was one of the youngest men involved in the case, if not the youngest, chosen as a high street solicitor to represent Robert because he had acted for one of his older brothers before. He did not have children of his own, though later when his sons would reach two – like James was – he would mark it off in his head and think, 'Jesus, imagine losing him now…' Lloyd was 22 years old when he lost a brother and had witnessed the impact of that death on his mum and dad. 'That, then, was my understanding of what it was like to lose a child.'

He had been driven towards the legal system partly because of his mother's litigation worries after the landlord who owned her shop passed away. He did not like the conversion course after finishing university, and it was only when he entered practice that he realised how much he actually enjoyed the profession.

'Everyone else involved in this case was older than me. The QC and the junior barrister, for example, both had kids who were older than Robert. I watched Robert respond to them as many kids would with teachers. I think I managed to avoid that with him, largely because I wasn't very experienced talking to kids of his age. I had to try and negotiate a new way of talking. So rather than going into parent mode, it had to be something different. I can't say whether it was the right or wrong thing to do but he didn't shut down. If he didn't want to speak about something he'd say, "I don't want to talk about it."

'You never really know what is going on behind someone else's eyes, but you try and satisfy yourself that there's some evidence they understand what you're saying. You repeat yourself a lot at the risk of turning them off. We reached an understanding that allowed us to work. All you can do is try and explain in simple terms the consequences of reaching one decision and the consequences of reaching another. But I don't know for certain how much he understood everything. He was ten years old.'

After two days of interviews, Robert and Jon were charged with the murder of James. Lloyd could feel a sense of relief in the room. But there was also revulsion. Phil Roberts, the sergeant in charge of Robert's interview, leaned over to Lloyd and said, 'I can't help but think the devil was in Bootle Strand last Friday.' The sergeant later recalled a chilling moment which shocked him and other detectives like Constable George Scott. As the boys left South Sefton Magistrates' court, after police applied for an extended warrant of detention, 'Thompson looked [across] at Venables and smiled. It was a cold smile – an evil smile. I believe the smile said they knew they were responsible... and thought they were going to get away with it.'

'I believe human nature spurts out freaks,' Roberts concluded. 'These two were freaks who just found each other. You should not compare these two boys with other boys – they were evil.'

He had known then about another chilling moment in the detention room, hours after Robert had been charged. With a couple of social workers and a police officer watching over him, he had fallen asleep only to be awoken by a passing train as it chugged past on the railway line just where James's decapitated body had been found just a few hundred feet away. Having asked whether he had heard a train and having had it confirmed, Robert lay down again before saying, 'I know all the times of them trains.'

'ONCE, OR MAYBE TWICE,' DOMINIC LLOYD WOULD SAY, WHEN ASKED whether defending Robert Thompson had caused him any problems, particularly as he still lived in Liverpool and the city was – and has been since – so emotionally connected with a case that would define his career. At a barbecue someone launched at him, but friends had seen the situation coming and were able to get in the way. Otherwise, interested people were generally respectful, knowing that if he didn't do the job, someone else would have to. 'It was more, "I don't know how you do it," rather than, "You should not be doing it,"' he reflected. 'You can have a civilised discussion, but it tends not to be a very deep discussion.'

In the moments after Robert and Jon left the youth court room, having been accused of James's murder and in passing each other exchanged what were interpreted to officers as 'evil' glances, the solicitor would retreat to his office just over the road from South Sefton Magistrates' in Bootle. Entry was though a side door, there was a chip-shop style counter and a narrow staircase which led to a higher floor space.

'Within minutes, the reception was filled with reporters,' he remembered. They wanted detail and colour. The identities of the boys would remain simply Child A and Child B until eight months later, when a judge at Preston Crown Court decided it was in the public interest to disclose them. All that was known then was their age and the extent of injuries they had inflicted, since described as 'absolutely horrific' by Albert Kirby, the detective superintendent, who held press conferences every morning at 11am in Bootle's Salvation Army Hall in front of a gallery of more than 200 reporters.

When there had been no arrests, Kirby warned: 'Poor James was missing from his mum for a few seconds and he was gone, disappeared. Parents must keep hold of their youngsters – we cannot guarantee their safety at the moment.'

By the end of that week CNN had flown in and a German television crew was stalking the police headquarters. In the panic, toddler harnesses were cleared in shop shelves across Merseyside. The Strand's Mothercare store waited for an order of 70 to arrive. Another police superintendent asked for community leaders and the clergy to help abate the sense of fear. When the fear was replaced by fury, Denise Bulger, James' mother, was left staring in front of the television cameras, begging for calm.

There was nothing Dominic Lloyd could tell reporters as they huddled around him, hurriedly arranging their filming and recording equipment. He was preparing for a criminal trial asking a really narrow question. The context behind his client's life did not really matter. Robert Thompson either committed the crime or he did not. That was his focus. A pre-sentencing report would reveal more accurate information about the background of the family involved. He was trying to get to grips with the evidence and the facts of the case.

'I could have spent every night out for the next few years eating and drinking on newspaper expense accounts,' he admitted. 'I did meet with some journalists to try and explain my position. There was a major demand for me and that wasn't something I was used to or felt was warranted. Some of journalists seemed nice people and they were interesting. But I was up to here with it pretty quickly.'

Lloyd had avoided the angry scenes outside his office, which involved five demonstrators being detained by police, having thrown missiles and launched themselves at the vans supposedly carrying the suspects away – though those vans were later revealed as decoys. The tension had been similarly raw six days earlier when detectives believed they had found James's killer at a house on Snowdrop Street in Kirkdale after being tipped off by the boy's father, only to discover that he had not been in The Strand when James was taken. Camera crews filmed the gathering crowd and an older teenager compared the energy around him to 'a Liverpool match', where kids hung out of trees like animals to get sight of the offender and 'the noise of them all screaming for blood'.

The case would bring three periods of press coverage. From the point of the abduction, the story built across five days, when the question being asked was, 'Who did it?' Therefore, there were no real restrictions on journalists, who were able to work with rumours which in turn became part of myth. Then came an eight-month wait for the trial, where the vacuum was filled by a sharp focus on Liverpool itself. Part three involved the boys being found guilty of the crime, their identities being revealed and the conversation around the leniency of their eight-year sentence subsequently seized upon by opportunists and loathsome strategists like the editor of the *Sun* newspaper, Kelvin Mackenzie.

Lloyd was one of those rare people in Liverpool who does not have any interest in football. He went to one Everton match as a child and after a tremendous win asked father what the score was, at which point, 'I knew it wasn't for me.' He did appreciate, however, its relevance to other people in the city and its links to a wider social feeling.

'I had no doubt then and I have no doubt now that the reporting of the *Sun* on this case was calculated to try and improve its position on Merseyside and that relates back to the way it disgraced itself,' he said.

In the five years between 1987 and 1992, the paper lost 400,000 readers from its overall circulation and many of those readers had come from Liverpool, the city which had boycotted the paper since 1989 when it printed lies about the role of Liverpool supporters at Hillsborough.

Mackenzie orchestrated a campaign, backing the Bulger family in their quest for harsher punishments after convictions were made and this led to Michael Howard, the Home Secretary, illegally extending the sentences imposed on the children. Elsewhere in the paper, Richard Littlejohn had screeched: 'This is no time for calm. It is a time for rage, for blood-boiling anger, for furious venting of spleen,' and this sort of comment enabled Lloyd to make an application to stay the indictment on the basis of the prejudicial publicity received. Though his application was rejected, the *Sun*, he said, 'got plenty of mentions', which could have halted the proceedings altogether. Mackenzie, it seemed, could not lose with this case. Liverpool's boycott had cost the paper close to £15million a year. By simultaneously attempting to win readers back, he was also able to stick the knife firmly where it hurt the most, presenting the city again in a negative light.

Initially, stories flew across Merseyside and reached beyond. In reality, Denise Bulger was a cautious young mother, who nearly always took James out shopping in a buggy. But not that day, so the rumours went. Instead, it was whispered, she was out shoplifting that afternoon and had to delay reporting James missing while she disposed of stolen goods which was a malicious falsehood. The killers had taken him to a house and tortured him, apparently. They had abducted him for a paedophile ring, it was also wrongly said. They had tied him to a tree and set him on fire. 'I'd imagine the root of the stuff about Denise was based around preconceived ideas of how Liverpool people supposedly lived,' Lloyd said. 'It was total and utter nonsense.'

Three days after James's body was found, the Prime Minister John Major talked about the government's tough stance on crime, saying: 'Society needs to condemn a little more and understand a little less.' It was a message which seemed to manifest itself that afternoon in front of the court house in Bootle where there were calls for the two unknown boys to be hanged. This manifestation reached into the reports that followed, the most infamous of which was written by Jonathan Margolis and published in the *Sunday Times* under the headline of 'Self-Pity City'.

Liverpool's collective mood had been captured by the landlord of the Jawbone Tavern in Kirkdale when he spoke to the *Guardian* a few hours after the murder. 'We feel dirty, vulgar and vulnerable and it's like everyone is saying, "It's Liverpool again,"' he said. 'The press are crawling all over us like they did after Hillsborough.'

Liverpool felt like it was in the dock and there was not going to be a fair trial. 'The city with a murder on its conscience,' was a headline in *The Times* beneath the question, 'as James Bulger was led to his death, what were the people of Liverpool doing?' Walter Ellis, the author, droned on: 'The mob, as self-pitying as it is self-righteous, is a constant presence, whether on tour in the Heysel Stadium,

Brussels, or at home among the social dereliction of Liverpool 8, or, as this week, in the back streets of Bootle.' An article in the *Daily Express* headlined with, 'New Britain's Desolation Row,' before Peter Hitchens devoted a page to attacking Kirkby, the apparent link being that the Bulger family lived there. 'Its main army is a fearsome horde of burglars, glue-sniffers, vandals, drug addicts and joyriders,' he suggested. Then there was Crosby-born, Blundellsands-raised long-time London resident Anne Robinson, also writing about Kirkby in her column for the *Daily Mirror*, an area which she thought 'makes Alcatraz look like the Park Lane Hilton'.

A week after James Bulger was murdered, the European Commission ranked Merseyside alongside parts of southern Italy and eastern Germany as especially poor, signalling it would grant approximately £1billion in special grants. In 1992, unemployment in Liverpool was still almost treble the national rate. Outside the city, there were few sympathetic voices about what might have happened there; nobody asking what fourteen years of Conservative rule might do to the residents of a place which was later proven as being earmarked for decline; nobody asking what mass job losses might do to a collective psyche; nobody really asking why the extreme sort of changes that happened in Liverpool might provoke extreme – or unbelievable – actions or reactions.

Ian Jack, writing in the *Independent*, believed that Liverpool had 'lost everything' and 'was dying'. He also believed that Liverpool had separated itself from the rest of the country, suggesting the city's 'last function in British life' was to provide theatre. Jack claimed that Liverpool had learned to dramatise itself and to show its stigmata because of Heysel and then because of Hillsborough: because of responsibility and then because of anger and self-protection. The *Liverpool Echo* acutely appreciated sensitivities around headlines and their focus in the early weeks and months was around the misery of James Bulger's family. It was only when his murderers were convicted and their identities revealed that words on the front pages reflected the horror of what had happened.

Neither Jack, Margolis or any other of the writers lining up to have their say about Liverpool stopped to think about its history in sympathetic terms. Nobody stopped to think that the angry young man crashing through a police cordon and getting arrested for public order offences was a form of expression; that Catholic guilt applied and it was a working class way of screaming, 'the murder of James Bulger does not represent the place I come from,' a place which had not only been abandoned by the state and reputationally scalded for attempting to shout about this injustice but scalded also by the memory of tragedies, one of which remained raw, to a large extent unexplained and otherwise totally misunderstood.

If the reaction outside the court was disproportionate – according to Margolis, 'an orgy of crude hatred' – why was he so surprised? A week earlier, in an article entitled, 'Are our children spinning out of control?' he had asked whether perceptions of normality were rattled because of the unprecedented nature of the crime: 'We'd never seen this before,' he wrote. Would it then be actually quite normal to expect an unprecedented reaction?

Basic research may have given him a more balanced perspective because children had always murdered other children, even extremely young ones. Just twenty years earlier – in Liverpool, indeed – an eleven-year-old boy pleaded guilty to the manslaughter of a two-year-old having accidentally hit him on the head with a stone. Rather than take him home, he held the child down in a pool of rainwater until he drowned. While the nineteenth century had seen boys and girls hanged by the British justice system, twelve months before James Bulger's murder, an eleven-year-old girl from Northumberland killed an eighteen-month-old she was supposed to be babysitting. She had beaten and suffocated him and was found guilty of manslaughter. Perhaps, instead, we hadn't seen it *like this* before, with the moment of abduction caught on CCTV; the victim so small, so angelic – the images of him being taken away to his death so evocative, so chilling, so desperate and sad.

The judge would eventually label this crime as 'an act of unparalleled evil and barbarity'. At the same time, the case of Suzanne Capper was being heard, a sixteen-year-old from Manchester who was kidnapped, tortured, set-alight and murdered just two months before James Bulger's death. Yet this trial did not receive the same level of focus and there was no social commentary or psychobabble about crime rates in Manchester, which exceeded Liverpool's at the time.

Maybe it suited Liverpool for this crime to be described as evil, because evil includes a supernatural component and it has the potential to remove place from discussion about roles. When something bad happens in Liverpool, it nevertheless feels like the whole of the city is on trial and this goes some way towards explaining why people react the way they do.

Margolis used the 1,086 death notices placed in the *Liverpool Echo* in memory of James Bulger as proof of the city's maudlin state, while he also suggested Anfield was 'getting off' on mourning as Liverpool Football Club held a minute's silence ahead of their game with Ipswich Town. He believed that Liverpool was a 'bit screwy' because Harry Rimmer, the council leader, had accused the London media of a racist attitude while the chairman of the police authority urged Merseysiders not to buy national newspapers. 'Like blacks in the USA, Scousers are now on the proscribed list,' Margolis wrote. 'You publicly find fault with them at your peril.' He then observed that the Liverpudlian mentality was similar to the Russian. 'You might be in a deluxe version of Moscow.'

Margolis, who apologised five years later when he came to Liverpool to promote a book, had realised too late of the damage he'd inflicted. 'My article seemed to release a Pandora's box of cold loathing from all over the country,' he admitted. It had not just been the anger of Liverpudlians that rocked him but the response of liberals and left-wingers elsewhere, who complimented him for 'sticking it to those whingeing Scousers'. He would supposedly tell them that was never his intention. 'But the thing built up its own malign momentum, exposing a quite shocking anti-Scouse racism.'

It was a shame that his more accurate conclusions should be lost in the storm. In the aforementioned previous article about youth crime, he had finished with a scene on a packed bus in Birkenhead, filled with children and old ladies. The driver had the radio playing and the song was Lonnie Donegan's 'My Old Man's a Dustman'.

'In 1993, a lot of youngsters would be grateful to have an old man, and the old man delighted to be a dustman,' he wrote. Was it too fanciful to suggest that if the world returned to that place, the tragedy of James Bulger would never have happened?

AT PRESTON CROWN COURT, IT WAS DECIDED THAT NEITHER BOY should give evidence in their trial and so, except for the tapes from police interviews, their voices remained unheard.

It emerged that on 12 February 1993, Jon Venables left his school bag in the bushes on the roundabout beneath the flyover on Queens Drive, which bisects County Road and Rice Lane. He met Robert Thompson and his little brother Ryan by the church that leads into Walton Village. Despite pressure to follow them, Ryan went to school because Friday was pottery class and he liked pottery.

Meanwhile Robert and Jon headed towards Bootle, where they were spotted by a classmate. Their classmate informed a teacher, who then informed the headmaster.

Accounts from other teachers told how it had taken two of them to separate Jon from another boy as he tried to choke him with a ruler. They also told how he used to headbutt the playground walls and cut himself with scissors. His behaviour had been disruptive at St Mary's, particularly the day before he helped commit this atrocious act. All of this explained why the headteacher called Jon's mum first. But there was no answer.

They were born a fortnight apart in 1982 and separated by two inches, Jon being the taller of the two. They were still wearing their school uniforms as they stole: from Clintons Cards, from Superdrug, from Boots, from Tandy and then from TJ Hughes where they beckoned a child from a mother, who recognised what was happening and called him back. This went on all afternoon: ducking and diving, pinching, running down the aisles, hiding behind the rails; getting told off, running away again.

James Bulger was eating Smarties when they took him from the door of butchers, A. R. Tym's, while James's mother Denise bought lamb chops. 'Let's get a kid lost,' Robert said Jon had suggested earlier that day in front of TJ Hughes. A woman sitting outside Sayers saw James and was reassured when she heard the boys say, 'Come on, baby.' CCTV images showed Robert walking just in front of Jon, who was holding James's hand.

At first, they went behind The Strand and along the walkway beside the Leeds Liverpool Canal. Robert and Jon spoke about pushing James into the water but instead, one of them dropped him on his head as he sat on the wall and he began to cry. Though a woman saw what was happening, she presumed they were brothers just mucking about.

In total, 38 people would see James as he was taken to Walton nearly two and a half miles away. It was a busy time of day: down Park Street, past the Employment Centre, right at the Atlantis Fish Bar, left at the Liverpool tax offices, past The Mons pub on the ring road jammed with traffic on a Friday evening and along Church Road.

When approached, witnesses said that Jon was usually the first to speak up, reassuring them with lies. The cut on James's head had been covered up by the hood of his jacket. But Jon and Robert always had some sort of explanation, even promising they would take him to Walton Lane, the police station they would bypass, sneaking behind the facility instead and onto the rail tracks.

The solicitor for Neil Venables, father of Jon, later denied the boy had watched an 18-certificate film his father had rented a month before. Jon, it was established, collected toy trolls, and *Child's Play 3* contained scenes in which an obsessed doll, Chucky, died after being splattered with blue paint and having its face pulped. (*Child's Play* would also feature in the court proceedings in the murder of Suzanne Capper).

James was exhausted by the time they began to torture him. First by flicking blue Humbrol modelling paint into his eyes, which they had stolen from a shop on County Road. He was kicked, stamped upon and had stones and bricks thrown at him. Batteries were placed in his mouth and it was thought that some had been entered into his anus, though this could not be proven. A heavy iron bar – a railway fishplate – was dropped on James's head and caused ten fractures to his skull. A pathologist explained that James had 42 separate injuries in total, though none could have been confirmed as the final blow.

James was motionless by the time Robert and Jon placed him across the railway line, covering his head with the trousers and pants they'd already removed; weighing his head down further with rubble. It was believed that James was already dead by the time a freight train came trundling along, cutting him in half. Five miles away in Blundellsands, Jim Fitzsimmons – the police officer trying to find James – was getting told of his disappearance. He did not know then that it was already a murder case.

Jon broke down in the police interviews, making the confession: 'I did kill him.' In court, he asked the social worker sitting next to him whether James, in heaven, could hear what was being said. He hated 'the baby smell' on his clothes and said that he fantasised about James growing inside him, being reborn. But Robert gave nothing away. Though James's blood was found in the welt of his shoe, he would never publicly admit his part.

THE PLACE MOST ASSOCIATED WITH JAMES BULGER IS BOOTLE. Except that is only where he disappeared. He was murdered in Walton by children who went to school in Walton. Though Jon Venables' parents were separated and his time was divided between both his father, who lived in Bootle, and his mother, who lived in Norris Green, Robert Thompson was from Walton Village and he knew the streets and its alleys best.

In 1993, Dominic Lloyd completed the same walk as James when he was dragged from The Strand to the railway line. What struck him the most then about the route was the level of traffic and the relentless noise. 'A really nasty environment, dual carriageway nearly the entire distance until you get to County Road,' he recalled. James was taken in the cold of winter as it was going dark. Cars with their lights will have rushed past, their exhausts emitting plumes of petrol and diesel. The whole world was going by. None of it stopping. None of it seeing. To an adult then, it felt industrial and uncaring. To a boy of two years, it must have been terrifying.

Down by the subways, where Robert and Jon both hid their bags before making their way into Bootle that morning, there is a stretch of Queens Drive after the flyover which feels like an aeroplane runway. Lloyd rode motorbikes in his spare time instead of following football teams. He grew up three miles closer to city centre in Tuebrook – another working-class area, but one where huge sycamore trees hang over the main roads that lead onto Liverpool's inner-ring. On one of his rides, Lloyd noticed that the cathedral of green that softens everything continues for miles, but stops just before the signs start appearing for Walton Jail, when vegetation is taken over by a long, straight strip of damp concrete and a strange hostility in the amount of brickwork.

Flanking those walls and behind the terraced houses is Walton Village, where Robert and Jon ran errands for a woman at a video shop in the hour after the murder until they were spotted by Robert's mum and told to go home. Ann Thompson's life had unravelled in the village, having been the victim of domestic abuse at the hands of her husband and prior to that, her father. Her marriage would breakdown after her husband left with a woman they both met on holiday at a caravan site, and from there she descended into an abusive relationship with alcohol, drinking at the Top House, where journalists would later pay regulars to tell stories about her. In the hours after Robert was charged, Ann was taken away along with her seven other boys under the cover of darkness and holed up initially in a city centre hotel, the Gladstone, and then in a flat attached to a residential care home for the elderly, before moving to a secret location outside of Merseyside.

There had, however, been two Waltons. There was the Walton of Goodison Park and Everton Football Club, whose fortunes in 1993 reflected the struggles of the district which surrounded it. That season, Everton's thirteenth placed finish was their lowest since 1981, but that did not entirely explain attendances, which had slipped almost by half in the six years since Kevin Ratcliffe lifted the club's last title. The gate of 3,039 at Wimbledon for Everton's visit in the inaugural Premier League season remains the competition's record low and this shows Everton had become a team few looked forward to facing, though not for the reasons Evertonians would prefer.

Peter Kilfoyle, who won the controversial Walton by-election of 1991 when the Monster Raving Looney Party's Screaming Lord Sutch was just a few hundred votes short of beating the Conservative candidate into third place, said that Walton in 1993 had become one of the poorest boroughs in the European Union, partly because of the area's loyalty to Labour during fourteen years of Tory rule.

'A lot of people were living way below the poverty line,' he said, 'and football was becoming more expensive to watch so something had to give.' This might explain why Everton's average home attendance in 1992/93 was 20,457 – the second worst figure since the World War One.

Liverpool City Council's Deprivation Index ranked Walton way below the bleakest areas of Toxteth. Unemployment had doubled in two decades and in 1993 were running at 40 per-cent, the same levels that had seen one of the most violent social disturbances in Toxteth eleven years earlier.

Many of the terraced homes near Goodison Park were owned. The same could be said of the terraced houses near to Bedford Road where Robert Thompson and Jon Venables met at St Mary's school. Cross back over County Road and into Walton Village, the situation changed, and this held significance according to a pupil who was in the same school year as Robert and Jon.

'Kids who lived on Bedford Road tended to do well,' he said. 'They had at least one parent who went to work and they had books at home. There was more of a nuclear family, though not in the sort of sense that someone from Middle England would recognise.'

In Walton Village, though, there were more signs of social breakdown. The bigger houses had been bought by private landlords and rented out. Parents tended to be single and if they did work – like Ann Thompson – they tended to be involved in menial jobs that involved long hours.

'This meant the kids could do what they wanted. You automatically get older when this happens. You don't have a childhood. You're becoming an adult far too quickly. You're looking after yourself. You're sorting out your own tea. You've got a key to the door. Or in Robert's case, you're climbing up the drainpipe and sneaking into the house late at night.'

Walton's crime was not significantly high but typical of most inner cities. Of the 650 crimes registered at Walton Lane per month, a quarter were committed by juveniles, though the majority of those juveniles were cautioned rather than prosecuted. Youth workers and liaison officers held a collective view that petty theft – the sort Robert and Jon were involved in as a matter of routine before taking James from The Strand – was endemic in 'street urchin culture', though they did recognise their jobs made them see the worst of what young people had to offer.

It was, according to one youth worker born outside of Liverpool, the lack of parental attention that stimulated this culture, though he had sympathy with the plight of a city which had its primary industry in the docks ripped from its heart, thus leading to an abandoned sense of purpose for workers no longer with any regularity in front of them. This, according to his observations, led to subsequent martial breakdowns and single parents trying to keep families afloat by taking whatever jobs they could find, even if it meant several children being left to figure out life for themselves at a time when the world was becoming more commercial and everybody – children included suddenly – were being encouraged what to buy. 'Children were becoming more independent in one sense but needier – or more wanting – in another,' he said.

Out of school, Robert and Jon were rarely seen on the side of County Road where life was tough, but easier than it might have been in Walton Village. 'Virtually every one of the kids that hung around with them from the village has ended up in prison, whereas me and my group of mates don't know anyone stopped by the police or arrested,' said the pupil from St Mary's. It had frustrated him that the word 'feral' kept appearing in the reports when describing children in Walton. 'I hung around on street corners, but that didn't make me feral,' he reasoned. At Christmas, the pupil would get pretty much what he asked for off his mother, but he wondered whether that was the case with any of the other children, and the Thompsons in particular.

'Yet in the writing about James's murder, we *all* had nothing,' he emphasised. 'We were all meffs. And we were all on the rob together. It just wasn't true. There was an element of it. But there was a bigger element of working-class values being in place across Walton. I used to go on holiday to Spain, for example – once to Florida. My mum was a single parent and we'd go with my auntie and uncle. If you're a meff or you're feral you don't go on holiday to Florida. And I wasn't the only one in our school that went to Florida.'

In 1989 Charles Murray, an American author on social policy, visited Britain in search of the 'underclass' and his conclusions in a *Sunday Times* article caused a furore. The term had first been coined in the US by Ken Auletta, who had seen the rust belt states and sympathised with the plight of the people. Murray disagreed, claiming unemployment, amorality and crime were norms to be accepted. It should be a community's reaction to the situation it finds itself in that defines its existence.

Four years later, Murray's writing would appear in a health and welfare review of Britain, which included conflicting viewpoints such as Frank Field's, the Labour MP for Birkenhead, who had identified the main 'forces of expulsion' in his own exposition, *Losing Out*, where he explained the rise in the British 'underclass', which by 1993 had been separated from the rest of society 'in terms of income, life chances and political aspirations'. This came through unemployment, widening class differences, the exclusion of the very poorest from rapidly rising living standards, and a hardening of public attitudes.

Britain's interpretation of what was coined 'the cycle of deprivation' was first put forward in 1972 in a speech by Sir Keith Joseph, before he became a key-Thatcherite who helped dismantle the notion of a post-war consensus and one-nation conservatism. His central idea was that poverty persisted because social problems reproduced themselves from one generation to the next and, specifically, that inadequate parents tended to rear inadequate children.

To paraphrase Richard Tawney, the socialist economic historian, what thoughtful rich people may refer to as the problem of poverty, thoughtful poor people may call the problem of wealth. By 1993, two extremes had been openly engineered by government policy and the enormous inequalities beneath them were two parts of the same problem. Thatcherism had adversely transformed British society, widening the gap between the haves and the have nots. In simple terms, Field believed the Thatcherites had rewarded the rich and punished the poor, increasing inequalities and hence, Britain had a growing underclass. 'Change the policies, and the underclass will diminish,' he wrote.

Though Murray and Field disagreed over the causes, it was clear that both could see the same evidence on the disastrous effects on children of absent fathers. It was a coincidence that around the time James Bulger went missing on that Friday, Murray was pulling out his briefcase in Baton Rouge, Florida, ready to tell a group of congressmen and senators about the social state of his nation.

The night before I met the pupil from St Mary's to discuss his memories from the period around James's death, he had watched a documentary about the murder which included a clip from an ITN news report in the days before Robert and Jon were arrested. It had reported that more than 300 juveniles had been questioned in relation to the offence, branding them as 'the usual suspects'.

'Imagine being a 12-year-old lad amongst the "usual suspects" in the murder of a two-year-old boy,' he said, wondering about the impact of presenting Liverpool as the sort of place that might actually have 300 child suspects in relation to one of the most significant crimes in modern history.

Then there was the interview with the group of kids who discovered James on the railway line. They had walked past the body at first because they wanted to see the 'big dogs' in the police compound. The reporter asked them what James looked like, but they could not see the face 'because it was wrapped up, like a coat... with house bricks all round it and bars on it'. They could see the body, though, 'all the organs hanging out from the waist'.

A crowd of twenty children had gathered by the end of the interview, several of them laughing nervously at the back – others mucking about. For the St Mary's pupil, the scene summed up how standards in so many ways had slipped. He imagined what it must have been like for them in those moments and then in the days, weeks, months and years after. 'These kids have just had the most horrific experience that they are ever, ever going to have,' he said. 'They've found a baby cut in half. And they're in the park with their mates wearing Berghaus jackets talking about it to adults with cameras shining on them.' Had he discovered James, he thought about how it would have affected him psychologically. 'They should have been whisked away. They'd have had police liaison officers now. They'd have had someone looking after them for a week at least or sent to counselling straight away. Can you imagine the horror of that experience? In front of the cameras they were acting hard but when they're alone at night and they close their eyes, they must think about it.'

One of the boys was Terence Riley, who was thirteen years old when he found James along with his brother. 'He has seen things which no young person should have to see,' his defence team argued when he was first jailed in 2009 for dealing drugs. 'Finding James Bulger's body on the railway line, without any counselling, was bound to have some effect on such a young person.'

By 2018, when Riley was in prison for a third time – this on money laundering charges, it was revealed that he was engaging with mental health authorities having been diagnosed with post-traumatic stress disorder. 'One wonders if he had undergone counselling got the help he needed after that incident, whether he would find himself in the position he is today,' his barrister asked.

The pupil from St Mary's thought back to what it was like in the Victorian school which is still there but has since been converted into an adult learning facility; still with its towering steel gates and railings, its high ceilings, its wooden floorboards and its wintery drafts, its playground where there are markings for hopscotch. He had 'loved the school'. There were hymns every morning and assemblies every week.

'It wasn't the rabble that's been painted,' he insisted. 'It was a nice school with nice kids apart from the few who didn't want to work and some who truanted. They came from the more deprived areas and turned out to be the badly behaved kids.'

Robert Thompson had been at St Mary's since the start of infant school, but Jon Venables joined later after being removed from other schools for behavioural problems. Both had been held back a year. Aged ten, they were learning with nine-year-olds and rather than approaching secondary school like other boys their age, they still had 18 months left at juniors. Stunted maturity was marked by appearance because while they had progressed from shorts to long trousers in the autumn of 1992, other ten-year old boys at St Mary's and other ten-year old boys they knew from the streets around Walton had made the same transition twelve months earlier. When Neil and Susan Venables separated, the locations of split homes placed Jon and Robert walking home together.

In police interviews, Jon came across as remorseful and Robert was cold. A feeling developed that Robert had led John. Yet the pupil at St Mary's saw their personalities differently.

'Jon was a lunatic, I didn't like him at all. He shouldn't have been in the school from day one, I thought. Weird. Then he became mates with Robert and from there, they'd always be together. At play time, it would just be those two. Jon sometimes tried to play football with us but he'd run on and boot the ball over the wall and act the clown. He was a clown basically, but an odd clown. Not someone who pissed about in school to make people laugh. There was something not quite right about this kid. It would have been diagnosed with Asperger's or ADHD by now, 100 per-cent. He'd have been on the spectrum. Maybe if he came along a few years later when New Labour started kicking in he'd have been taken care of. Instead, he got put into a mainstream school with mainstream children. I think it was because Mrs Slack was the headteacher and she was strict. I think they thought: "She'll be able to straighten him out..." She used to have a cane in her office hanging up. She never used to hit us with it. But it was there as a little reminder of what might happen.'

St Mary's had 260 pupils and two classes in each year. The classes in juniors were separated into the clever ones and the not-so-clever ones. The arrangement in infants – just one class per year – in theory brought the kids close together from the moment they joined.

'That's why a lot of relationships were so close from reception all the way up until we left junior school. Everyone knew each other. I could pick out everyone else's mum, but not Robert or Jon's. I couldn't say, "That's Robert's mum," or "There's Jon's mum." Jon's dad collected him from time to time. The mums would get together but they wouldn't see Robert's mum, certainly. She wasn't visible at all.

'Robert was always on his own. Before Jon joined the school, he was always with his little brother, Ryan. He never played footy with us. To me, he was just quiet. Maybe to lads who knew him out of school, they'd say differently. I can't remember any interaction with him. He wasn't my mate. He wasn't anyone's mate. He got left out of everything. He'd miss out on school trips because he never seemed to have any money. In infant school, I can't remember him being in trouble at all, but in juniors he'd regularly walk out of school. It was quite easy to get away if you wanted to. One fire exit and nobody there to stop you going through it. From there you were into the yard.'

In the academic year between 1992 and 1993, Thompson and Venables had truanted for half of the calendar and the school had alerted social services. Ofsted had confirmed that truancy in Liverpool's primary schools was above the national average and in secondary schools, well above. There were thirteen schools in special measures and the education authority blamed funding and a lack of support not only for literacy and numeracy but school management.

'By third year juniors, I was in Miss Helm's class. Robert and Jon were in Mrs Rigg's class. They got separated and Jon got put into Miss Helm's class with us. I got the impression it was the last roll of the dice for him. I don't think she'd have wanted him, but she got given him. She was a nice teacher so maybe she thought she could bring him along. Robert by then was viewed as a bit of a lost cause, really. I remember him being dragged by a teacher called Mr Dwyer down the corridor. Mr Dwyer ripped his jumper. You know Dennis the Menace's dad? Mr Dwyer looked like him: little moustache, going bald, but what hair he did have was slicked back. He must have been about 60 so he'd probably done national service. You didn't want to get told off by him. I have no idea what Robert had done that day but whatever it was it was enough to be seen by the headmistress.'

On the morning of James Bulger's murder, Robert had tried to encourage his younger brother Ryan to sag with him and Jon.

'Ryan was tiny. He used to have these huge glasses like Penfold. It was obvious that these were the only glasses he could afford – or the glasses that the NHS had given him. He was one of those kids with a patch on his eye. You'd see him and you'd think, "Fucking 'ell." Their uniforms would always be terrible. Hand-me-down shoes. Shorts that were too small. When one of the parents bought her kid some slightly longer shorts for the winter months, all of the other parents followed the trend. But Robert and Ryan were still wearing these tight shorts.

'We'd all go to school looking immaculate: bathed the night before, hair brushed, clean clothes. They'd have what they've been wearing all week. Maybe they hadn't had a bath. I remember Robert wearing a polo shirt underneath his jumper rather than a proper school shirt with a tie on.

'On days when we were invited to bring toys into school, they didn't bring in much. One of them might have one item and the other would have nothing. On own clothes day, Robert would come in wearing his school uniform either because he didn't have a pound or 50 pence or because he didn't have the clothes. There's us in our brand-new tracksuits and trainers. Loads of us would come in wearing our Liverpool or Everton kits. And there's him in his uniform.

'People came to my house and it was always tidy. Nobody would ever get invited to Robert's house for a birthday party. And that's another thing, nobody – including me – ever invited Robert to their birthday parties. The same goes for Jon. But they were never bullied and they never seemed to act as bullies. Boys will always fight over stupid things; Liverpool and Everton. But because Robert and

Jon weren't into footy, they were left alone. They were sort of separated from the rest of the kids in a social sense, a bit like the underclass.'

They had been introduced by chance, through circumstance. The fathers of both had lost their jobs through the depression of Liverpool and family separation followed. Both had siblings who earned more attention. There were warning signs at home with Jon, who was disruptive in school, but not so much with Robert. They gravitated towards one another across a playground because they were 'two loners together', though they were not especially good friends. To the classmate, Robert seemed to truant before Jon but it was hard to tell – 'you don't really know if someone is absent for a good reason until it becomes a pattern' – but Jon 'had more of a sadistic streak' because of the way he treated himself, 'banging his own head on the wall if he couldn't get what he wanted or when he was being told off.' Jon's behaviour deteriorated in a more dramatic way than Robert's, pulling down displays, standing on desks and throwing chairs.

When the pupil at St Mary's later saw the police interviews with Jon and Robert on television, Jon's behaviour particularly was familiar.

'Jon used to turn his crying on and off like a tap. It used to freak me out. He was disruptive. The teachers would tell him off and he'd start crying straight away. No one really bursts into tears at the age of ten when they're told off by a teacher. It was the sort of reaction you saw from a really young child they can't get what they want off their mum. He burst into tears whenever he wanted. Because he was crying his eyes out and Robert didn't cry, Robert gets the blame when they question which one led the other. Jon's remorseful because Jon's crying. Well he's not. Jon can cry when he wants to cry. I remember saying to my mum: "He does this all the time, he cries whenever he wants to." It was like a party trick. In my eyes, there was no remorse when he was crying. He's just crying because he knows he's in a bad situation and he'd better cry.'

It was the last day of term when Robert and Jon did not show up at St Mary's and James Bulger went missing. The pupil admitted there could be no rational explanation for what happened to James. He was not religious and he did not believe in evil. He would wrack his brain trying to figure out how it had come to this, stressing that by trying to explain what had happened on the streets of Walton was not an attempt to justify the appalling actions of two boys he once knew. That Friday in February, he had invited four friends around to his house – most likely because he had a new computer game. After visiting his nan's, an enormous fire was billowing from the windows of a flat above a William Hill bookies near the Glebe Pub. 'Being a little kid, it was exciting, all the fire engines flying past. "Mum, can we stay and watch it?" I asked...'

It was around this time, Robert and Jon were dragging James across County Road and towards his death, no more than 100 yards behind the gathering crowd.

The boy from St Mary's was now an adult and willing to consider imponderables. 'What if we'd been friendlier to Robert in school?' he'd asked himself, though not of Jon, who he insisted several times should have had been in special education. The fire on County Road which burned out the top floor of a building had taken everyone's attention: 'It was a busy time of day on a busy road which had lots of people coming home for the weekend – what if just a few of the people watching had turned around, then more than 38 would have seen what was happening...'

Finally, he would ask himself two questions without being able to answer them.

'Had we forgotten what real dangers actually looked like? Or had we become too busy to notice what was important?'

In a society which had been told it had the opportunity to gain a lot more, Liverpool had been the city which had the most to lose.

Now, it was made to feel as though it had lost everything.

Acknowledgements

I WAS FORTUNATE ENOUGH TO HAVE TWO GRANDPARENTS FOR most of the way through my childhood who would tell me about Liverpool's deep past. Thank you firstly, then to Etta and Jo who sadly will never really appreciate their influence. My mum and dad too played a role here, Sue and Peter. They made me proud to come from Liverpool. My wife Rosalind has amongst many things helped round off rough edges and increased my understanding in the art of argument. (She might not thank me for saying that but it is meant as a compliment). Thanks to James Corbett at deCoubertin for a great idea and thanks to Jack Gordon Brown and Megan Pollard for their assistance, as well as Leslie Priestley for his diligence and Thomas Regan for brilliant artwork. Thank you also to Peter Hooton and Brian Reade for all their time and assistance. Andy Taylor, nice one for letting me kip at yours on my way to meet Tebbit. We have Mark, Ian, Matt, Howie, Billy and Jay who are always there.

Bibliography

Books

Beckett, Andy; *Promised you a Miracle* (Penguin, 2015)

Belchem, John; *Liverpool 800* (University of Chicago, 2012)

Crick, Michael; *March of Militant* (Faber, 1986)

Dodd, Jegsy and Sampson, Kevin; Here we go Gathering Cups in May (Canongate, 2008)

Du Noyer, Paul; *Liverpool Wondrous Place* (Virgin, 2007)

Frost, Diane and North, Peter; *Militant Liverpool* (April, 2013)

Frost, Diane and Phillips, Richard; *Liverpool '81* (Liverpool University Press, 2011)

Gayle, Howard; *61 Minutes in Munich* (deCoubertin, 2016)

Gilmour, Ian; *Dancing with Dogma* (Simon & Schuster, 1992)

Hart, Simon; Here we Go (deCoubertin, 2016)

Hatton, Derek; *Inside Left* (Bloomsbury, 1988)

Heseltine, Michael; Life in the Jungle (Hodder and Stoughton, 2000)

Horrie, Chris and Chippendale, Peter; *Stick it up Your Punter* (Faber, 1990)

Jones, Owen; *The Establishment* (Penguin, 2015)

Kilfoyle, Peter; *Left Behind* (Politico, 2000)

Lane, Tony; *Liverpool, City of the Sea* (Liverpool University Press, 1997)

Macefield, MWl; *In Search of The La's* (Helter Skelter, 2003)

McClure, James; *Spike Island* (Macmillan, 1981)

McSmith, Andy; *No Such Thing as Society* (Constable, 2011)

Mulhearn, Tony and Taffe, Peter; *Liverpool, a City that Dared to Fight* (Fortress, 1988)
Paul, David; *Liverpool Docks, a Short History* (Fonthill, 2016)
Parker, Howard; *Living with Heroin* (Open University, 1988)
Parkinson, Michael; *Liverpool on the Brink* (Policy, 1985)
Reade, Brian; *43 years with the Same Bird* (Pan, 2009)
Sandbrook, Dominic; *Seasons in the Sun* (Penguin, 2013)
Smith, David James; *The Sleep of Reason* (Faber, 2007)
Tempany, Adrian; *And the Sun Shines Now* (Faber, 2017)
Turner, Alwyn; *Crisis, What Crisis?* (Aurum, 2013)
Turner, Alwyn; *Rejoice! Rejoice!* (Aurum, 2010)

Newspapers

Liverpool Echo
Liverpool Daily Post
Guardian
Observer
The Times
The Sunday Times
Sheffield Star
The Daily Telegraph
Daily Mail
Daily Express
The Sunday People

Index

About the Author

Simon Hughes is a journalist and award-winning author. He writes about football for *The Athletic*. His books include *Red Machine*, *Men in White Suits* and *On The Brink*.

www.decoubertin.co.uk